*A threefold cord is not
easily broken.*
-ECCLESIASTES 4:12

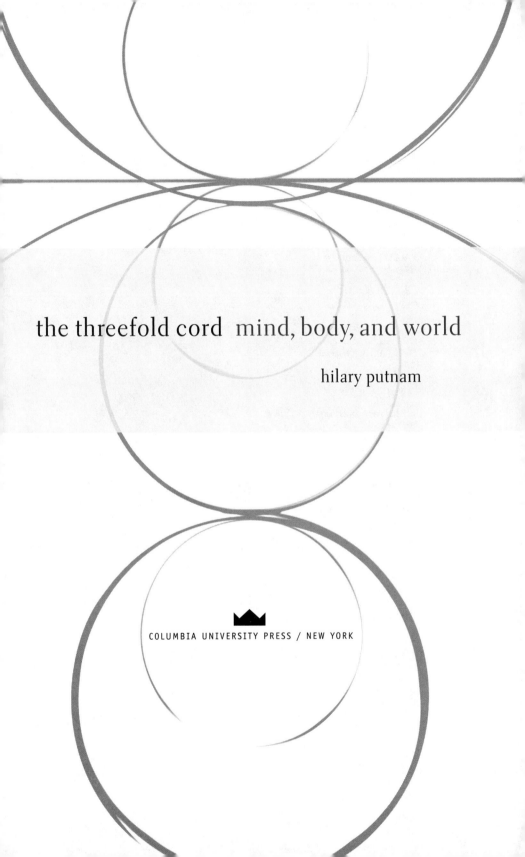

the threefold cord mind, body, and world

hilary putnam

COLUMBIA UNIVERSITY PRESS / NEW YORK

Columbia University Press
Publishers Since 1893
New York   Chichester, West Sussex

Part 1 first appeared in the
Journal of Philosophy 91:9 (September
1994).
Reprinted by permission
of the *Journal of Philosophy.*

Library of Congress
Cataloging-in-Publication Data

Putnam, Hilary
The threefold cord: mind, body,
and world / Hilary Putnam.
p.   cm. — (The John Dewey essays
in philosophy; no. 5)
Includes bibliographical
references and index.
ISBN 0–231–10286–0 (cloth)
ISBN 0–231–10287–9 (paper)
1. Perception (Philosophy)
2. Mind and body.
I. Title.
II. Series
B945.P873T47   1999
128'.2—dc21
99-38458

Casebound editions of
Columbia University Press books
are printed on permanent and durable
acid-free paper.

Printed in the
United States of America

c 10 9 8 7 6 5 4 3
p 10 9 8 7 6 5 4 3 2 1

to george boolos, 1940–1996

Think where man's glory most begins and ends
And say my glory was I had such friends.

—W. B. YEATS

contents

preface

Part 1 of this book was presented as a series of three John Dewey Lectures (of the same title: "Sense, Nonsense, and the Senses: An Inquiry Into the Powers of the Human Mind") at Columbia University, March 22, 24, and 29, 1994. In September of the same year a revised version of the three lectures appeared by permission of Columbia University as an issue of the *Journal of Philosophy*. Apart from copy-editing, I have not further revised them for this publication.

An invitation from the committee of the American Philosophical Association that chooses the Josiah Royce lecturer (with the participation of the Brown Philosophy Department) led to part 2 of the book being presented as a series of three Josiah Royce Lectures (of the same title: "Mind and Body") at Brown University, November 3, 5, and 7, 1997.

Together these two parts lay out my view on perception (hence the Mind and the World) and on the ancient Mind-Body puzzles. Trying to think of a book title that covered both topics, the reference to the "three-fold cord which is not easily broken" came to mind. Some have objected to the third part of the title, "Mind, Body, and World" as redundant, on the ground that the mind and the body are *parts* of the world, but this objection would, if allowed to stand, also rule out such familiar titles as "Mind and World," so I have decided to ignore it.

After I had delivered the Royce Lectures at Brown, I became aware of an interesting article on the topic of explanation by Jaegwon Kim, who graciously accepted the role of my "stalking-horse" in those lectures, and I felt that it would clarify the position I take in those lectures if I added a discussion of his distinction between "internalist" and "realist" views of explanation. This became the first of the two afterwords that make up part 3. Discussions about "qualia" with various people (including a memorable lunch with Tyler Burge) led me to write the second afterword.

My thanks to a number of other people who have made valuable suggestions and criticisms are given in footnotes to individual lectures, but I want to give a special mention to my old friend, Ben-Ami Scharfstein, who gave the entire book a close reading at a late stage, and I also want to thank Cesar Gomez (one of the world's leading mathematical physicists in the esoteric field of "string theory" and a fine "amateur" philosopher). During the discussion of my model-theoretic argument in *Reason, Truth, and History* at a conference in Madrid in 1988 Gomez made a remarkable suggestion. He suggested that "perhaps John Austin's *Sense and Sensibilia* contains the way out of the whole problem." I disagreed on that occasion, but in a few years I came to see that Gomez had been exactly right. (The fact that I was studying the philosophy of William James, who was a powerful advocate of "natural realism," was a big factor.) Part 1 of this volume is my way of working out the Austinian insights that Gomez recalled to my attention.

part one sense, nonsense, and the senses

an inquiry
into the powers
of the human mind

the antinomy of realism

*No theory is kind to us that
cheats us of seeing.*
—HENRY JAMES TO ROBERT LOUIS
STEVENSON, JANUARY 12, 1891

The besetting sin of philosophers seems to be throwing the baby out with the bathwater. From the beginning, each "new wave" of philosophers has simply ignored the insights of the previous wave in the course of advancing its own. Today we stand near the end of a century in which there have been many new insights in philosophy; but at the same time there has been an unprecedented forgetting of the insights of previous centuries and millennia.

At the same time, it would be absurd to make the reactionary move of trying to believe what philosophers who lived two hundred or two thousand years ago believed. As John Dewey would have told us, they lived under wholly different conditions and faced wholly different problems, and such a return is impossible in any case. And even if it were possible to go back, to do so would be to ignore the correct criticisms of the abandoned positions that were made by later generations of philosophers. But I want to urge that we attempt to understand and, to the extent that it may be humanly possible, to overcome, the pattern of "recoil" that causes philosophy to leap from frying pan to fire, from fire to a different frying pan, from different frying pan to a different fire, and so on, apparently without end.[1] In these lectures I will try to show what such understanding and overcoming might involve by examining the central metaphysical issue of realism.

That issue is especially suited to this purpose, because current examples of the recoil phenomenon are so plentiful in connection with the topic. Philosophers who recoil from the excesses of various versions of metaphysical realism have recoiled to a variety of very peculiar positions—deconstruction being currently the most famous, but one could also mention Nelson Goodman's "irrealism" or Michael Dummett's "antirealism" as examples of a similar recoil on the part of some analytic philosophers. And philosophers who recoil from what they see as the loss of the world in these antirealisms have embraced such mysterious notions as "identity across metaphysically possible worlds" and the "absolute conception of the world."[2] Today the humanities are polarized as never before, with the majority of the "new wave" thinkers in literature departments celebrating deconstruction cum Marxism cum feminism . . . and the majority of the analytic philosophers celebrating materialism cum cognitive science cum the metaphysical mysteries just mentioned. And no issue polarizes the humanities—and, increasingly, the arts as well—as much as realism, described as "logocentricism" by one side and as the "defense of the idea of objective knowledge" by the other. If, as I believe, there is a way to do justice to our sense that knowledge claims are responsible to reality without recoiling into metaphysical fantasy, then it is important that we find that way. For there is, God knows, irresponsibility enough in the world, including irresponsibility masquerading as responsibility, and it belongs to the vocation of the thinker, now as always, to try to teach the difference between the two.

I began by saying that we have lost insights as well as gained them in the course of the philosophical debate (indeed, that is an essential part of the phenomenon I am calling recoil—when one is dominated by the feeling that one must put as much distance between oneself and a particular philosophical stance as possible, one is not likely to acknowledge that the defenders of that stance possess *any* insights); and, as my reference to previous millennia was meant to suggest, some of those insights are very old. Indeed, I might have titled these lectures "Aristotelian Realism Without Aristotelian Metaphysics." But I could equally have titled them "Deweyan Realism." For Dewey, as I read him, was concerned to show that we can retain something of the spirit of Aristotle's defense of the commonsense world, against the excesses of both the metaphysicians and the sophists, without thereby committing ourselves to any variant of the metaphysical essentialism that Aristotle propounded.[3] I am therefore delighted to give these lectures under the rubric "Dewey Lectures." For I am convinced that my concern in these lectures—the search for a middle way between reactionary metaphysics and irresponsible relativism—was also one of Dewey's concerns throughout his exemplary philosophical career.

the assumptions of traditional realism

Dewey's realism was influenced, in turn, by that other great American pragmatist, William James. James aspired to a kind of realism in philosophy that was free of the excesses of traditional forms of metaphysical realism.[4] This has made it difficult for philosophers to read James as a kind of realist at all. Toward the end of his life William James wrote a letter to a friend in which he bitterly complained of being misread.[5] James wrote that he never denied that our thoughts have to fit reality to count as true, as he was over and over again accused of doing. In the letter he employs the example of someone choosing how to describe some beans that have been cast on a table. The beans can be described in an almost endless variety of ways depending on the interests of the describer, and each of the right descriptions will *fit* the beans-minus-the-describer and yet also reflect the interests of the describer. And James asks, Why should not any such description be called true? James insists that there is no such thing as a description that reflects no particular interest at all. And he further insists that the descriptions we give when our interests are not theoretical or explanatory can be just as *true* as the ones we give when our interests are "intellectual." "And for this," James wrote "we are accused of denying the beans, or denying being in any way constrained by them! It's too silly!"[6]

A traditional realist philosopher might reply to James as follows: "If that is *all* you are saying, then I do not see that any of your fulminations against philosophers who believe in a 'ready-made world' are in order. And if you have been misunderstood, it is your own rhetoric that is at fault. The

Scholastic realists had the matter just right in their rejoinders to their nominalist opponents," my imaginary traditional realist might continue. "Suppose you decide to classify the beans by color, or by whether they are next to a bean of the same size, or in any other way. The reason that such a classification is possible, and can be extended to other similar collections of beans in the future, is that there are such *properties* as colors, sizes, adjacency, etc. Your beloved 'interests' may determine which combinations of properties you regard as worth talking about, or even lead you to invent a name for things with a particular combination of properties if there is no such name already in the language, but it does not change the world in the slightest. The world is as it is independently of the interests of any describer."

As will become clear, I do not, myself, side completely with James, nor do I side completely with his traditional realist critic. I agree with the critic that the world is as it is independently of the interests of describers.[7] James's suggestion that the world we know is to an indeterminate extent the product of our own minds is one I deplore.[8] But the traditional realist's way of putting what is wrong with James's position involves a metaphysical fantasy.

The metaphysical fantasy is that there is a totality of Forms, or Universals, or "properties," fixed once and for all, and that every possible meaning of a word corresponds to one of these Forms or Universals or properties. The structure of all possible thoughts is fixed in advance — fixed by the Forms. James rightly rejected this picture — but his recoil from its metaphysical excess drove him to question the independence of the world, which in turn caused his opponents to recoil either back to this picture or to the differently extravagant picture proposed by James's Absolute Idealist opponents.

One problem with the traditional view is its naïveté about meaning. One tends to think that the meaning of a word is a property shared by all the things denoted by the word. Now, there is indeed a property that all instances of pure gold have in common, namely consisting of (a mixture of isotopes of) the element with atomic number 79, but the English word *gold* is not synonymous with "element with atomic number 79." Indeed, the ordinary meaning of the word *gold* cannot be expressed as a property or a conjunction of properties at all.[9] As Wittgenstein pointed out, there are many words we can use perfectly well — one example, which has become famous, was the word *game*—although there is no one property common to all the things to which the word correctly applies.

Another problem with this traditional sort of realism is the comfortable assumption that there is one definite totality of objects that can be classified and one definite totality of all properties.[10] These two problems are related. It is true that a knowledge claim is responsible to reality, and, in most cases, that means a reality independent of the speaker. But reflection on human experience suggests that neither the form of all knowledge claims nor the ways in which they are responsible to reality is fixed once and for all in advance, contrary to the assumptions of the traditional realist.

Traditional forms of realism are committed to the claim that it makes sense to speak of a fixed totality of all "objects" that our propositions can be about. We can speak about wars, but is the Second World War an *object*? According to Donald Davidson, events are objects, and so the answer is "yes," but few traditional metaphysicians would have included events as objects. And the criteria for identity of these objects are obscure indeed.[11] We can speak about the color of the sky, but is the sky an *object*? We can speak about mirror images, but are mirror images *objects*? We can speak of "objects of desire," such as the novel I wish I had written; are such "intentional objects" really objects? And the list goes on and on . . . Indeed, what these examples suggest is that the widely held view (among analytic philosophers) that whenever I use the words *all, some, there are, there aren't any* (the so-called quantifiers) in such phrases as "all numbers," "there are some mirror images," "all of the characters in *Moby Dick*," and I am not prepared to provide a "translation" of the offending phrases into the preferred vocabulary of spatiotemporal objects and sets, I have "committed myself" to the existence of some objects (possibly "abstract" ones) is radically misguided.[12]

In fact, problems start even before we consider such problematic "objects" as wars, the sky, or mirror images. One ancient criterion for being a single object is that the parts of a single object move with the object when the object is moved. But I have a lamp in my house that violates *that* criterion. The shade falls off whenever the lamp is moved! Is the lamp then not an object? Although it was not the motive for the original invention of what philosophers call "mereological sums," that is, objects that have arbitrary objects as parts, it may seem that that invention does make sure that the totality of "objects" is large enough to handle such cases as my lamp. If the "sum" of *any* two (or more) objects is an object, if there is even an "object" consisting of my left ear and your nose, then it is *guaranteed* that there is such an object as the mereological sum of the body of the lamp (and the bulb) and the shade. But the metaphysical price is high![13]

Some philosophers may not care about such examples as the sky or mirror images, because they may be prepared to say that these things don't really exist (but is describing the color of the sky just making a false claim, then?); but they will say that all scientifically important objects can be identified with mereological sums of molecules—and ultimately particles. But here they fail to remember that the particles of modern physics are not little billiard balls and thus miss the fact that yet another extension of the notion of "object"—in fact, the most radical extension to date—has taken place within physics itself.

The reason that quantum mechanical "particles" are not objects in the traditional sense is that in contemporary quantum mechanics particles have no definite number at all! (in most "states"). But traditional objects always have definite number. This means that if our familiar tables and chairs (and my lamp) are mereological sums it cannot be quantum mechanical particles that they are mereological sums *of*. And the logical properties of quantum mechanical "fields" are equally bizarre. (Incidentally, adopting an ontology of spacetime points is no panacea for these problems; for the problems posed by quantum mechanical "superpositions of states" affect spacetime itself, not just its "material content.") Thus quantum mechanics is a wonderful example of how with the development of knowledge our idea of what counts as even a *possible* knowledge claim, our idea of what counts as even a *possible* object, and our idea of what counts as even a *possible* property are all subject to change.[14] The traditional realist assumes that general names just correspond more or less one-to-one to various "properties" of "objects" in some sense of "property" and some sense of "object" that is fixed once and for all, and that knowledge claims are simply claims about the distribution of these "properties" over these "objects."

The traditional metaphysician is perfectly right to insist on the independence of reality and our cognitive responsibility to do justice to whatever we describe; but the traditional picture of a reality that dictates the totality of possible descriptions once and for all preserves *those* insights at the cost of losing the *real* insight in James's pragmatism, the insight that "description" is never a mere copying and that we constantly add to the ways in which language can be responsible to reality. And this is the insight we must not throw away in our haste to recoil from James's unwise talk of our (partly) "making up" the world.

But, in the light of my criticisms, might it not be suggested that even my employment of the term *reality* is misleading and a potential source of philosophical puzzlement? It is of course true that such general terms as *reality*, *reason* (and one might add *language, meaning, reference* . . .) are sources of deep philosophical puzzlement. Yet the solution is not simply to jettison these words. The notion that our words and life are constrained by a reality not of our own invention plays a deep role in our lives and is to be respected. The source of the puzzlement lies in the common philosophical error of supposing that the term *reality* must refer to a single superthing instead of looking at the ways in which we endlessly renegotiate—and are *forced* to renegotiate—our notion of reality as our language and our life develop. Similar remarks apply to the other terms just listed.[15]

why has realism become a problem?

Let us now ask just why realism about "the external world" came to seem problematical. Early modern philosophers assumed that the immediate objects of perception were mental, and that mental objects were nonphysical.[16] What is more, even their materialist opponents often put forward accounts of perception that closely paralleled these "Cartesian" accounts.[17] Even in contemporary cognitive science, for example, it is the fashion to hypothesize the existence of "representations" in the cerebral computer. If one assumes that the mind is an *organ*, and one goes on to identify the mind with the brain, it will then become irresistible to (1) think of some of the "representations" as analogous to the classical theorist's "impressions" (the cerebral computer, or mind, makes *inferences* from at least some of the "representations," the outputs of the perceptual processes, just as the mind makes inferences from impressions, on the classical story) and (2) to think that those "representations" are linked to objects in the organism's environment only causally, and not cognitively (just as impressions were linked to "external objects" only causally, and not cognitively).[18]

In his 1991 John Locke Lectures[19] John McDowell argues persuasively that this picture, whether in its classical version or in its modern materialist version, is disastrous for just about every part of metaphysics and epistemology. In McDowell's view the key assumption responsible for the disaster is the idea that there has to be an interface between our cognitive powers and the external world—or, to put the same point differently, the idea that our cognitive powers cannot reach all the way to the objects themselves.

Accounts of perception that reject this claim are conventionally referred to as "direct realist" accounts (although this is certainly an unhappy name).[20] But there is less to some versions of direct realism than meets the eye. Sometimes the term is applied to any position that denies that the objects of "veridical" perception are sense data. Such a usage makes it much too easy to be a direct realist. All one has to do to be a direct realist (in *this* sense) about visual experience, for example, is to say, "We don't *perceive* visual experiences, we *have* them." A simple linguistic reform, and, *Voila!* one is a direct realist.[21]

To avoid the suggestion that philosophical progress is so easily achieved, it may be helpful to distinguish between what is commonly called "direct realism" and what I shall call from now on "natural realism." (I take the label from William James's expressed desire for a view of perception that does justice to the "natural realism of the common man.") A natural realist, in my sense, does hold that the objects of (normal "veridical") perception are "external" things, and, more generally, aspects of "external" reality.[22] But the philosopher whose direct realism is just the old causal theory of perception with a bit of linguistic cover-up can easily go along. "We perceive external things—that is to say, we are caused to have certain subjective experiences in the appropriate way by those external things," such a philosopher can say. The natural realist, in William James's sense, holds, in contrast, that successful perception is a *sensing* of aspects of the reality "out there" and not a mere affectation of a person's subjectivity by those aspects.[23] I agree with James, as well as with McDowell, that the false belief that perception *must* be so analyzed is at the root of all the problems with the view of perception that, in one form or another, has dominated Western philosophy since the seventeenth century. James's idea is that the traditional claim that we must conceive of our sensory experiences as *intermediaries* between us and the world has no sound arguments to support it and, worse, makes it impossible to see how persons can be in genuine cognitive contact with a world at all.[24]

The tendency in the last thirty years to repress what continues to puzzle us in the philosophy of perception obstructs the possibility of progress with respect to the broader epistemological and metaphysical issues that do preoccupy us. To illustrate how severe this repression presently is, let me offer an anecdote. Shortly after I began writing these lectures in the Berkshires, I went to the excellent bookstore on Water Street in Williamstown and looked at the collection of philosophy books on display there. What I wanted to see was what was available about *perception*. Although Wittgenstein was well represented, and Ayer (and not just *Language, Truth, and Logic*), and such contemporaries as Colin McGinn and Peter Unger, there was not a single book by John Austin—the philosopher whose *Sense and Sensibilia* represents the most powerful defense of what I am calling "natural realism" in the history of philosophy. Nor (apart from Wittgenstein, whose concern with these issues is underappreciated, even if his work as a whole is not) was there any other work by a natural realist, nor, for that matter, was there a single book devoted to perception as a topic (although the topic, of course, "comes up"—usually in a very naive way—in works about "cognitive science").

It was not always so. At the turn of the century the question of direct realism was a burning one. Not only William James, but the American New Realists and, in different ways, Moore and Russell were deeply exercised by it for a time. But after the mid-1930s the traditional conception of perception as requiring an interface between the perceiver and the "material objects" once again became coercive.[25] This conception was subjected to a further round of scathing criticism in Austin's *Sense and Sensibilia* (published posthumously after Austin's death in 1960) and, in a much less satisfactory way, in Gilbert Ryle's *The Concept of Mind*. But, perhaps because Austin was not

alive to explain and defend his views, Anglo-American philosophers responded to Austin and Ryle rather minimally. They stopped talking about "sense
data," of course, and spoke of "experiences" (or some such)—and they adopted the linguistic reform I described a moment ago. Even Peter Strawson, a
great philosopher who frequently shows a profound concern for these issues,
frequently mixes a genuine strain of natural realism with a wholly incompatible "causal theory of perception."[26] But, for the most part, philosophy of
perception became a nontopic for analytic philosophers. And, with the movement of interest away from phenomenology after the 1950s, it became, for the
most part, a nontopic for "continental" philosophers as well.

Why did I say that this has a great deal to do with the "realism issue" in the
philosophy of language? Just think: How could the question "how does language
hook on to the world?" even appear to pose a difficulty, unless the retort: "How
can there be a problem about talking about, say, houses and trees when we *see*
them all the time?" had not already been rejected in advance as question begging or "hopelessly naive." The "how does language hook on to the world" issue
is, at bottom, a replay of the old "how does perception hook on the the world"
issue. And is it any wonder if, after thirty years of virtually ignoring the task taken
up by my handful of philosophical heroes—the task of challenging the view of
perception that has been received since the seventeenth century—the very
idea that thought and language do connect with reality has come to seem more
and more problematical? Is it any wonder that one can't see how thought and
language hook on to the world if one never mentions perception?

the "antinomy of realism"
For approximately the first twenty-five years of my professional life as a
philosopher I shared with my contemporaries a conception of what the real
metaphysical and epistemological issues were and a conception of what (little) bearing the philosophy of perception had on those issues. However, in the
course of the past fifteen years I have come increasingly to appreciate the
degree to which our present view of what the live philosohical alternatives are
depends precisely on a very broad, if vague, consensus on the nature of perception. My strategy for the remainder of this lecture will be briefly to

describe how I came to this conclusion by offering a synopsis of my own intellectual history in the last twenty years, though I should confess that I have additional motives for engaging in this bit of intellectual autobiography. First, in philosophy, it is necessary to distinguish one's position from other positions, and I especially want to make clear what I am keeping from my own past positions and where I feel I went wrong in the "internal realism" that I have been defending in various lectures and publications over the last twenty years. Indeed, if I fail to do this, then my position in these lectures is bound to be badly misunderstood. Second, before I go on in the later lectures to sketch a direction in which I think a solution to the philosophical problems I shall be discussing here lies, I want in this first lecture to try to bring out what I take the problems themselves to be. What I want to lead up to, therefore, is not a just a description of my previous views but a depiction of the philosophical state of mind that led me to them. That state of mind was one in which the whole realism problem came to look to me like one giant antinomy of reason. It is that view of the realism problem that I want to draw you into now. In doing this, I know that I will be going against the grain for many of you. Many philosophers want to dismiss traditional problems in the philosophy of perception as if too much time had already been wasted on them and as if we were simply beyond them now. (To such philosophers what I am calling for will seem a reinfantilization of philosophy.) Many philosophers today are utterly comfortable either with a dogmatic realist view or with an equally dogmatic antirealist view. I believe that progress with respect to these problems will only come when we appreciate how each of these views is equally unsatisfactory, each is made in the mirror image of the other, and each depends on the idea that the other is the only alternative. Indeed, I believe that *deep* philosophy always begins with an appreciation of difficulties that appear to preclude *any* path to clarity, with the sense of paradox, and the best way I know to convey that sense of paradox in the case of the realism issue is to describe the way in which I came to experience it.

First of all, in the mid-1970s, when I wrote "Realism and Reason"[27] and "Models and Reality,"[28] my first two publications about the realism issue, I did not see that issue as closely involved with issues about perception, or with a particular set of assumptions about the powers of the human mind, and, if I had, I would not have been content with the appeals to what I called "verificationist semantics" in those essays. At that time I argued that our understanding of our language must consist in our mastery of its use. And I went on to say, "To speak as if *this* were my problem, I know how to use my language, but, now, how shall I single out an interpretation? is nonsense. Either the use of the language *already* fixes the 'interpretation' or *nothing* can."[29]

I still agree with those *words*. But I would say them in a rather different spirit now. The difference has to do with how one hears what is involved in an appeal to "use." The notion of use that I employed then was a "cognitive scientific" notion, that is, use was to be described largely in terms of computer programs in the brain. To be sure, even then I did not think it could be exhausted by reference to computer programs in the brain. For a variety of reasons that it would take too long to review now, I thought one would not only have to talk about the functional organization of the language user's brain but one would also have to specify the sort of environment in which the language user was embedded.[30] My picture of use was a portmanteau affair. There was the computer program in the brain and there was the description of the external causes of the language user's words.

But I later came to see that there is another, fundamentally different way to conceive of "use." On this alternative picture (which, as I have argued elsewhere, was that of the later Wittgenstein) the use of words in a language game cannot, in most cases, be described without employing the vocabulary of that game or a vocabulary internally related to the vocabulary of that game.[31] If one wants to describe the use of the sentence "There is a coffee table in front of me," one has to take for granted its internal relations to, among others, facts such as that one perceives coffee tables. By speaking of perceiving coffee tables, what I have in mind is not the minimal sense of "see" or "feel" (the sense in which one might be said to "see" or "feel" a coffee table even if one hadn't the faintest idea what a coffee table is), I mean the full achievement sense, the sense in which to see a coffee table is to see that it is a coffee table that is in front of one.

There is, of course, a sort of cultivated naïveté about the move I just ascribed to Wittgenstein—the Israeli philosopher, Avi Sagi, suggested to me that what I am advocating is "second naïveté," and I happily accept that description. The difference between the scientistic and the Wittgensteinian purport of the slogan "Meaning is use" is stark. Taken in the scientistic way, the slogan fits perfectly into the Cartesian cum materialist picture I described before: the "use" of language in this sense is something that can be described in terms of dispositions to respond to "mental representations." If I am right about where the appearance that "How can we so much as perceive things outside of our own bodies?" and "How can we so much as refer to things outside of our own bodies?" are deep problems comes from, then the slogan "Meaning is use" will not help one bit if one understands the notion of "use" in *that* way.

Of course, there are also problems if one understands the slogan in the way I attributed to Wittgenstein. (And the slogan should not really be "Meaning is use" but *Understanding is having the abilities that one exercises when and in using language*.) The difficulty will be in seeing how a deliberate move in the direction of "second naïveté" can possibly help after three centuries of modern philosophy, not to mention a century of brain science and now cognitive science. The problem for my philosophical "heroes" and myself is to *show the possibility* of a return to what James called natural realism.

To explain why I think such a return is called for, I will continue to recount my own former confusions in connection with these problems. I started seeing difficulties with realism—difficulties that depend on assumptions introduced into philosophy in the early modern period—a few years before I started to see any alternatives to that sort of realism. Before I wrote "Realism and Reason" and "Models and Reality," in particular, I did not see either how to defend realism or how there could be any *other* way of understanding the relation of language to reality. It seemed to me that I had become entangled in hopeless antinomies! (I subsequently became dissatisfied with my solution to the problem in those articles, but it was in those articles that I first came to appreciate the depth of the problem.)

One of the considerations that led me to see things in this way was the so-called Skolem Paradox in the philosophy of mathematics, the paradox that every consistent theory has an enormous number of different possible interpretations, even nonisomorphic interpretations.[32] Thus, the totality of truths about mathematical "objects" expressible in the language of mathematics cannot fix which objects we are referring to *even up to isomorphism*.[33]

I argued that by the use of the same tool Skolem used to prove the theorem that is now called the Skolem Löwenheim Theorem (or, alternatively, by the use of other theorems from the same branch of logic, the branch called "model theory"), one could prove similar results about *any* language, including everyday language or the language we use in empirical science.[34] My thought was that Skolem's argument (and the other "model theoretic" arguments) still goes through if one adds constraints to the admissible interpretations specifying that certain predicates must apply to certain objects whenever the "inputs" to the neural computer (say, the outputs of the "perception modules") are of a specified kind. For obvious reasons, I called these constraints "operational constraints." To be sure, such operational constraints restrict the permitted interpretation of predicates pertaining to the "perceptual inputs" themselves; but all other predicates in the language excepting only those explicitly definable by means of the operationally constrained predicates will still have a huge multiplicity of unintended interpretations, including quite bizarre ones.[35]

The reason I thought this posed a problem is that on the "Cartesian cum materialist" philosophy of perception (as well as on the Cartesian dualist conception, of course) the perceptual inputs are the outer limit of our cognitive processing; everything that lies beyond those inputs is connected to our mental processes only causally, not cognitively. Even if one puts the "inputs" as far out as the surface of our body (as Quine does with his talk of "surface neurons" and "surface irritations"), everything outside our skin is also outside our cognitive processing. But what my "model theoretic argument" showed was that interpretations of our language—even ones that make true the very sentences that are "really true," true from a "God's eye view" (assuming, as realism traditionally does, that the notion of a God's eye view makes sense)—can agree on what those inputs are while disagreeing wildly on what our terms actually refer to. Thus I concluded that if the sort of realism we have been familiar with since the early modern period, including the causal theory of perception, is right, then everything that happens *within* the sphere of cognition leaves the objective reference of our terms, for the most part, almost wholly undetermined.

This argument occured to me two or three years before my first two "anti-realist" publications. At the same time, I argued, "Either the use of the language *already* fixes the 'interpretation' [of our words] or *nothing* can." A world that interprets our words for us, a world in which there are, as it were, "noetic rays" stretching from the outside into our heads (remember, I still thought of the mind as a thing, and, hence saw no recourse but just to identify it with the brain) is a magical world, a fantasy world. I could not see how the fantasy even made sense, but at that point I also did not see how reference was possible unless the fantasy made sense. Hence my feeling that I was confronted by a genuine antinomy. My early formulations of internal realism were an unsatisfactory attempt to resolve that antinomy.

"internal realism"

In 1975–76 the work of Michael Dummett, a philosopher who has done an enormous amount to bring issues about realism back into the center of philosophical attention, suggested what I thought was a "way out" of the antinomy. In the publications I mentioned I called that way out—that is, the idea that our understanding of our language consists in our mastery of such skills as the ability to assign degrees of confirmation to sentences—"verificationist semantics."[36] But the publications I mentioned did not explain what I proposed to do about the notion of *truth*. That was saved for *Reason, Truth, and History*. There I proposed to identify being true not with being verified, as Michael Dummett does, but with being verified to a sufficient degree to warrant acceptance under sufficiently good epistemic conditions.[37]

Although this early version of "internal realism" was inspired by the position Dummett calls "global antirealism,"[38] it had two major differences from that position. Unlike Dummett's "global antirealist," I did not suppose that empirical propositions could be *unalterably* verified or falsified.[39] And I was bothered from the start by the excessively "idealist" thrust of Dummett's position, as represented, for example, by Dummett's flirtation with strong antirealism with respect to the *past*, and I avoided that strong antirealism by identifying a speaker's grasp of the meaning of a statement not with an ability to tell whether the statement is true now, or to tell whether it is true under circumstances the speaker can actually bring about, as Dummett does, but with the speaker's possession of abilities that would enable a sufficiently rational speaker to decide if the statement is true in sufficiently good epistemic circumstances.

To the objection that this is still an idealist position I replied that it certainly is not, on the ground that while the degree of confirmation speakers actually assign to a sentence may simply be a function of their sensory experiences (note that I still had the standard—i.e., the early modern—conception of sensory experiences!), the notion of *sufficiently good epistemic circumstances* is a "world involving" notion.[40] That is why the totality of actual human sense experiences does not, on this position, determine the totality of truths, even in the long run.

But the "antinomy" was still there, just under the surface. If, on the picture we have inherited from early modern philosophy, there is a problem about how, without postulating some form of magic, we can have referential access to external things, there is an equal problem as to how we can have referential or other access to "sufficiently good epistemic situations." On my alternative picture (as opposed to Dummett's) the world was allowed to determine whether I actually am in a sufficiently good epistemic situation or whether I only seem to myself to be in one—thus retaining an important idea from commonsense realism—but the conception of an epistemic situation was, at bottom, just the traditional epistemological one. My picture still retained the basic premise of an interface between the knower and everything "outside." But while the need for a "third way" besides early modern realism and Dummettian idealism is something I feel as strongly as ever, such a third way must, as McDowell has repeatedly urged, *undercut* the idea that there is an antinomy and not simply paste together elements of early modern realism and elements of the idealist picture. No conception that retains anything like the traditional notion of sense data can provide a way out; such a conception must always, in the end, leave us confronted by what looks like an insoluble problem.[41]

where i went astray

That I was still assuming something like the sense datum picture can be seen from remarks I made in the course of offering a brief characterization of functionalism in *Reason, Truth, and History* (pp. 78–82). Having explained that a "functionalist," in my sense, identifies mental properties with computational properties of the brain, I wrote,

> Today I am still inclined to think that that theory is right; or at least that it is the right *naturalistic* description of the mind/body relation. There are other, "mentalistic" descriptions of this relation which are also correct . . . (indeed the notions of "rationality," "truth," and "reference" *belong* to such a mentalistic version). I am, however, attracted to the idea that *one* right version is a naturalistic version in which thought-forms, images, sensations, etc., are functionally characterized physical occurrences. (p. 79)

In the discussion that follows the passage just cited from *Reason, Truth, and History* I also explained that in my view sensations have a 'qualitative' aspect that cannot be characterized functionally, and that aspect was to be identified with some physically characterized aspect of our brain functioning.[42]

It is not that I was unaware of the possibility of taking perception as being perception of things rather than "sense data." For example, I considered such a possibility in the course of discussing "operational constraints" on the interpretation of our language. But that possibility, though mentioned, remained largely unexplored. The emphasis in that paper is primarily on the possibility of retreating to a conception in which we perceive only our own sense data. The reason is not hard to find: my picture of our mental functioning was just the "Cartesian cum materialist" picture, a picture on which it has to seem magical that we can have access to anything outside our "inputs"—those "qualia" that I thought could be identified with "physical occurrences."[43] To the extent that I was aware of something that could be called "direct realism," the direct realism that I was aware of was only the superficial linguistic reform that does nothing except to make a verbal modification in the way the traditional picture is presented. If one holds that traditional picture fixed, as I did, then the verbal modification (the modification that consists in allowing that we can *say* we "observe" external things, but which of course must be *understood* as meaning that those things cause us to have certain "qualia" and that they do so "in the appropriate way") seems, at bottom, just a way of hiding a problem, the problem of how even our perceptions can be determinately of particular external things, a problem I saw myself as "uncovering" when I pointed out that we could take the operational constraints on the interpretation of our language to refer just to our sense data.

The alternative to the early modern picture that I have begun to lay out today does not involve "feigning anesthesia."[44] It does not involve denying, as Daniel Dennett sometimes seems to do, that phenomenal consciousness, subjective experience with all its sensuous richness, exists.[45] It involves, instead, insisting that "external" things, cabbages and kings, can be *experienced*. (And not just in the Pickwickian sense of *causing* "experiences," conceived as affectations of our subjectivity, which is what qualia are conceived to be.) In my next lecture I shall try further to convince you that that alternative is necessary and feasible.[46]

In my next lecture I shall also have to consider the objection that there is something "unscientific" — in the sense of *antiscientific* — about natural realism, the illusion that we have labored under since the beginning of the seventeenth century, that the mathematization of nature *forces* the traditional view of perception upon us. Seeing that there is no conflict between natural realism and science, and no conflict between a suitably commonsensical realism about our conceptual powers and science, will require us to return to the discussion of the other traditional realist assumptions that I mentioned at the beginning of this lecture, the persistent assumptions that the form of all knowledge claims and the ways in which they are responsible to reality are fixed once and for all in advance.

the importance of being austin: the need for a "second naïveté"

The metaphysics of realism traditionally included the idea that there was a definite totality of all objects (in a sense of "object" that was imagined to have been fixed, at least in philosophy, once and for all) and a definite totality of all "properties."[1] A general name referred to objects that have some property in common. This picture is by no means a mere item in the dustbin of history; it underlies, for example, the theory of reference very recently advanced by Jerry Fodor, according to which all words (even the word *witch*) correspond to "properties," and there are "laws" connecting those properties with the use of the corresponding words. In a variant that shows a slight influence of nominalism, properties are foresworn in favor of classes. For example, David Lewis believes that at least the basic cases of reference involve what he has called "elite classes" or "natural classes," classes of objects not only in the actual world but in other "possible worlds" as well that are singled out by reality itself.[2] These classes of things in different possible worlds are clearly just Lewis's substitute for the older "properties." Since knowledge claims are claims about the distribution of properties over the objects, and logical functions (negations, disjunctions, conjunctions, and multiple generalizations) of such claims, it follows, on this picture, that there is a definite totality of all possible knowledge claims, likewise fixed once and for all independently of language users or thinkers. The nature of the language users or the thinkers can determine which of the possible knowledge claims they are able to think or verbalize but not what the possible knowledge claims are.

The epistemology that goes with this position most commonly involves a causal theory of perception. On that theory the objects we perceive give rise to chains of events that include stimulations of our sense organs, and finally to "sense data" in our minds.[3] In materialist versions of the theory "sense data" are assumed to be identical with physical events in our brains; in recent variations on the materialist theme inspired by cognitive science, these events in our brains are said to be a subset of the "mental representations" or to be the outputs of certain "modules," etc.

Before the seventeenth century the dominant account of perception was Aristotle's (as interpreted by Aquinas and other Scholastic philosophers).[4] That account had strong (if puzzlingly stated) elements of direct realism. For example, in book 3 of *De Anima* Aristotle writes that the "thinking part of the soul, while impassible, must be capable of receiving the form of an object; that is, must be potentially the same as its object without being the object."[5] For Aristotle, the form of a perceptible may be a perceptible property, for example "hot" or its privation, "cold," the form of a bronze sphere may be its shape, the form of a human being may be rational animality. And we are puzzled by Aristotle's theory because we don't understand in what sense the mind "becomes" hot or cold (even "potentially" if not actually hot or cold) when it perceives something hot or cold, or in what sense the mind becomes "potentially" spherical when it perceives a bronze sphere or becomes "potentially" a particular rational animal when it perceives a man. But the thrust of Aristotle's doctrine is clear: what we perceive is the external warmth and coldness, the external shape, the intelligence and the animality of the person with whom we are talking, etc. The idea that we only experience events inside ourselves, events whose only relation to the warmth and the coldness, the shape, the intelligence, and the animality is that they are *caused* by them, is wholly foreign to this older way of thinking. Only after Berkeley and Hume has this come to seem the only *possible* way to think.[6]

Just *why* this became regarded as the only possible way to think is a difficult question. On the empiricist side, the new psychology of the "association of ideas" undoubtedly played a role.[7] On Descartes's side, there was also a reaction against the Aristotelian tradition precisely on account of that tradition's emphasis on perception and Descartes's own need to allay his skceptical worries by minimizing the role of perception in knowledge.[8] Indeed, the rise of a concern with scepticism among both empiricists and rationalists is a feature of the age. But one factor that has been repeatedly advanced as at least a part of the explanation is the new *mathematization of nature*.[9] For the first time "nature" in the modern sense (*that* sense hardly existed before the seventeenth century) became conceived of as the realm of mathematical law, of relations expressible *more geometrico*—soon to become: of relations expressible by means of algebra and calculus. Color and warmth seemed to have no place in such a conception of nature and were banished to the status of mere subjective affections of the mind (or, in the case of La Mettrie and perhaps of Hobbes, the brain).[10] The idea that the description of nature by means of mathematical formulas leaves us with no option but to say that our everyday descriptions of things cannot possibly apply to the things "as they are in themselves" was soon to become coercive.

Early modern realism's philosophy of mind was an attempt to save some room for our everyday descriptions while fully accepting that idea. According to this new philosophy of mind, our "experience" is entirely a matter taking place within the mind (or within the brain), within, that is to say, a realm conceived of as "inside," a realm where there are certainly no tables and chairs or cabbages or kings, a realm so disjoint from what came to be called the "external" world that (as Berkeley insisted) it makes no sense to speak of any experience as *resembling* what the experience is "of."[11] Nevertheless, according to those philosophers who were not willing to follow Berkeley into idealism, "external" things are the *causes* of our "inner" experiences, and, while the person on the street is mistaken in thinking that he or she "directly perceives" those things, still, we "indirectly perceive" them in the sense of having experiences caused by them. Moreover, even color and warmth and the other "secondary qualities" (as they came to be called) can be granted a derivative sort of reality—they do not exist as "intrinsic properties" of the things "in themselves," but they exist as "relational properties," as dispositions to affect our minds (or brains) in certain ways.

In the last lecture I argued that this philosophy of perception makes it impossible to see how we can so much as *refer* to "external" things. And I argued that we need to revive direct realism (or, as I prefer to call it, natural realism)—more precisely, we need to revive the spirit of the older view, though without the metaphysical baggage (e.g., the mind "becoming" its objects, though only "potentially," or the mind taking on the "form" of the object perceived "without its matter"). I mentioned William James as the first modern philosopher to unambiguously call for such an account of perception and I listed Edmund Husserl, Ludwig Wittgenstein, and John Austin as among those who shared James's sense that progress in philosophy requires a recovery of the "natural realism of the common man."

austin versus the traditional refutation of "naive realism"

But is natural realism so much as a tenable position? Have not the arguments rehearsed by epistemologists from the seventeenth century to Russell's *The Problems of Philosophy* and after effectively blocked the possibility of any revival of what I was taught in college to call "naive realism"? Even to rehearse briefly the diagnoses and discussions of all four of these philosophers would take a series of lectures much longer than these. Moreover, in spite of their striking partial convergence with respect to the philosophy of perception, in other respects their broader philosophical programs are remarkably different. James's discussion[12] is set in the context of a grand metaphysics of "pure experience"; Husserl's discussion[13] is set in the context of the grand project of a pure phenomenology (and includes the important idea that the "primary qualities" of physics are not a set of "properties" that we have discovered things to have but a set of *idealized abstractions*);[14] Austin's discussion is set in the context of an ambitious project of trying to convince the philosophical world of the importance of a close examination of the ways in which concepts are deployed in ordinary language (as well as in philosophy); and Wittgenstein's discussion is set in the context of a profound reflection on the nature and source of philosophical perplexity. Moreover, the parallelism between Wittgenstein's thought and that of the three others has been largely missed, because the celebrated Private Language Argument (which, in my view, is scattered through most of part 1 of *Philosophical Investigations*), while deeply relevant to our subject, was misread, first as a defense of some version of behaviorism and later[15] as a denial that our knowledge claims are responsible to any reality external to communal approval or sanction—a swamp of misreadings too wide and boggy to wade through at this moment without losing our thread completely. The topic of how to interpret Wittgenstein on these matters is one that I shall come back to in the third of these lectures.[16] I will therefore restrict myself here to saying a few words about one or two of John Austin's arguments. I pick Austin because, of the four philosophers I just listed, he is the one who most carefully replies to each of the traditional (i.e., the early modern) arguments against naive realism. Indeed, *Sense and Sensibilia* is one of the most unjustly neglected classics of analytic philosophy, and I strongly urge all of you to read or reread it with care.

As Austin points out, one strategy used by the early modern epistemologists, and followed in the present century by Russell, Ayer, Price, etc., was to begin by "establishing" that there are "visual experiences" ("auditory experiences," "tactile experiences," etc.) that are not "veridical." For Descartes, dreams were an especially compelling example.

Descartes's choice of dreams was, in a way, a happy one for his purpose. For the examples, abundant as they are in epistemological writing (including Descartes's own), of ordinary illusions (the stick in water that looks bent but is straight, the mirror image that is mistaken for the object itself, etc.) are much less convincing as proofs that "what we observe is, at least some of the time, mental." Such examples do show that perception is not infallible; but the inference from "perception is not infallible; therefore it cannot be direct" is a peculiar one, and clearly needs premises that are going to be problematic. I am, after all, perceiving something "out there" when I see a stick in water (and even when I see a mirror image); it is just that it looks like something else, and that is why I take it *for* something else. If we did not have the experience of dreaming, hallucination should also seem a problematic example of the "perception of something mental"; most of us, thank God, never experience a hallucination. And, if it were not that we all dream, I wonder what we would *make* of people who hallucinate? Someone who obviously does not have a dagger in front of him says, "Is this a dagger I see before me, the handle toward my hand?"This is bizarre enough behavior, but would it, of itself, even suggest the notion of perceiving "sense data"?

However, we all do dream, and when our dreams are vivid and realistic enough they give us a paradigm of an experience in which it is *as if* we were seeing or hearing or feeling something or other when nothing of that kind is physically present for us to see or hear or feel. It is true, as Austin emphasizes, that dreams are normally not "just like" our daily perceptual experiences, and not just because the dream events are (usually) "incoherent"; as a rule, the very phenomenology of dream experience is somehow different, and when we say that some experience is "like a dream," or that our state of mind on some occasion is "dreamlike," we are saying that that experience or that state of mind is somehow *different* from a normal perceptual experience or a normal state of mind; different in a way that reminds us of the "quality" of a dream.[17] Still, some dreams are much less "dreamlike" than others, and we sometimes are confused for a moment on awakening as to whether we are still dreaming. If someone claimed to have had a dream that was "so real that it was exactly like being in such and such a place," we could not, after all, dismiss his description a priori. And these considerations are not just considerations that move philosophers; the question "Is it all a dream?" is an old one, and has fascinated artists too. Calderon's great line "La vida es sueño y sueño de un sueño" is one that almost every Spanish speaker has known for centuries.

But let us suppose that someone, call her Helen, does have the (perhaps impossible, but let us assume it is possible) experience of having a dream that is so real it is exactly like being in a place — but a place that person has never been, say, in front of the Taj Mahal. The traditional sense datum epistemologist argues thus: "Helen is certainly experiencing *something*; what she is experiencing is certainly not the Taj Mahal (that is thousands of miles away) or indeed any physical object (her eyes are closed, and the pillow is over her head); therefore, what she is experiencing is something mental. So the immediate object of a perception is, at least *some* of the time, something mental."[18]

Next let us imagine that a year later Helen has "exactly the same visual experience" but is actually in India and looking at the Taj Mahal. "We agreed that what Helen was immediately perceiving when she dreamt was something mental," the traditional sense datum epistemologist continues. "Is it not implausible, to say the least, that things as different in nature as a physical building and a mental sense datum could seem exactly alike? Should we not conclude that on the second occasion too she was immediately perceiving sense data, mental entities, indeed sense data exactly like the ones she was aware of on the first occasion, but with the important difference that on the second occasion they were actually caused (in the appropriate way for a case of visual perception) by the Taj Mahal and on the first occasion they were not? On the second occasion she was indirectly perceiving the Taj Mahal and on the first occasion she was not even indirectly perceiving it, but what she immediately perceived on both occasions was her sense data."

Austin devotes a marvelous chapter of *Sense and Sensibilia* to pointing out all the things that are wrong with this "argument."[19] To begin with, there is the gratuitous assumption that the dreamer is perceiving *something*. If no physical objects are being perceived, then objects of some other sort must be being perceived (or "experienced"). Then there is the assumption that whatever is not physical must be "mental" (Russell and Moore questioned that one, while accepting pretty much the rest of the argument.) There is the strange use of "direct" and "indirect" (as if seeing an object that is right in front of one were really seeing its image on an inner television screen). Moreover, there is the assumption that waking and dreaming experiences are "qualitatively indistinguishable." And finally, even if one grants this latter assumption, there is the wholly unsupported claim that objects with radically different "natures" cannot *appear* exactly alike. In fact, both James and Austin argue that even if cases of dreaming, illusion, etc., *were* perceptions of something nonphysical, and the experience of someone who dreams *were* more or less exactly like a "veridical experience" of, say, Harvard's Memorial Hall (one of James's favorite examples), there is simply no argument that the object of the veridical experience cannot *be* Memorial Hall itself.[20]

a possible rejoinder

Originally, doctrines of sensory ideas or sense data were put forward as philosophically sophisticated descriptions of the phenomenology of ordinary perceptual experience. In this century, as they came increasingly under fire as *mis*descriptions of that experience, sense datum theory was sometimes invoked not as a mere description of experience but as the best available explanation of a variety of well-known facts about perception.[21] What I want to consider for a few minutes is whether—once we give up on the idea that such theories can be justified by reflection upon facts provided by mere introspection—we can really find in such theories any kind of explanation at all.

Consider a sense datum epistemologist who attempts the following rejoinder to Austin: "You are right that it is not *deductively* inconsistent to maintain that in some cases we immediately perceive parts and/or properties of material things and in other cases, e.g., dreaming, we perceive subjective things (call them 'sense data,' without prejudice to the question of their ultimate metaphysical nature).[22] But we sense datum epistemologists did not claim that our argument amounted to a *deductive* proof. Indeed, if you look at the very passages Austin cites from Ayer and Price, you will see that this strong claim is avoided. You yourself, in paraphrasing the argument, used the words 'implausible, to say the least,' which are not words one uses in a deductive argument."

(I pause to observe that once the sense datum epistemologist admits that the claim that we immediately perceive sense data and only sense data is less than deductively certain, the claim that our sense data are what we know about *noninferentially* is already abandoned. Room is left, to be sure, for "coherentist" versions of traditional epistemology, but hardly for the high foundationalist projects.)

"The problem with the position that James and Austin entertain as an alternative to ours," my imaginary spokesperson for sense datum epistemology continues, "is that it utterly fails to explain why it would so much as *seem* to the dreamer, say, Helen, in the case of your example, that she is actually seeing the Taj Mahal. Even if Austin is right, and the quality of the dream experience is not exactly the same as that of her later veridical experience, it is utterly unexplained why the quality of the two experiences should even seem *similar*. The hypothesis that in both cases the same (or at least similar) sense data are immediately perceived *explains* why the experiences are similar."

Notice how peculiar the suggested "explanation" is, however. Let us first consider its immaterialist version. It is not, after all, as if the "Cartesian" epistemologist had any mechanism to offer to explain just *how* events in the brain produce "sense data," or of how the mind "immediately observes" the postulated objects. Indeed, there was not even agreement among (immaterialist) sense datum epistemologists as to whether "sense data" were *parts* of individual minds (as in Hume's account), or somehow belonged to those minds without being parts of them (note the possessive case in Berkeley's talk of "spirits and *their* ideas"), or as to whether they were particulars or qualities (Nelson Goodman even thinks qualities *are* particulars),[23] or, in the twentieth century, as to whether the same sense datum could conceivably be "immediately perceived" by more than one mind, or even as to whether it was conceivable that some sense data could exist unperceived. As an "explanation" of the fact that when she dreamed it seemed to Helen as if she were actually perceiving the Taj Mahal, the immaterialist version of the sense datum theory is a nonstarter. The explanation begins with a familiar fact, the fact that when I am dreaming it seems to me as if I were seeing this or that, and offers an "explanation" in terms of utterly mysterious entities and processes—one that lacks all detail at just the crucial points and possesses no testability whatsoever. Such an "explanation" would not even be regarded as *intelligible* in serious natural science.[24] Of course, if the claim that "Helen had qualitatively identical sense data on the two occasions" is no more than philosophical newspeak for "It seemed to Helen when she dreamt as if she were seeing just what she later saw when she actually saw the Taj Mahal," then (apart from the problem as to whether a dream and actual seeing ever really are "qualitatively" indistinguishable) the claim is perfectly intelligible, but a mere restatement of a fact in a special jargon cannot claim to be an *explanation* of that fact.

the emptiness of "identity theory"

Although sense datum theory itself has fallen into disrepute, the assumptions that underlie it remain very much in vogue. These include the assumption that there is a self-standing realm of experiences or mental phenomena; that these phenomena take place in the mind/brain; that the locus of this drama is the human head; and, finally, that perception involves a special cognitive relation to certain of these "inner" experiences as well as the existence of "causal chains of the appropriate type" connecting them to "external" objects.

I have had occasion to remark more than once that Cartesianism cum materialism, a materialist version of modern realist metaphysics and episte-mology, goes back almost as far as Cartesianism itself (one thinks of Diderot and La Mettrie); however, the "identity theory," the theory that sensations and thoughts are just brain processes, did not become a truly major topic of dis-cussion until the second half of the twentieth century. The passage about the nature of "qualia" in my *Reason, Truth, and History* that I read to you last time was written when I still subscribed to this theory. Does the identity theory avoid the objections to the sense datum theory we just rehearsed?

If sense data ("qualia") are themselves brain events, rather than the imma-terial effects of brain events, then the problem of just how a material event in the brain is supposed to cause an immaterial event in the mind is certainly avoided. Whether the second of the problems I just mentioned, the problem as to how these qualia are supposed to be *observed*, that is to say, how we become *conscious* of them, is also avoided is more doubtful. In *The Modularity of Mind* Jerry Fodor calls the outputs of his hypothetical "per-ception modules" *appearances*. This assumes that when one of these hypo-thetical pattern recognizers produces "outputs" the event is ipso facto a con-scious event. But this is hard to swallow. If, for example, we say that the mod-ules for visual "appearances" are in the visual cortex, which is where they have been hypothesized to be, then we run up against the fact that parts of the visual cortex (say, the parts that service one side of the visual field) can be *dis-associated* from the "speech areas." Are we to say that in such a case—a case of "blind sight," or a case of a "split brain"—there are *visual sense data* (*"appearances"*) *of which the person is not aware*? And what would happen if our technology advanced to the point at which we could remove the "module" involved in the visual recognition of, say, chairs from the brain and keep it alive and functioning in a vat (in response to stimuli provided by a computer)? Would one then have "chair sense data" without any *person* to experience those sense data? If there can be "sense data" (or "appearances") in a small group of neurons, why should we not speak of the sense data of a *thermostat*? This way madness lies.

On the other hand, it will do no good to search the brain for a "grandmother neuron"—a point such that the messages from the visual cortex become *transformed* into sense data or qualia when they arrive *there*. Brains have speech centers, areas for different sorts of memory, etc., but not consciousness centers. (If there are doubts in your mind, the data beautifully laid out in Dennett's *Consciousness Explained* should convince you. It is, I suspect, just because consciousness and reference cannot be identified with a definite brain function [respectively, a definite physical relation] that Dennett is led to the denial of both subjective consciousness and objective reference—this is another instance of the phenomenon of "recoil" in philosophy, this time from Cartesian dualism all the way to "the absence of phenomenology.")

Thus the problem that the "immediate perception" of a sense datum is an utterly unexplained process still survives in the materialist version of the theory. But there is an even more serious problem with identity theory, I believe—namely, what "identity" is supposed to mean in this context.

Back in the 1950s a widely heard argument against identity theory was that sense data (the typical example was a visual sense datum of a homogeneous kind, say, the appearance of a large area of blue sky) and neural processes have a very different "grain"—neural processes are discontinuous, have many different parts of many different sorts, and the blue sky sense datum is utterly uniform and undifferentiated. It makes no sense, it was claimed, to say that things so different are "identical."[25]

This "grain argument" against identifying sense data (assuming their existence, for the sake of argument) with brain states was a bad argument but a good "intuition pump," for consideration of this argument leads us to pose the following question: What sort of "identity" are we talking about when we claim that a sense datum and a brain state are "identical"? If the identity is sui generis, and the "correlation" postulated by the theory of "psychophysical parallelism" is equally sui generis, then it is an illusion that "identity," on the one hand, and "parallelism," on the other, are mutually exclusive alternatives (it looks as if they come to the same thing in different words).

The two currently most popular proposals for making sense of the notion of identity required by the theory that sensory experiences are identical with brain processes are:

(1) The "identitity" is the identity of theoretical identification; and
(2) The "identity" is "anomalous token identity."

Let us briefly consider each of these alternatives.

(1) *The "identity" is the identity of theoretical identification* (compare: "Light is identical to electromagnetic radiation of a certain kind"). This is the alternative that I favored in *Reason, Truth, and History*.[26] There I distinguished between two notions of what I have just been calling "sense data" (there I referred to them as "qualia"): a functional notion (in this sense, to have a "blue sense datum" would be to have the sort of sense datum that one normally has when one sees something that is—by public standards—blue) and a "qualitative" notion (in this sense to have a "blue sense datum" would be to have a "quality" that I privately associate with the word "blue," one that may or may *not* be the one you associate with the word).[27] And I described myself as attracted to the view that sense data are simply states of the brain. On this view, when we group sense data together on the basis of their functional characteristics, we use the functional notion (so that, in this case, we are speaking of computationally characterized states of the brain), and when we group them together on the basis of what appear to us to be their qualitative properties, we are grouping them together on the basis of certain neurological characteristics (although, in ordinary use, that is not what it seems to us that we are doing).

This alternative presupposes (as do many versions of the identity theory), that terms for sense data (or qualia) belong to a scientific or potentially scientific theory that can be "reduced" to physics, or physics cum computer science, with the aid of such "theoretical identifications."

But it is not clear that there is a *theory* of sense data (in either sense). If we suppose that when people ordinarily talk about "seeing," "dreaming," etc., they are describing *sensations* (a term in everyday language whose use has been heavily influenced by modern philosophy), and we equate sensations in this sense with sense data, then we may be able to regard our everyday beliefs about seeing, dreaming, imagining, hallucinating, about something's "looking like" something else, etc., as a rude "theory" of sense data. But the separating out of this supposed special "qualitative" sense of *sense datum* seems more like a bit of fancy philosophical speculation than a part of a theory that is supposed to yield explanations and predictions. But let us, for a moment, grant the extremely questionable presupposition that it *can* somehow be made out that there is such a theory, and that the theory can be made continuous with the web of our ordinary psychological beliefs (otherwise it is hard to imagine what the "theory" could look like). Granting the presupposition, the question I now wish to consider is whether we can make sense of the putative "identity" in question with the aid of the notion of theoretical identification.

Now, the web of our ordinary psychological beliefs involves—indeed, it mainly consists of—intentional notions and propositional attitudes. (Example of a connection between "sensation" concepts and propositional attitudes: "When I have the visual experience of seeing a green field, I normally believe that I am seeing a green field.") Now, a claim to have "reduced" a notion in one science—say, the science of optics—to a notion in a different science— say, the science of physics—*via* a "theoretical identification" stands or falls with the possibility of showing that the approximate truth of the laws of the former science can be *derived* from the laws of the later science (the more "basic" one) with the aid of the proposed system of theoretical identifications, the system to which the proposed identification (say, "Light is electromagnetic radiation of such and such wavelengths") belongs.[28] To reduce the term *light*, for example, we have to also reduce talk of *shadows, penumbras, reflection, refraction,* etc. Similarly, if this model of "theoretical identification" applies to talk of sense data, then it must be possible to reduce the concepts that figure in laws involving sense data (i.e., laws involving *sensations*)—to reduce talk of a sensation's *seeming* to be of such and such, for example. If a term really functions as part of a theory, then to show that the term is reducible one has to reduce the theory. If intentional talk and "sense datum" talk are really as connected as intentional talk and ordinary language talk of what one sees and what one thinks one sees are connected, then success in the project of reducing qualia talk (if there really is a body of "qualia talk" to reduce) presupposes success in the project of reducing intentional talk to physical cum computational terms.

In recent years I have devoted a good deal of my writing to showing that that project is not the straightforward scientific project it might seem at first blush to be, but a chimera.[29] That project takes two forms. The simpler form involves identifying the intentionality of our thoughts (where these are conceived of as a sort of *inner writing*) simply with their *causal covariation* of what they are about, at least in basic cases. I believe that, in different publications, Barry Loewer and I have shown that the various attempts to spell this out are subject to disastrous counterexamples.[30] The more complex form was my own idea of "functionalism." This idea employed the notion of theoretical identity just explained, and involved seeking computational states that could be identified with our various propositional attitudes. In fact, at the beginning I hoped that the required notion of a computational state *had already been made precise by the preexisting formalisms for computation theory, e.g., the Turing formalism or the theory of automata.* When it became clear that the formal properties of these states are quite unlike the formal properties of psychological states,[31] the original idea of functionalism quickly was replaced by an appeal to the notion of an ideal "psychological theory." But this ideal psychological theory was conceived of as having just the properties that formalisms for computation theory possess.

A formalism for computation theory *implicitly defines* each and every computational state by the totality of its computational relations (e.g., relations of succession, or probabilistic succession) to all the other states of the given system. In other words, the whole set of computational states of a given system are *simultaneously implicitly defined*, and the implicit definition *individuates* each of the states, in the sense of distinguishing it from all other computational states. But no psychological theory individuates or "implicitly defines" its states in this sense. Thus, functionalism conceived of what it called an ideal psychological theory in a very strange way. No actual psychological theory has ever pretended to provide a set of laws that distinguish, say, the state of being jealous of Desdemona's fancied regard for Cassio from every other actual or possible propositional attitude. Yet this is precisely what the identification of that propositional attitude with a "computational state" would do. Thus functionalism brought to the study of the mind strong assumptions about what any truly scientific psychological theory must look like.

There is no reason to think that the idea of such a psychological theory (today such a theory is often referred to as "conceptual role semantics") is anything but utopian. There is no harm in speculating about scientific possibilities that we are not presently able to realize. But I came to see that the possibility of an ideal psychological theory of this sort is nothing more than a "we know not what." No one has the slightest idea as to how one might go about constructing such a theory. No one has any conception of what such a theory might look like. One hears a lot of talk about cognitive science nowadays, but one needs to distinguish between the putting forward of a scientific theory, or the flourishing of a scientific discipline with well-defined questions, and the proffering of promissory notes for possible theories that one does not even in principle know how to redeem. If I am right, the idea of a theoretical reduction in this case—the reduction of the entire body of psychology implicit in our ordinary practices of mental state attribution to physics cum computer science—is without any clear content. One cannot make the unexplained notion of "identity" of "sense data" with "functionally characterizes states of the brain" precise with the aid of the concept of the reduction of one theory to another if one has no idea of the nature of the theory *to which we are supposed to do the reducing* (and only a very problematic idea of *what theory we are supposed to reduce*).

This objection seems to me to be decisive if our notion of a sense datum is the supposed "functional" one. What of the supposed "qualitative" sense, the sense in which sense data are supposed to be directly physically characterized?

In this case we know what theory we are supposed to do the reducing *to*, namely, the physics and chemistry of the brain, but, once again, *what "the-*

ory" *are we supposed to reduce?* Consider, for the moment, just the assumed "visual sense data." If all we have to reduce are the relations among the colors, then there are many possibilities. Indeed, there are relations among processes in the *eye* that correspond to just about all the color relations we can detect,[32] and there are doubtless such relations among various processes in the visual cortex as well (Fodor's "perceptual modules"). But we would not identify sense data with processes in the eye, simply because one can have color sensations even after one has lost one's eyes. This suggests that the constraint on any account of "qualitative" sense data should include the fact that we are *conscious* of them: but how plausible is it that one should be able to reduce (hypothetical) "laws" involving the notion of *consciousness* without becoming involved in "reducing" the propositional attitudes? The concept of consciousness (certainly the concept of consciousness that is relevant for *epistemology*) is the concept of *availability to thought*. Once again, it seems that either we do not know what theory it is that we are speaking of "reducing" or else the theory includes a substantive portion of our talk of propositional attitudes. But these latter cannot be reduced to the physics and chemistry of the brain for a variety of reasons—among these, the now familiar "externalist" reasons: the dependence of the content of our propositional attitudes on what is outside the organism (but present in the organism's environment), the familiar variable realizability issues, etc.[33] In sum, the notions of "reduction of theories" and "theoretical identification" lack any real content in the present context.

(2) I now want to consider the other proposal for making sene of the notion of "identity" presupposed by mind/brain identity theory, namely: *The identity is Donald Davidson's "anomalous token identity."*[34] Theoretical identities, e.g., Light is electromagnetic radiation of such and such wavelengths, identify all events falling under one description (events of one "type") with events falling under another description (events of another "type"). Davidson believes that, as I just argued, there are no "type-type" identities to be found between events falling under a psychological description and events falling under a physical description, but he claims that, nevertheless, each individual event of someone's thinking so and so or experiencing such and such is

"identical" with some physical event.[35] In Davidson's jargon, each "token" mental event is identical with a "token" physical event.

Davidson's criterion for this sort of identity is *two events are the same if they have the same causes and the same effects.* But this criterion is hopelessly circular (as Quine has pointed out). Quine's point is that to tell whether "token event A" *has* the same effects (or causes) as "token event B" one has to know whether they are *identical* or not—Davidson's criterion is "viciously circular," Quine claimed.[36]

To see that Quine is right, imagine that we want to decide if the firing of a small group of neurons—one of Jerry Fodor's "modules"—is or is not "token identical" with an "experience of blue." The firing of the group of neurons will have a host of effects that we would not ordinarily think or speak of as effects of my experiencing blue; for example, the excitation of other neurons. If the experience of blue is identical with the firing of the group of neurons, then those other excitations are "effects of the experience of blue"; if, however, the experience of blue is identical with the activity of a larger part of the brain, including the other neurons in question, then those other excitation events will be *part* of the event that is "the experience of blue" and not *effects* of it. There is no way in which one can decide a group of excitation events is identical with "the experience of blue" by employing Davidson's criterion. We are left with a criterionless and sui generis sort of "identity."[37]

Much of the appeal of the identity theory has always had its source in the fear of being driven to the supposed opposite horn of a specious dilemma—the dilemma that either we must opt for some form of identity theory (or perhaps eliminative materialism) or else be forced back to the dark old days of dualism. But does abandoning "identity theory" commit us to a dualism? Not at all. The way out of the dilemma I would like to propose requires an appreciation of how sensory experiences are not passive affectations of an object called a "mind" but (for the most part) experiences of aspects of the world by a living being. Mind talk is not talk about an immaterial part of us but rather a way of describing the exercise of certain abilities we possess, abilities that supervene upon the activities of our brains and upon all our various transactions with the environment but that do not have to be reductively explained using the vocabulary of physics and biology, or even the vocabulary of computer science.[38] The metaphysical realignment I propose involves acquiescence in a plurality of conceptual resources, of different and not mutually reducible vocabularies (an acquiescence that is inevitable in practice, whatever our monist fantasies) coupled with a return not to dualism but to the "natural realism of the common man."

the arguments from perceptual relativity

The debate we just reviewed concerning the need to posit "sense data" centered on the argument from—as it was traditionally put—"the similarities between veridical and nonveridical experiences." But there is another strategy employed by traditional epistemologists from the seventeenth century to Russell's *The Problems of Philosophy* and after; the strategy of denying that most of the *properties* of external things we ordinarily think of ourselves as perceiving (in particular the so-called secondary qualities of color, texture, warmth, and coldness, etc.) are really "out there" to *be* perceived. From the (alleged) fact that these qualities are not "properties of the things as they are in themselves," it was traditionally concluded that they are "in the mind."[39] The first strategy—the strategy of identity theory—works from "inside out"; it argues against natural realism as an account of what is in our minds; the second strategy works from "outside in"; it argues against natural realism as an account of what is "out there." Both strategies, of course, flow from the background assumptions bequeathed to us by the metaphysical pictures of early modern realism (and its materialist and "neutral monist" variants).[40]

In the brief space remaining I cannot review the various natural realist rejoinders to this strategy in detail. However, let me first remind you of my earlier brief allusion to Husserl's important idea that the so-called primary qualities of physics are not a set of "properties" we have discovered things to have, but a set of *idealized abstractions*. When Husserl denies that the primary qualities are properties, he does not mean to deny that physical objects really have, say, mass and charge, but does mean to deny that the notion of a "perfectly precise mass" and a "perfectly precise charge" (or position, etc.) is more than a useful idealization. This claim of Husserl's fits well with the idea one finds already in James (which is enthusiastically adopted by Dewey),[41] that there is nothing "secondary" about such experienced attributes of things as color, but this is not a literature I can discuss here. A more contemporary treatment of the same issue can be found in Peter Strawson's "Perception and Its Objects," which speaks beautifully to this issue. Although I do not agree with absolutely everything Strawson says in it, its influence will be evident in the few remarks I shall make on this venerable issue.[42]

As I just remarked, the traditional dichotomy of primary and secondary qualities rested upon a metaphysical picture according to which the primary qualities represented the ways in which real things are in themselves, while the secondary properties represented the ways in which they affect the human sensorium. Secondary qualities were thus secondary in the sense that they were merely *apparent* properties of the real world. I have devoted much effort to attacking the assumptions that underlie this picture elsewhere.[43] Here I shall confine myself to making a few remarks about the case of color. According to the traditional picture, the things in front of me do not really have contrasting colors at all. But, if (as has been recognized since Berkeley) the arguments against the idea that things are colored in the way they seem to be also cut against the idea that they are *shaped* in the way they seem to be, *solid* in the way they seem to be, etc., then my description of the *data* for whatever scientific account of the world I may accept consists of a mass of *falsehoods*.[44] If traditional epistemology is right, science (and the epistemological sophistication that allegedly comes from science) *undercuts its own data*. But let us consider the argument against the idea that things are actually colored.

For me, the most memorable encounter with the argument dates back to my student days, when I first read Russell's *The Problems of Philosophy*. Russell points to the fact that the shaded parts of a table have a different look from the parts that are in glare, and concludes that the colors we see when we look at the table cannot be properties of the table in itself but can only be dispositions to produce certain sense data "under normal conditions." This account suggests that when a part of the table is viewed "under normal conditions" it will produce one definite sort of "color sense data."

But colors are more abstract than traditional writers on perception—including Russell—generally acknowledge. A color—say, the color of the roof of the house down the street—does not look the same in direct sunlight and in the shade, but neither condition is "abnormal." (If you were to rule out seeing objects in shade as not "seeing them under normal conditions," you would have to say that whenever I am inside a room—which is being out of direct sunlight, for the most part—I am seeing objects under "abnormal" conditions.) And the condition one might think of as ideal—seing an object in a room with a "good north light" set in the ceiling!—is surely a very rare and abnormal one (and colors looks somewhat different then than they do either in direct sunlight or in shadow). Every color has a number of different "looks."

If you like, you may say that the color is the potentiality of having those "looks" under those various conditions. And the "looks" themselves are certainly *relational* properties. But Russell himself succesfully polemicized against the long-standing tendency of metaphysicians to regard relational properties as *therefore* "mental." The relational nature of the looks of colors does not require us to say that the color is the potentiality of causing certain sense data in human beings, where "sense data" are conceived of as mere affectations of our subjectivity.[45] For that account would only help to explain the nature of colors (scientifically) if sense data themselves were better off, as scientific entities, than colors, or than talk of the "looks" of things. But, as we have seen, they certainly are not.

Is the situation, then, a "standoff" in the sense that it is equally metaphysically advantageous (1) to think of the looks of things as irreducible (though relational) aspects of reality that depend upon the way those things reflect light, the conditions under which they are viewed, etc., or (2) to think of the looks of things as dispositions to produce certain sense data, and to think of sense data as irreducible aspects of reality correlated to brain states? No, because colors and the looks of colors, thought of in the first way, are perfectly describable (public), and so are the empirical dependencies in question, while if they are thought of in the second way, all of the sceptical problems described in my first lecture inevitably arise.[46] Epistemologically, we have every reason to prefer an account under which our experiences are ab initio encounters with a public world.

The famous "inverted spectrum" puzzle can serve as an example here. The puzzle cannot be that someone who has a defect in his eyes or his optic nerves or a miswiring in his brain might see colors in a way different from the way they actually look (or the "way we normally see them," as it is misleadingly put sometimes). For such a defect could be discovered, and perhaps the best explanation of the patient's behavior might involve such a mis-seeing. But rather the puzzle is traditionally supposed to be that someone with normal eyesight, brain, optic nerve, etc., might have different "visual qualia"—and this supposed possibility depends entirely on the conception of the mental as a self-standing realm (sealed off within the head), a conception encouraged by the questionable assumptions drawn from the philosophy of perception that it has been my concern to combat here. If we adopt the natural realist account and reject the traditional modern realist account, then the supposed sceptical possibility seemingly forced on us by this puzzle does not arise. (This is, I think, a consequence of a proper understanding of the Private Language Argument. If this is right, it is an unnoticed way in which Austinian concerns about perception are relevant to Wittgensteinian ones about the nature of mental states.)

In the course of the last few minutes I have allowed myself to speak as if the question were one of choosing between two "accounts." But that concedes too much. As we saw in our discussion of the problems of the "sense datum theory," with or without the epicycle of "identity theory," the traditional epistemological story postulates "entities" whose behavior is unexplained and, indeed, inexplicable, and whose "postulation," in the end, provides us with no more than an alternative jargon in which we can restate such garden variety facts as the fact that on certain occasions it seems to one that one is seeing (hearing, feeling, smelling, etc.) something that is not there, and the fact that the look of something is not a property it has independently of the conditions under which it is perceived. "The natural realist account" urged on us by Austin and Wittgenstein, is, in the end, not an "alternative metaphysical account," although, in James's case, it had pretensions to become that. Winning through to natural realism is seeing the *needlessness* and the *unintelligibility* of a picture that imposes an interface between ourselves and the world. It is a way of completing the task of philosophy, the task that John Wisdom once called a "journey from the familiar to the familiar."

the face
of cognition

In the last two lectures I argued that our difficulty in seeing how our minds can be in genuine contact with the "external" world is, in large part, the product of a disastrous idea that has haunted Western philosophy since the seventeenth century, the idea that perception involves an interface between the mind and the "external" objects we perceive. In dualistic versions of early modern metaphysics and epistemology, that interface was supposed to consist of "impressions" (or "sensations" or "experiences" or "sense data" or "qualia"), and these were conceived of as immaterial. In materialist versions the interface has long been conceived of as consisting of brain processes. The position I described as "Cartesianism cum materialism" simply combines the two versions: the interface consists of "impressions" or "qualia" *and* these are "identical" with processes in the brain (as I mentioned earlier, I endorsed the latter of these in *Reason, Truth, and History*).

Once one has been persuaded, as we were in the seventeenth century, that this is the only *possible* way to think about perception, one is left—if one does not wish to think of "intentionality" as a magical power—with the task of trying to show that the referential directedness of our thinking at the objects we think about can be constituted out of or in some way "reduced to" the *causal* impacts of those objects upon us; a task so hopeless that philosophers have repeatedly been led to recoil to one or another version of idealism—to deny that the idea of objects that are not perceived or at least thought of by someone so much as makes sense, or to hold that that idea is no more than an intellectual construct that helps us to "cope" in one way or another.[1] Since the seventeenth century, philosophy has oscillated between equally unworkable realisms and idealisms.

Drawing on ideas of Austin and William James, I argued that the way out requires the achievement of what I called a "second naïveté," of a standpoint that fully appreciates the deep difficulties pointed out by the seventeenth-century philosophers but overcomes those difficulties rather than succumbing to them—a standpoint that sees that the difficulties do not, in the end, require us to reject the idea that in perception we are in unmediated contact with our environment. We do not have to accept the interface conception.

Rejecting "Cartesianism cum materialism" does not, of course, mean going back to Cartesian dualism itself. We should not think that if we refuse to identify the mind with the brain we will find ourselves committed to thinking of it as an immaterial part of us;[2] mind talk, I urged, is best understood as talk of certain abilities we possess, abilities that depend upon our brains and upon all the various transactions between the environment and the organism but that do not have to be reductively explained using the vocabulary of physics and biology, or even the vocabulary of computer science.[3]

"naive realism" with respect to conception

In my first lecture I also said that the threat of a loss of the world that accompanied the acceptance of early modern metaphysics and epistemology will not finally be put to rest until we arrive at what I called a commonsense realism about conception to accompany the "second naïveté" about perception that I have been defending. I now want to explain what I meant by that remark, and here too I shall follow a lead pioneered by Wittgenstein, whom I have been praising in these lectures. Here, however, I shall be running against a powerful current of Wittgenstein interpretation, one that sees Wittgenstein precisely as the father of the new *anti*realism.[4] Since my own realism has, in recent years, been increasingly inspired and influenced by my reading of Wittgenstein, I shall try, in the course of this lecture, to indicate how I find a "second naïveté" about our conceptual access to the things we talk and think about, coupled with an enormous sophistication about the varieties of that access, in the writings of the later Wittgenstein.

To begin our move away from an exclusive focus on the issues about perception, let us consider a case of *imagining*. Suppose that someone imagines deer grazing on the meadow and goes to look for them there. What is the traditional picture of such a "mental event"?

Imagining the deer—let us assume that "visual imagery" is involved—is traditionally conceived of as the formation of something in every way analogous to a picture, except that the picture happens to be "mental." This "mental picture" is supposed to play exactly the role that "impressions" (conceived of as an interface) played in the traditional account of perception. It is conceived of as entirely "inside the mind" (or "inside the head")—a realm where, of course, there are no *deer*—and as connected—causally or mysteriously—with the deer and the meadow "out there." *Early modern epistemology and metaphysics saddled us with an interface conception of conception as well as an interface conception of perception.* And, once again, Cartesianism cum materialism has simply retained the interface while identifying it with something in the brain; current talk of "mental representations" in "cognitive science" represents just this conception.[5]

I believe that Wittgenstein's celebrated discussion of the "duck-rabbit" drawing[6] is directed, inter alia, against the interface conception. The physical sketch is not intrinsically a drawing of either a duck or a rabbit; it can be seen as either. But it is very hard to form a "mental image" that is ambiguous in the way the duck-rabbit drawing is ambiguous. (I find that with effort I can form a mental image of a "duck-rabbit drawing"—but that image is not ambiguous; I experience it as an image of a "duck-rabbit drawing," not as an image of a living thing, either duck or rabbit.) It has been pointed out that one of Wittgenstein's reasons for pointing out that when one sees the duck-rabbit drawing one typically sees it *as* a duck drawing or *as* a rabbit drawing (but not both) was to get us to see that "visual experiences" are not at all like the physical pictures that we might draw to convey "what they are like" and thereby to undermine one classical conception of what a "sense datum" is.[7] That is indeed part of what Wittgenstein was doing, but it is also true that the "mental images" we sometimes form when we *think* or *remember* something are also not all like physical pictures. We should not think of the "mental image" involved in imagining the deer on the meadow as a picture into which an interpretation has to be *read*, any more than we should think of the "visual experience" of the duck-rabbit drawing as if it were a *second* duck-rabbit drawing, one that happens to be "mental" instead of physical.

Wittgenstein makes a similar point about the role of *words and sentences* in thinking.[8] It is a truism that words and sentences in a language do not have their meaning intrinsically; the words "snow is white" could have meant "the carburetor is clogged" had the history of English been different. But the truism is less than half of the truth. When we know and use a language well, when it becomes the vehicle of our own thinking and not something we have to mentally translate into some more familiar language, we do not, pace Richard Rorty,[9] experience its words and sentences as "marks and noises" into which a significance has to be read. When we hear a sentence in a language we understand, we do not associate a sense with a sign design; we perceive the sense *in* the sign design. Sentences that I think, and even sentences that I hear or read, simply do refer to whatever they are about— not because the "marks and noises" that I see and hear (or hear "in my head," in the case of my own thoughts) intrinsically have the meanings they have but because the sentence in use is not just a bunch of "marks and noises" (*Philosophical Investigations* 508).

That Wittgenstein should have made this point may seem surprising, especially if one allows the debate about realism to be structured in the way in which Dummett has proposed. Dummett sees the philosophical options as follows: either our sentences have only assertability conditions or they have something mysterious floating above them and connecting them with reality. But, as I will argue, we do not have to accept the idea that one is forced to choose between just these two options.

It is, of course, undeniable that a large part of the point of the meditations on "following a rule" in *Philosophical Investigations* is to warn us away (or, better, to wean us away) from the seductions of Platonism, from the idea that thinking about something can be a freestanding activity, unsupported by many other activities, linguistic and nonlinguistic.[10] But there is no real contradiction between rejecting that sort of Platonism and respecting the commonsense idea that we can conceive of how, say, some past event was, and not just in the sense of conceiving of what it would be to verify *now* that that is how it was. If someone is able, for example, to imagine seeing Eisenhower receive the German surrender that ended the war in Europe in 1945, then that person must possess a whole range of other abilities, intellectual and practical. In particular, the person must know who Eisenhower was, what the war in Europe was, etc.[11] Mimicking what Wittgenstein says about following a rule, one might say that *thinking* is not something only one person could do, and then only once.

In a lecture we have in the form of notes taken by one of the people present,[12] Wittgenstein used the example of thinking about his brother in America. Wittgenstein emphasized both that the words *reach* to his brother in America—there is simply no sense to the supposition that I only *think* I am thinking about my brother, if I am in Wittgenstein's position—and that this is not because there is some sort of supercausal connection that reaches (faster than light, as it were) from the thought to his brother in America; the thought is about his brother in America because a "technique of usage" is in place. Many interpreters think of the thought as an object to which an interpretation is *added* by "assertability conditions," that is, by a method of verification, e.g., saying, "My brother has a concert in New York" when one's brother has told one that he is going to play a concert in New York on the day in question, etc. Such interpreters identify the "technique of usage" Wittgenstein speaks of with such assertability conditions;[13] their analysis leaves no room for the truistic thought that one of the *uses* of the sentence "My brother has a concert in New York" is *to recount what one's brother is doing in New York.*[14] Once one rules this truistic thought out, one cannot help reading Wittgenstein as some sort of antirealist. But Wittgenstein wrote[15] that "when we say, and *mean*, that such-and-such is the case, we— and our meaning—do not stop anywhere short of the fact; but we mean *this—is—so.*" I believe that this is a central element in Wittgenstein's thought from the *Tractatus* on.

Our ability to think about what is or what may be going on at a distance will seem more mysterious than it is if one overemphasises the differences (enormous and important as they are) between our cognitive abilities and those of animals.[16] The cognitive states of animals lack anything like the determinacy of human cognitive states,[17] yet a wolf could expect to find deer on a meadow, and its ability to expect that is a primitive form of our ability to expect to find deer on the meadow. Our highly developed and highly discriminating abilities to think about situations that we are not observing are developments of powers that we share with other animals. But, at the same time, one must not make the mistake of supposing that language is merely a "code" that we use to transcribe thoughts we could perfectly well have without the "code." This is a mistake, not only because the simplest thought is altered (e.g., rendered far more determinate) by being expressed in language[18] but because language alters the range of *experiences* we can have.[19] But the fact remains that our power of imagining, remembering, expecting what is not the case here and now is a part of our nature.

It will be objected that what I have offered (and what Wittgenstein offered) is not a "scientific" picture. That is quite true. But our purposes in speaking of perception and conception, thought and imagination, etc., are only occasionally scientific (and "You still owe me a definition of 'scientific,' " one might say). Aristotle[20] reminded us long ago (and Dewey repeated the reminder) that discourses must seek their own levels of both certainty and precision. There is nothing in our commonsense realism about both perception and conception that is "antiscientific" in the sense of *standing in the way* of serious attempts to provide better models, both neurological and computational, of the brain processes upon which our perceptual and conceptual powers depend, processes concerning which we still know very little. Moreover, it is a profound mistake to equate serious science with the Cartesianism cum materialism that has for three centuries tried to wrap itself in the mantle of science. Today that attempt often takes the form of empty talk about "the conceptual structure of the mind"[21]—talk that simply takes for granted the idea that thinking *is* syntactic manipulation of symbols. Nothing in the successes of serious psychology or linguistics endows that view with content. Instead, such talk frequently lowers the level of philosophical discussion to that of popular "scientific" journalism.

dummettian antirealism

What I now propose to do is to show how this way of looking at the matter — the way I have just attributed to Wittgenstein—undercuts the objections to realism advanced by Michael Dummett, the objections that so concerned me at the very beginning of what has proved to be a long journey from realism back to realism (but not, as will be seen, back to the metaphysical version of realism with which I started).

As I explained in the first lecture, Michael Dummett sees the problem of realism as having to do with the "recognition transcendence" of truth. Either truth is simply the state of being verified or it transcends what the speaker can verify, he argues, and if it transcends what the speaker can verify, it is not a property whose presence the speaker can "recognize." And if truth is a property whose presence (in some cases, at least) the speaker cannot recognize, then the speaker's alleged "grasp" of the notion of truth becomes a mystery. In effect, Dummett is telling us, if truth is not verifiable, then, short of postulating magical powers of mind, we will not be able to explain how we understand the notion. The rejection of magical powers of mind requires the acceptance of a very radical form of verificationism, according to Dummett's line of thinking—one so radical that it requires us to revise a number of the laws of classical logic, beginning with the Principle of Bivalence.[22]

There is a rejoinder to Dummett's argument that Dummett himself anticipated from the beginning, one that he discusses at length in *The Logical Basis of Metaphysics*. That rejoinder, which in essence goes back to Tarski's celebrated essay on the concept of truth[23] runs as follows: "What is your problem? Take any sentence you like—take a sentence whose truth value we may not be able to find out, if you please. For example, take the sentence:

(1) Lizzie Borden killed her parents with an axe.

"Even if the truth of this sentence is 'recognition transcendent', surely you understand what it *means* to say that (1) is true. For you understand (1) itself, and the chief logical principle governing the use of the word 'true' is:

[Tarski's Convention T:] *If S is the name of any sentence, and we write that sentence[24] in the blank in:*

(2) *S is true if and only if* . . . .

then the resulting sentence will be true.

[Less formally: a sentence that says of another sentence S that S is true is equivalent to S itself. Tarski's famous example was:

(3) 'Snow is white' is true if and only if snow is white.]

In short, you understand 'Lizzie Borden killed her parents with an axe' and you know that

'Lizzie Borden killed her parents with an axe' is true if and only if Lizzie Borden killed her parents with an axe.

So you do understand what it means to say that (1) is true; *it means that Lizzie Borden killed her parents with an axe."*

I want also to note the fact that some philosophers who offer this account of how we understand sentences of the form "S is true"—but not Tarski himself[25]—add the claim that truth is not a "substantive property." These philosophers—I shall refer to them as "deflationists," in order to distinguish their position from Tarski's own (unmodified) position—claim that the predicate "is true" is just "a logical device."[26] I shall say something about this "deflationist" position shortly.

However, Dummett's reply to the (unmodified) "Tarskian" argument takes us to the heart of his philosophical concerns. "Granted that I understand sentence (1), and other sentences with an unknown truth value, e.g., undecided conjectures in mathematics," he answers (in effect—I am formulating his reply in my own words), "the philosophical problem is *to give an account of what that understanding consists in.*" In short, if you appeal to an *unexplicated* notion of "understanding a sentence," then you are simply ducking all the philosophical problems.

According to Dummett, my understanding of the sentence (1) (i.e., of any sentence) consists in my ability to *recognize if (1) is verified.* In other words, *if* (1) *should* be verified (by data that I myself perceive), then I *would* be able to tell that it was, and the ability or system of abilities that enables me to do this *constitutes* my understanding of (1). Similarly, I possess the ability to recognize proofs in mathematics, and this allows me to say that if I were given a proof of the conjecture that there are infinitely many twin primes (primes such that one is obtained by adding or subtracting two to a prime), I could recognize that it *was* a proof. And that is how I can say that I *understand* the Twin Prime Conjecture.

Dummett, of course, would concede the "Tarskian" points that he also understands the statement that (1) is true and the statement that the Twin Prime Conjecture is true, and that he knows that the statement that (1) is true is equivalent to (1) itself, etc. "But notice," he will point out (my words again!), "If my account is right, a speaker's understanding of the statement that (1) is true involves the speaker's understanding what it is for (1) to be verified—and this property, being verified, is a property that (1) and its negation may *both* lack; it does not require the speaker to know anything about a property—call it 'classical truth'—that must be possessed either by (1) or else by (1)'s negation, independently of whether anyone can tell which one possesses it, as is postulated by classical logic." In short, if Dummett's verificationist account of *what constitutes understanding* is right, then either truth is a useless metaphysical abstraction or else there is nothing to the claim that *truth is a bivalent property*, the claim that characterizes "two-valued" logic. (It is thus that Dummett is led to the radical claim that a sound philosophy of language requires the revision of classical logic itself.)

I want now to consider the response of the "deflationist philosophers" I mentioned a few moments ago. These philosophers agree with Dummett in thinking of our understanding of our sentences as *consisting in* our knowledge of the conditions under which they are verified, although they reject Dummett's notion of "conclusive verification," replacing that notion with a notion of degrees of verification.[27] They also reject Dummett's claim that we must not think of truth as a bivalent property, although they do agree that it is not a "substantive property" about which some metaphysical story needs to be told; rather they claim that rejecting that metaphysical picture of what truth is does not require us to give up the Law of the Excluded Middle, "$p \lor \lnot p$." As just mentioned, the deflationists even allow us to assert Bivalence:

(3) "Either p is true or the negation of p is true,"

where p is any declarative sentence,[28] but they interpret the assertion of (3) as a mere linguistic practice, free of commitment to the existence of a property "truth" that is determinately possessed either by the sentence or else by the negation of the sentence. That is, if we put sentence (1) for p, what (3) means, they say, is

(4) Either Lizzie Borden killed her parents with an axe or Lizzie Borden did not kill her parents with an axe.

—and (4), it will be noted, does not contain the word *true*.

But why should we accept (4)? Deflationists give different answers. Carnap and Ayer said that the acceptance of sentences of the form "p or not-p" is a linguistic convention; Quine, rejecting that answer, says simply that such sentences are "obvious" (sometimes he says "central" to our reasoning). But does not the "obviousness" of (4) depend on our belief that there is a fact of the matter as to whether Lizzie Borden did or did not administer the famous "forty whacks"? And if uttering a sentence (whether or not I also employ the "logical device" of saying that the sentence "is true") is just following a communitywide practice of assigning it a degree of assertability "as a function of observable circumstances," how do we so much as make sense of the idea of a fact of the matter as to the rightness of statements that are *neither* confirmed nor disconfirmed by those observable circumstances?

If we structure the debate in the way in which both Dummett and the deflationists do, then we are left with a forced choice between (a) either Dummettian antirealism or deflationism about truth, or (b) a retreat to metaphysical realism. Both Dummett's "global antirealist"[29] and the deflationist advertise their accounts as rescuing us from metaphysical realism. But surely one of the sources of the continuing appeal of metaphysical realism in contemporary philosophy is a dissatisfaction with the only apparent alternatives. The metaphysical realist will want to reply to the deflationist (and the antirealist) as follows:

"Realism requires us to say that either (1) or the negation of (1) is true. If a philosopher advises us to retain 'Either (1) is true or the negation of (1) is true' as something we are permitted to say while reinterpreting *what we are doing when we say it* in such a way as to deprive us of what we ordinarily mean (when we say of a sentence that it is true), then he is disguising the radically revisionary character of his theory through a terminological sleight of hand. That is what the deflationist, in effect, does. He allows us to hold on to the thought that 'Either (1) is true or the negation of (1) is true' only in the attenuated sense that he advises us to follow a policy of assigning all grammatical sentences of the syntactic *shape 'p v $-p$'* the degree of assertability (the "level of confidence," in Horwich's phrase) one. This attenuated sense in which the deflationist continues to permit us to speak of a sentence's being true fails to capture what is significant about true sentences (as opposed to false ones): true sentences possess a substantive property that false sentences lack—namely, the property of corresponding to a reality. Deflationism is thus unable, for example, to acknowledge the reality of past events (as things that truly happened), even though it retains the old form of words ('It happened or it didn't happen') as a *mere* form of words. Deflationism, in effect, follows the lead of logical positivism[30] in refusing to think of our sentences as subject to serious terms of normative appraisal, of appraisal in terms of the possession or absence of a substantive property of rightness that is different from verifiability. On the deflationist account, when one asserts the whole sentence '(1) is true or the negation of (1) is true' one is not saying that one of the *disjuncts* possesses the relevant sort of substantive rightness. The deflationist is unable to do justice to the sense in which one of the disjuncts of this sentence possesses the same sort of substantive rightness as does (if you are presently reading this essay) the sentence 'You are right now reading these words in front of you.' The deflationist (by regarding degree of assertability, but not truth, as a property that is more than just a logical device)[31] is therefore unable to capture the sense in which certain statements about the past (namely, the true ones) are fully as *right* as statements about the present. Dummett perceives the situation more clearly than the deflationists in that he at least recognizes—indeed emphasizes—that his account of understanding commits him to antirealism about the past (and not only about the past). Neither Dummet nor the deflationist, however, can accommodate the ordinary sense in which certain statements about the past are substantively true."

What is the difference between the realism of the metaphysical realist (whose response to deflationism I just sketched) and the commonsense realism that I wish to attribute to Wittgenstein? In a different context (in response to a Platonist about rule following) Wittgenstein writes,

> Really the only thing wrong with what you say is the expression "in a queer way." The rest is all right; and the sentence only seems queer when one imagines a different language-game for it from the one in which we actually use it.[32]

Wittgenstein would, I believe, reply to the metaphysical realist's response to the deflationist (which I have sketched above) by saying, "Really the only thing wrong with what you say is the expression 'substantive property' (and related uses of 'substantive', as in 'substantive sort of rightness' and 'substantively true')." Thus, from Wittgenstein's point of view, most of the words that the metaphysical realist finds himself moved to say (in reponse to the deflationist) are perfectly all right. But the metaphysical realist makes these words seem fated to say something *queer* by calling upon them to bear an explanatory burden—to bear metaphysical weight—in accounting for the relation between Thought and Reality. The metaphysical realist feels that the deflationist has drained our ordinary ways of speaking and acting of their substance, and so he seeks to reinfuse them somehow with substance. It is to this end that he ineffectually invokes the notion of a "substantive property." The metaphysical realist (in trying to do justice, for example, to our ordinary realism about the past) feels compelled to appeal to something that *underlies* our language games: a mysterious property that stands behind—both in the sense of remaining invisibly in the background and in the sense of guaranteeing—our ordinary ways of speaking and acting. The metaphysical realist and the deflationist share a common picture in that it seems to both a queer thing that certain statements (for example, about the past) can be said to be true.

the error (and the insight) in verificationism

Part of what is right in the metaphysical realist's response to the deflationist is the realization that that view does not (as advertised) successfully undercut

Dummettian antirealism. On the contrary, deflationism about truth—as long as it involves (as it has since Ramsey introduced the position in the 1920s) a verificationist account of understanding—adopts the most disastrous feature of the antirealist view, the very feature that brings about the loss of the world (and the past). It differs from antirealism in this regard only in that it attempts to disguise that feature by means of a superficial terminological conservatism. The metaphysical realist is thus to this extent right: to undercut Dummett's antirealism requires challenging his account of understanding, not adopting it. But what makes the metaphysical realist's response *metaphysical* is its acceptance of the idea (which it shares with the Dummettian antirealist) that our ordinary realism—for example, about the past—presupposes a view of truth as a "substantive property." The metaphysical realist, in wanting a property that he can ascribe to all and only true sentences, wants a property that corresponds to the assertoric force of a sentence. But this is a very funny property. To avoid identifying this property of "truth" with that of assertability, the metaphysical realist needs to argue that there is something we are saying when we say of a particular claim that it is true over and above what we are saying when we simply assert the claim. He wants Truth to be something that *goes beyond* the content of the claim and to be that in virtue of which the claim is true. This forces the metaphysical realist to postulate that there is some single thing we are saying (over and above what we are claiming) whenever we make a truth claim, no matter what sort of statement we are discussing, no matter what the circumstances under which the statement is said to be true, and no matter what the pragmatic point of calling it true is said to be.[33]

The right alternative to thinking of truth as a "substantive property" à la the metaphysical realist is *not* to think of our statements as mere marks and noises that our community has taught us to associate with conditions for being conclusively verified (as in the account of Dummett's "global antirealist") or to associate with "betting behavior" in a way that is "a function of observable circumstances" (as in Horwich's account). The right alternative is to recognize that empirical statements already make claims about the world— many different sorts of claims about the world—whether or not they contain the words *is true*. What is wrong in deflationism is that it cannot properly accommodate the truism that certain claims about the world are (not merely assertable or verifiable but) *true*. What is right in deflationism is that if I assert that "it is true that *p,*" then I assert the same thing as if I simply assert *p*. Our confidence, when we make statements about the past, that we are saying something whose rightness or wrongness depends on *how things were back then* (when we claim, for example, that "It is true that Lizzie Borden killed her parents with an axe") is not something that requires the metaphysical idea that there is a "substantive property" whose existence underwrites the very possibility of using the word *true*.

In order to see more clearly the difference between the commonsense realism I am defending and the kind of metaphysical realism we are right to recoil from, let us shift our attention for a moment from discourse about observable things, such as deer grazing on the meadow, to discourse about unobservables, e.g., microbes. In the first lecture I remarked that the use of instruments should be viewed as a way of extending our natural powers of observation. But the use of language is also a way of extending our natural powers of observation. If I could not understand talk about "things too small to see with the naked eye," the microscope would be at best a toy (like the kaleidoscope); what I saw when I looked through the eyepiece would mean nothing to me. However, it would be a mistake to conclude that the dependence goes both ways. The phrase "too small to see with the naked eye" does not depend for its intelligibility on the invention of an instrument that allows us to see things smaller than the things the naked eye can see (nor did we regard it as changing its sense when the microscope was invented). What is mistaken about verificationism is the claim that the meaning of an expression like "things too small to see with the naked eye" depends on there being methods of verifying the existence of such things, and the related claim that the meaning of such an expression changes as these methods of verification change (e.g., with the invention of the microscope). However there is a philosophical danger of rejecting what is right in verificationism in the course of rejecting what is wrong with it. What is right in verificationism is that a great deal of scientific talk does depend for its full intelligibility on the provision of the kind of thick explanatory detail that is impossible if one has no familiarity with the use of scientific instruments. For example, in Democritus's writings, as we know of them, the notion of an atom was a metaphysical one, but one to which *we* can give a sense, even if Democritus himself could not.[34] Thus scientific instruments and scientific ways of talking are both ways of extending our perceptual and conceptual powers, and those ways are highly interdependent; indeed, they can fuse into a single complex practice.

The ways in which language extends the mental abilities that we share with other animals are almost endless; our ability to construct sophisticated scientific theories is only one example. A very different sort of example is provided by the role of logical constants, for example, the words *all* and *no*. An animal or a child that has not yet learned to use these words may have expectations that we who have acquired them can and do describe with the aid of these words. For example, imagine that someone with modest skills at sleight of hand causes a handkerchief to "vanish" in front of a child's very eyes, and the child displays astonishment. We might say that the child believes (believed) that "handkerchiefs do not vanish into thin air just like that"—i.e., that *no* handkerchiefs vanish into thin air just like that. Of course, that generalization does not have any consequences that the child can understand not possessed by the generalization: "*Observed* handkerchiefs do not vanish into thin air just like that." Yet we would not dream of using the latter words to describe the child's attitude to the event. We would not know how to make sense of the suggestion that a child is only concerned to make a judgment about the behavior of *observed* hankerchiefs. This is the case *not* because we take the child to be concerned with making judgments about both observed *and* unobserved hankerchiefs; the distinction between the two generalizations is not one that belongs to the child's intellectual repertoire. It is a part of *our* repertoire (and which description we use may make a difference to *us* under certain circumstances: "Fine shades of behavior. Why are they *important*? They have important consequences." *Philosophical Investigations*, p. 204). We describe even primitive preverbal attitudes as attitudes toward objects of which people may or may not be aware, and not just toward the part of the world that the child (or we) can "verify." Our sophisticated adult talk about certain features of the world (such as "those that are observable to us") rests upon—is parasitic upon—just such a primitive preverbal attitude toward the world.

A quite different aspect of the extension of our conceptual abilities brought about by the possession of words for generality is the possibility of formulating conjectures that transcend even "ideal verifiability," such as "There are no intelligent extraterrestials." The fact that this conjecture may not be verifiable even "in principle" does not mean that it does not correspond to a reality; but one can only say what reality corresponds to it, if it is true, by using the words themselves.[35] And this is not deflationism; on the contrary, deflationism, by identifying understanding with possession of verification abilities, makes it mysterious that we should find these words intelligible. Once again, the difficulty here lies in keeping what is right in verificationism (or in this case in deflationism) while throwing out what is wrong.

Nothing in what I just said requires us to think of our ability to conceive of such things as microbes (or of our ability to think that there are no intelligent extraterrestials) as a freestanding ability, independent of a great many other abilities and independent of scientific and other institutions and practices.[36] But, conversely, nothing in Wittgenstein's insistence on the ways in which conception and practical interaction with the world depend upon one another, and on the plurality of kinds of conception and practice involved, requires us to think of conception as the mere manipulation of syntactic objects in response to perceptual "inputs" (as "cognitive scientists" tend to do. I do not wish to accuse Michael Dummett of consciously holding that picture of conception, but his emphasis on *formal proof* as a model of verification, and his insistence that the goal of philosophy of language should be to *specify recursively* how the sentences of the language can be verified, suggest to me that his picture of language use is closer to the "cognitive scientific" version of the Cartesian cum materialist picture than he himself may realize.[37] Dummett has been primarily concerned to combat "holistic" versions of that picture— versions in which the unit of significance is the whole network of sentences rather than the single sentence—in favor of a "molecular" version—a version in which each sentence has its own isolated method of verification; but this is a debate about the *details* of the picture. Dummett sees no alternative to the picture as a whole except to postulate mysterious mental acts; and that is because he has from the beginning felt obliged to regard his own thoughts as if they were syntactic objects that require rules of manipulation. But there is an alternative, as more than one philosopher has recently pointed out[38] — namely, to distinguish carefully between the activity of "representation" (as something in which we engage) and the idea of a "representation" as an *interface* between ourselves and what we think about, and to understand that giving up the idea of representions as interfaces requiring a "semantics" is not the same thing as giving up on the whole idea of representation.[39]

"things too small to see" and Cora Diamond's thought experiment

I first met Michael Dummett in 1960, and our earliest discussions concerned my attack on the positivist's "observational/theoretical" dichotomy in the lecture I delivered at the Congress on Logic, Methodology, and Philosophy of Science at Stanford in August of that year.[40] Dummett (perhaps not surprisingly, given his later development) was a staunch defender of the dichotomy, and he took particular exception to an example I used in that lecture. The point I was making even then was that our ability to refer to unobservables is best seen as a natural extension of our ability to refer to observables, and I said in passing that even small children can understand talk about things too small to see (I imagined a child enjoying a story about "little people too small for us to see"). My claim was that the words *small, thing, see*, etc. have the same meaning in talk of "things too small for us to see" (or in the talk of particles much too small to see that figured in nineteenth-century atomic theory) than they have in describing observables, and I concluded that the so-called observation terms in science can typically be used to describe *un*observables as well as observables, and that such a use does not involve any change of meaning. Dummett's view was that this is a totally different meaning of the words (he said, "a different use," but this clearly had the force of a different *meaning*).

Today it seems to me that both of us were being somewhat simplistic. I still believe both (1) that talk of things too small for us to see does not depend for its intelligibility on scientific theories or the invention of such instruments as the microscope, and (2) that the intelligibility of such talk does not involve a change in the meaning of the terms *small*, etc. I *was* ignoring the difference between scientific talk that depends for its full intelligibility on the provision of coherent explanatory detail (as contemporary talk of subatomic forces depends on a structure of laws and explanations as well as connections to experiments) and talk that we are not able to make sense of, because such detail is lacking (e.g., what is the *metabolism* of the "little people too small to see" supposed to be? Are their *cells* also supposed to be correspondingly smaller than ours?). Talk of "little people too small to see" is, indeed, a "different use"—a *fictional* use of the idea of *people* (not of *small*). But Dummett could not see what was right in what I was saying: that we do see the word *small* (and the comparative *smaller*) applied to, say, *molecules*, as having exactly the sense that it bears in talk of a small animal or a small piece of stone, etc.

The point is not affected by the fact that we no longer conceive of quantum mechanical particles as *literally* "particles." Indeed, at the moment we do not know how to conceive of them at all, apart from their interactions with our measuring instruments.[41] But that is for empirical reasons—nature has proved to be far less "visualizable" in the ultrasmall than we expected, and not because talk of "things too small for us to see" has no application. Microbes are *literally* things too small for us to see. And we do not see ourselves as forcing an arbitrary new meaning on the word *small* when we so describe them.

But does what we *see* as having the same meaning have anything to do with what does have the same meaning? For Dummett (early and late) the answer is "no." Our natural picture of what we are doing with our words and our thoughts has no philosophical *weight*, in his eyes. Dummett's rejection of our commonsense realism about our conceptual powers is of a piece with the tradition's rejection of "naive realism" about our perceptual powers.

But Dummett faces an obvious problem—one of which he is well aware. He cannot, after all, say that we change the meaning of our words whenever a new way of verifying a sentence is accepted. To do so would be to abandon the distinction between changing our beliefs and changing the meaning of our words—for just about any belief implies some new way of verifying *some* sentence. So Dummett has to show that he can distinguish methods of verification that are constitutive of a sentence's meaning from mere collateral information, a task that, Quine has convincingly argued,[42] there is no reason to believe can be successfully carried out.

Interestingly enough, Dummett himself criticizes Wittgenstein, whom he reads as holding that every new theorem in mathematics changes the meanings of mathematical expressions (by providing a new criterion for determining that one has made a mistake somewhere).[43] In a brilliant critique of this reading of Wittgenstein,[44] Cora Diamond develops this issue with the aid of a very simple thought experiment.

She asks us to "consider . . . the case of a man who has yet to learn to recognize *any* results of counting things as discordant. He has been taught the following kind of game (it could easily be part of another game, e.g., one kind of task in a game with a variety of tasks). Pencils are arranged in rows on a table. When you point to a row of pencils, he says the cardinal numbers in order from 1, one number for each pencil, as he touches them in order from the left. Then you say, 'Outcome?' and he gives the last number. He has been taught that he must not count any pencil more than once, and he must not omit any, or repeat any, or get them in the wrong order." The man is supposed to know that these count as mistakes in the game, and there is a penalty for making them. (The pencils are in plain view, and he is able to see that no pencils are added to any of the rows or removed while the game is going on.)

"Now I might well say that if the man carries out the procedure he was taught with the same row twice and says one number at 'Outcome?' the first time and another the second, then he must have made a mistake," Diamond continues. "Or I might say there is a result which is *the* result if the procedure is carried out correctly. Let us see what it might be to get the man himself to recognize the necessity I just spoke of." She imagines a case in which the man gets two different results and we say, "You've made some mistake," and he denies that he has. Then we count a row together with him, emphasizing the fact that we always get the same number for each pencil. "Of course," Diamond remarks, "this may not lead him to do or say or see anything. But let us suppose that he says 'Aha!' and now acts and speaks in such ways as to enable us to say that he must have made a mistake if he gets two such results" (pp. 246–247).

Following Diamond, let us refer to the game as described, but with the proviso that the player says, "I've made a mistake" only when it is called to his attention that he has counted some pencil twice, or counted them in the wrong order, or skipped a pencil, activity C. After his "Aha!" experience he plays a game D in which he is allowed to say "I have made a mistake" in these same circumstances but also whenever two different numbers are reached in counting the same row.

At this point Diamond turns to Dummett's interpretation of Wittgenstein's views on the philosophy of mathematics.

"It will be useful to ask exactly what is wrong with the following kind of account [roughly the kind of account given by Dummett's Wittgenstein]. What our "proof" did was to get the man to switch . . . from C to D, where . . . we have a pair of slightly different activities—the rules are slightly different—just as a game would be slightly different from chess if the rules differed in not permitting an option at the first move of a pawn. If the rules of C are different from those of D, "what we are talking about is something else." And so, if we look at the matter in this way, "There must be a mistake if I get first 7, then 8 for a row" would be *merely* a way of putting an arbitrary rule of a new game; and what the player goes on to say in this new game, D, has not the sense which "I made some mistake" has in the first game, C" (p. 247).

In discussing this, Diamond points out that in the case of card games we sometimes do and sometimes do not see one game as a form of another: in particular, she contrasts someone who sees an activity as playing Hearts or chess or Monopoly by oneself and someone who sees no relation between this activity and playing the same game with several players. She refers to this as a difference in the "sense" that the activity has for the players. And she compares saying that two activities have the same sense to saying that two picture faces have the same expression. "This is not like saying the mouths are the same length, the eyes the same distance apart; it is not that kind of description. But it is not a description of *something* else, the expression, distinct from that curved line, the dots, and so on" (p. 249).

Diamond's purpose in introducing the notion of sense is, of course, to explain the significance of taking activity D as "really the same" as activity C; "and the player's doing that," she writes, "characterizes the sense engaging in [D] has for him" (p. 249).

The analogy between seeing the same facial expression in two different configurations of lines and dots and seeing a necessity common to different practices of counting and calculating is an illuminating one. Seeing an expression in the picture face is not just a matter of seeing the lines and dots; rather it is a matter of seeing something *in* the lines and dots—but this is not to say that it is a matter of seeing something *besides* the lines and dots. Both sides in the debate between "realists" and "antirealists" about mathematical necessity believe that we are confronted with a forced choice between saying either (1) that there is something *besides* our practices of calculation and deduction that underlies those practices and guarantees their results; or (2) that there is *nothing but* what we say and do, and the necessity that we perceive in those practices is a mere illusion. Wittgenstein, here as elsewhere, wants to show us that it is a mistake to choose either the "something besides" or the "nothing but" horn of the dilemma. Diamond's example brings out how both the "realist" and the "antirealist" (in the fashion of Dummett's Wittgenstein) share the same picture of mathematical necessity, one according to which there must be *something* forcing us—the necessities that our rules reflect, conceived of as something external to our mathematical practices and the ways of thinking internal to them. The realist tries to make sense of such a something; the antirealist concludes that no sense can be made of it, so there is no necessity either. The philosophical task here lies in seeing that giving up on the picture which both the realist and and the antirealist share is not the same thing as giving up on our ordinary logical and mathematical notion of necessity.

Briefly put, the difference between Dummett's Wittgenstein and Diamond's Wittgenstein can be characterized thus: for Dummett, any change in the *rules* of a language game is a change in the meaning of the words. Since he shares this premise with the Wittgenstein he imagines, the only way he can criticize that Wittgenstein is to deny that proving a theorem in mathematics is in any way changing the rules. For Diamond, the question is not one of distinguishing between the "rules" of an activity and components of the activity that are not "rules"; for Diamond—and for Wittgenstein as Diamond reads him—the question is one of our "natural reactions," of our ways of "seeing the face" of one activity in another.

The difference between Dummett's Wittgenstein and Diamond's Wittgenstein parallels the difference we saw earlier between Dummett and myself. Dummett wants to say that the rules for the application of expressions such as "too small to see" change with the invention of the microscope, and therefore the meaning of the expressions change, or rather they are given new meanings in their new contexts of use. I want to say that the question is not one of distinguishing between the "rules" of the activity of using words and components of the activity that are not "rules," and that here too the question is one of our ways of "seeing the face" of one activity in another. It is true that for the person who cannot see the connection between the activities C and D the words "I have made a mistake" change their meaning depending on which game the person is playing; but such a person would be regarded as "stupid." Activity D would not have the sense for this person that it has for us. Someone for whom talk of things too small to see had a totally different meaning after the invention of the microscope would resemble the person just described. Thus the problem with Dummett's account is that it fails to properly describe who we are and the sense that our practices have for *us*. It fails to capture the way in which we "see the face" of the activity of seeing something with our eyes in seeing something with a microscope, and in which we "see the face" of using a magnifying glass to look at something very small in using a microscope to look at something "too small to see with the naked eye." And like Diamond, I am suggesting that the sameness of the "sense" of *small* in these cases is not an identity of "rules," nor yet a "description of *something* else" than the way we use the words in these cases.

wittgenstein on truth

How, then, do we understand "recognition transcendent" uses of the word *true*, as, for example, when we say that the sentence "Lizzie Borden killed her parents with an axe" may well be true even though we may never be able to establish for certain that it is? Tarski (who was not a deflationist in my sense, because he did not subscribe to the verificationist account of understanding[45] in any of its versions) expressed a genuine insight in pointing out (as Frege had before him) that there is an intimate connection between understanding a sentence and understanding the claim that that sentence is true. If we accept it that understanding the sentence "Lizzie Borden killed her parents with an axe" is not simply a matter of being able to recognize a verification in our own experience—accept it, that is, that we are able to conceive of how things that we cannot verify *were*—then it will not appear as "magical" or "mysterious" that we can understand the claim that that sentence is *true*. What makes it true, if it is, is simply that Lizzie Borden killed her parents with an axe.[46] The recognition transcendence of truth comes, in this case, to no more than the "recognition transcendence" of some killings. And did we ever think that all killers can be recognized as such? Or that the belief that there are certain determinate individuals who are or were killers and who cannot be detected as such by us is a belief in magical powers of the mind?

There is, however, something that Tarski ignores, and that is the fact that there are perfectly well-formed declarative sentences that are *neither* true nor false; indeed, in Tarski's theory, it was supposed to be a theorem of logic (given what Tarksi calls an "adequate definition" of the truth predicate)[47] that each sentence is either true or false (has a true negation). But there are many reasons why a sentence may fail to have a truth value: for example, the vagueness of some of its terms ("The number of trees in Canada is even") or the failure of the world to behave the way it should if the terms it employs are to work (e.g., many sentences about the simultaneity of events were *discovered* to lack a truth value when relativity theory appeared on the scene; this is quite different from ordinary vagueness, of the kind that it requires only "linguistic intuition" to perceive). The use of true and false in "Such and such a sentence is *neither true nor false*" is inadmissible in Tarskian semantics. Those who regard "true" as a mere "device for disquotation" (e.g., asserting sentences without actually using them) also ignore or deny this clearly predicative use of *true* and *false*.

One thinker who did *not* ignore or deny this was Wittgenstein. In an important (but frequently misunderstood) section of *Philosophical Investigations* (§136), he writes:

"At bottom, giving 'This is how things are' as the general form of proposition[48] is the same as giving the definition: a proposition is whatever can be true or false. For, instead of 'This is how things are,' I could have said 'This is true.' (Or again, 'This is false.') But we have

'p' is true = p

'p' is false = not-p

And to say that a proposition is whatever can be true or false amounts to saying: we call something a proposition when *in our language* we apply the calculus of truth-functions to it.

Now it looks as if the definition—a proposition is whatever can be true or false—determined what a proposition was, by saying: what fits the concept 'true,' or whatever the concept 'true' fits, is a proposition. So it is as if we had a concept of true and false which we could use to determine what is and what is not a proposition. What *engages* with the concept of truth (as with a cogwheel) is a proposition.

But this is a bad picture. It is as if one were to say 'The king in chess is *the* piece that one can check.' But this can mean no more than that in our game of chess we only check the king. Just as the proposition that only a *proposition* can be true or false can say no more than that we only predicate 'true' and 'false' of what we call a proposition. And what a proposition is is in one sense determined by the rules of sentence formation (in English, for example), and in another sense by the use of the sign in the language-game. And the use of the words 'true' and 'false' may be among the constituent parts of the game; and if so it *belongs* to our concept 'proposition' but does not '*fit*' it. As we might also say, check *belongs* to our concept of the king in chess (as so to speak a constituent part of it). To say that check did not *fit* our concept of the pawns, would mean that a game in which pawns were checked, in which, say, the players who lost their pawns lost, would be uninteresting or stupid or too complicated or something of the kind."

Kripke, who quotes only "But we have

'p is true = p' "

—sees *PI* §136 as a clear expression of deflationism. But I do not believe this can be what Wittgenstein intended for the following reasons:

(1) We know that Wittgenstein does not oppose the idea that empirical propositions "correspond to realities"; indeed, he elsewhere discusses the sense of this correspondence and distinguishes it from the very different sense in which mathematical propositions correspond to reality;[49] rather the thrust of the whole passage is clearly directed against the metaphysical realist's understanding of such platitudinous thoughts as the thought that "This chair is blue" can correspond to the fact that a particular chair is blue. The essential point Wittgenstein makes in *PI* §136 is that we do not recognize that something is a proposition by seeing that it "fits" the concept "truth," where truth is conceived of as a freestanding property.[50] But it would be just as much of a mistake to think that we can explain what truth is by saying that for any *proposition* p, p is true = p, as it is to think that we can explain what a proposition is by saying that a proposition is what is true or false. In both cases we are simply making grammatical observations; we must not confuse what are virtually tautologies for metaphysical discoveries. The notion of truth and the notion of a proposition mesh together like a pair of gears in a machine; neither is a foundation on which the other rests. Our understanding of what truth comes to, in any particular case (and it can come to very different things), is given by our understanding of the proposition, and that is dependent on our mastery of "the language-game," by which Wittgenstein means here "the whole, consisting of language and the actions into which it is woven."[51] There is a certain "holism" here; knowing what truth is in a particular case depends on knowing the *use* of signs in the language game just as knowing what checking is depends on knowing the use of the various pieces in chess.

(2) When we *ourselves* are willing to apply truth functions to a sentence—note how Wittgenstein emphasizes *in our language*—we regard the sentence as true or false, as a genuine *Satz*.

(3) A grammatical string of sounds or marks that is *neither* true nor false

is simply not a sentence (*Satz*) in Wittgenstein's sense.[52] This is what Wittgenstein means by speaking of "*the definition*—a proposition is whatever can be true or false" (my emphasis). There is no suggestion in this that adding the words "is true" is a "logical device" that we can apply to "declarative sentences" ad libitum.[53]

The possibility that I see in Wittgenstein's writings, of doing full justice to the principle that to call a proposition true is equivalent to asserting the proposition (doing full justice to what I called "Tarski's insight") without committing the errors of the deflationists, is a condition of preserving our commonsense realism while appreciating the enormous *difference* between that commonsense realism and the elaborate metaphysical fantasy that is traditional realism—the fantasy of imagining that the form of all knowledge claims is fixed once and for all in advance. That fantasy goes with the equally fantastic idea that there must be just one *way* in which a knowledge claim can be responsible to reality—by "corresponding" to it, where "correspondence" is thought to be a mysterious relation that somehow underwrites the very possibility of there being knowledge claims. Indeed, a rejection of the idea that we can speak once and for all of "all propositions" as if these constituted a determinate and surveyable totality, and of one single "truth predicate," whose meaning is fixed once and for all, is also one that the later Wittgenstein shared with Tarski.[54]

Instead of looking for a freestanding property of "truth," in the hope that when we find what that property is we will know what the *nature* of propositions is and what the *nature* of their correspondence to reality is, Wittgenstein wants us to *look* at ethical language (and not the kind of ethical language that only occurs in philosophy),[55] to look at religious language,[56] to look at mathematical language, which is itself, he says, a "motley,"[57] to look at imprecise language that manages to be perfectly "clear" in context ("Stand roughly here"),[58] to look at talk that is sometimes nonsensical and to look at the very same sentences when they function perfectly well (talk of "what is going on in so-and-so's head" is an example of this),[59] to look and *see* the differences in the way these sorts of discourse function, all the very different ways in which they relate to reality.

If Wittgenstein was right, how should his reflections affect our view of the concept of truth? On the one hand, to regard an assertion or a belief or a thought as true or false *is* to regard it as being right or wrong; on the other hand, just what sort of rightness or wrongness is in question varies enormously with the *sort* of discourse. *Statement, true, refers*, indeed, *belief, assertion, thought, language* — all the terms we use when we think about logic (or "grammar") in the wide sense in which Wittgenstein understands that notion — have a plurality of uses, and new uses are constantly added as new forms of discourse come into existence. On the other hand, that does not mean that any practices at all of employing "marks and noises" can be recognized by us as adding up to a form of discourse — for not every way of producing marks and noises is "one in which there is the face of meaning at all."[60] Part of what I have been trying to show in these lectures is that what we recognize as the face of meaning is, in a number of fundamentally important cases, also the face of our natural cognitive relations to the world — the face of perceiving, of imagining, of expecting, of remembering, and so on — even though it is also the case that as language extends those natural cognitive relations to the world, it also transforms them. Our journey has brought us back to the familiar: truth is sometimes recognition-transcendent because what goes on in the world is sometimes beyond our power to recognize, even when it is not beyond our power to conceive.

In the course of these lectures I have had occasion to discuss not only perception and understanding but a number of topics that are usually thought to be far removed from the philosophy of mind: such topics as truth (and deflationism about truth), necessity, and the realism/antirealism debate. But it should be clear by now that a nice allocation of philosophical problems to different philosophical "fields" makes no real sense. To suppose that philosophy divides into separate compartments labeled "philosophy of mind," "philosophy of language," "epistemology," "value theory," and "metaphysics," is a sure way to lose all sense of how the problems are connected, and that means to lose all understanding of the sources of our puzzlement. Indeed, we have seen how the arguments in the realism/antirealism debate over the very possibility of representing a reality "external" to our minds (or to our brains) constantly appeal to assumptions about perception and to assumptions about understanding—in particular, the assumption that we face a forced choice between explaining the very possibility of understanding by appeal to one or another metaphysical mystery, on the one hand, and accepting a verificationist account of understanding, on the other—and how that assumption in turn support deflationist and antirealist accounts of truth. At the very beginning of these lectures I spoke of the need to get a deeper understanding of the causes of our tendency to "recoil" from one horrendous position to another in philosophy. In this concluding lecture I have focused on what seem to me to be the two principle causes of this tendency. The first of those causes is a certain kind of reductionism, the kind of reductionism that makes it impossible to see that when concepts are interlinked, as *perception, understanding, representation, verification, truth* are interlinked, the philosophical task must be to explore the circle rather than to reduce all the points on the circle to just one point. The second of these causes is the prevalence of the sort of assumption just mentioned—the all too seductive assumption that we know what the philosophical options are, and that they amount in each case to a forced choice between a funny metaphysical something standing behind our talk (whether it be talk of "truth" or "reference" or "necessity" or "understanding") and "tough-minded" reductionism (verificationism, or deflationism, or antirealism, or whatever). No matter which of these causes is responsible for any given case of the tendency—and usually they operate in tandem—the surest symptom of their presence is an inability to see that giving up on the funny metaphysical somethings does not require us to give up on concepts that, whatever our philosophical convictions, we employ and must employ when we live our lives. Until now I have not mentioned the word *pragmatism* in these Dewey Lectures. But if there was one great insight in pragmatism, it was the insistence that what has weight in our lives should also have weight in philosophy.

part two mind and body

"i thought of what i called 'an automatic sweetheart'"

William James at one point makes the remarkable thought experiment of imagining a human being who (undetectably) lacks all mental properties:

> I thought of what I called an "automatic sweetheart," meaning a soulless body which should be absolutely indistinguishable from a spiritually animated maiden, laughing, talking, blushing, nursing us, and performing all feminine offices as tactfully and sweetly as if a soul were in her. Would anyone regard her as a full equivalent? Certainly not.[1]

But James was not the first philosopher to have this worry. The philosopher who more than any other fixed the shape of our subsequent worries about mind and body, René Descartes, considers it too. In the *Discourse on Method* Descartes even proposed a kind of "Turing test":

> For we can certainly conceive of a machine so constructed that it utters words, and even utters words which correspond to bodily actions causing a change in its organs (e.g., if you touch it in one spot it asks what you want of it, if you touch it in another it cries out that you are hurting it, and so on).

But it is not conceivable that such a machine should produce different arrangements of words so as to give an appropriately meaningful answer to whatever is said in its presence, as the dullest of men can do.[2]

The worry certainly seems far-fetched. Yet the issue has arisen again in a recent debate between two of our leading philosophers of mind, Jaegwon Kim and Donald Davidson.

In the essays collected in his book *Supervenience and Mind*, Kim devotes an extraordinary amount of attention to the philosophy of mind of Donald Davidson.[3] The reason is not hard to guess: Davidson's view is diametrically opposed to Kim's on the issue of what Kim calls "strong supervenience"[4] and what I shall refer to for the time being simply as reductionism. (However, Kim is impressed by Davidson's arguments against the existence of the sorts of psychophysical laws required for strong supervenience, and even includes a paper that appears to defend them in *Supervenience and Mind*.)[5] Although Davidson is a materialist to the extent of believing that each individual mental event is *identical* with an individual physical event, there are, according to Davidson no psychophysical laws. However (in most of the papers in *Supervenience and Mind*), Kim defends the possibility of finding such laws. As he puts it, even if certain arguments of mine[6] show that we aren't going to find any *unrestricted* laws of the form P↔M, where P is a physical property, M is a mental property, and the law quantifies over all physically possible organisms, still, there may well be "species-specific bridge laws," i.e., laws of the form $S_i \rightarrow (M \leftrightarrow P_i)$ "which, *relative to a species or structure* S_i, specifies a physical state P_i *as both necessary and sufficient* for the occurrence of mental state M."[7] Indeed, Kim's position in "The Myth of Nonreductive Physicalism" is that *only if there are such laws* can it be the case that mental properties have genuine causal efficacy.

First, here is Kim's description of Davidson's position:

Mental events, Davidson observed, enter into causal relations with physical events. But causal relations must be backed by laws; that is, causal relations between individual events must instantiate lawful regularities.[8] Since [according to Davidson] there are no laws about the mental, either psychophysical or purely psychological, any causal relation involving a mental event must instantiate a physical law, from which it follows that the mental event has a physical description, or falls under a physical event kind. For an event is physical (or mental) if it falls under a physical event kind (or a mental event kind).

It follows then that all events are physical events—on the assumption that every event falls into at least one causal relation.[9]

And here is Kim's criticism:

Davidson's ontology recognizes individual events as spatiotemporal particulars. And the principal structure over these events is causal structure; the network of causal relations that interconnects events is what gives intelligible structure to this universe of events. What role does mentality play, on Davidson's anomalous monism, in shaping this structure? The answer: None whatever.

For anomalous monism entails this: *the very same network of causal relations would obtain in Davidson's world if you were to redistribute mental properties over its events in any way you like; you would not disturb a single causal relation if you randomly and arbitrarily reassigned mental properties to events, or even removed mentality entirely from the world.* Remember: on anomalous monism, events are causes or effects only as they instantiate physical laws, and this means that an event's mental properties make no causal difference.[10]

davidson defended

I shall begin by defending Davidson against Kim's argument.[11] It isn't, let me say at the outset, that I share Davidson's anomalous monism or Davidson's view on causality. On anomalous monism, my position is that mental events aren't "identical" or "not identical" with physical events; I don't believe that the notion of "identity" has been given a sense here.[12] And I also believe that Elizabeth Anscombe's "Causality and Determination"[13] contains conclusive counterexamples to Davidson's claim that every true singular causal statement must be backed by a strict law.[14] However, I believe that the above objection to Davidson's position can be answered, and that trying to answer it is an excellent way to come to grips with a number of central issues in the philosophy of mind.

Kim's argument evidently turns on the following remarkable conditional:

Kim's conditional (assuming that Davidson's views are correct): *You would not disturb a single causal relation if you randomly and arbitrarily reassigned mental properties to events, or even removed mentality entirely from the world.*

An immediate consequence of this conditional is the following:

(AUTOMATA) (assuming that Davidson's views are correct): *Even if certain people did not have any mental properties, as long as all of their physical properties were the same and their physical environments were the same, the same physical events would happen.*

In effect, Kim has invited us to make the same thought experiment as James (assuming Davidson's philosophy of mind is correct): imagine that there were a world in which some body just like mine (just like yours) were in exactly the same physical state and exactly the same physical environment as mine (as yours), but lacked all mental properties. Would it not behave exactly as mine (as yours) does? The body would be exactly like the body of James's imagined "automatic sweetheart," an automatic me or an automatic you. And from the fact (as Kim must claim it to be) that the automatic Hilary Putnam would turn on the water just as efficiently even though the mental event, the "decision to turn on the water for a bath," did not take place, Kim concludes that (if Davidson's philosophy of mind is correct) the mental event is *without causal efficacy.* Mental properties are mere "epiphenomena," just as Santayana supposed them to be.[15]

Of course, the argument can be blocked by denying that the counterfactual "makes sense." And, for the counterfactual not to make sense, Kim thinks that it would have to be the case that our mental properties are somehow reducible to our physical properties (or more precisely, "strongly supervenient" on them in some satisfactory way).[16] But reduction (including "strong supervenience") requires psychophysical laws, which Davidson's position rules out. Thus Kim's conclusion is disjunctive: *either* Davidson is wrong, and there are psychophysical laws, or else our mental properties are ephiphenomenal. (I leave out a third alternative, that it is an illusion that we have mental properties, since neither Davidson nor Kim—nor I, for that matter—take that one seriously.)

setting the stage:
finding fault with jaegwon kim's counterfactual

Suppose I am running water for a bath. If someone asked me "Why is the water running in the bathroom?" I might reply, "I'm running the water in order to take a bath," but I might also say simply "I decided to take a bath." And no one would doubt that I have *explained* why water is running in the bathroom. To be pedantic about it, water is running in the bathroom *because* I decided to take a bath, and because I decided to take a bath in *this* particular bathtub at this particular time, and I decided to take a "real" bath as opposed to a shower, and I know full well that to fill the tub for a "real" bath I need to turn the faucet, and I know how to turn the faucet to the right position, and I acted on my decisions and my knowledge.

John Haldane has wisely remarked[17] that "there are as many kinds of cause as there are senses of 'because.' " (He added that "Aristotle's doctrine of four causes was only a preliminary classification.") If the "because" in the preceding explanation is correct, then in some sense of "cause" my decision to turn that faucet to the middle position (between hot and cold) is the *cause* of water (of a certain comfortable temperature) running right now. Decisions (which are among the things that philosophers refer to as mental or psychological events) can be the causes of water runnings (which are among the things that philosophers refer to as physical events). And to suppose (as Santayana would have done) that the "because" is not correct—that is, to suppose that it *isn't* because of my decision that water of that comfortable temperature is now running, that indeed my decision was totally "inefficacious"—would be to reject ways of talking that are essential to our whole conception of ourselves as beings in a world; ways of talking even Santayana (who constantly offers advice as to how to live, advice that would make no

"i thought of what i called
'an automatic sweetheart'"

sense if decisions were causally inefficacious) was unable to do without or to offer a coherent alternative to. Epiphenomenalism is C-R-A-Z-Y.

Does it then follow that our mental properties must in some way be reducible to physical ones? Before we try to crack *that* chestnut, let us first look into the question of how we might defuse Kim's counterfactual.

Well, we don't want to simply accept the antecedent as a fully intelligible possibility (*Certain people do not have any mental properties, but all of their physical properties are the same as if they did and their physical environments are the same as if they did*) while denying the consequent (*The same physical events would happen*); i.e., we do not want to assert:

(NOT-AUTOMATA) *If certain people did not have any mental properties, but all of their physical properties were the same as if they did and their physical environments were the same, DIFFERENT physical events would happen.*[18]

(NOT-AUTOMATA) is not something that we find believable.

Of course, the fact that we do not find (NOT-AUTOMATA) believable has everything to do with the fact that we no longer find strong Cartesian dualism ("interactionism") believable. For (NOT-AUTOMATA) is exactly what Descartes himself believed: he believed that the mind, conceived of as an immaterial entity that "bears" all of our mental properties, causes our bodies to act in a way in which they would not act if the mind were taken away.

In these lectures I shall be arguing that neither the classical problems in the philosophy of mind nor the "philosophical positions" they give rise to are completely intelligible. I think this whole idea of the mind as an immaterial object "interacting" with the body is an excellent example of an unintelligible position in the philosophy of mind, but this is not the customary criticism of interactionism.

The customary criticism was beautifully and trenchantly stated by Bertrand Russell.[19] If dualist interactionism is true, then my body must have a trajectory that is different from the trajectory that would be predicted for it by the laws of physics on the basis of the totality of the physical forces acting upon it. Descartes himself was aware of this, and since even he did not want to postulate that when human bodies are involved in physical interactions such basic laws as the Conservation of Momentum are violated, he posited that although the mind can alter the *direction* in which the body moves (by acting on the body in the region of the pineal gland), it cannot alter the "quantity of motion" (this is more or less what we today call "total scalar momentum"). But shortly after Descartes's time it was realized that *total momentum in each direction in space is also a conserved quantity. Thus, if interactionism is true, some conservation laws of physics are violated when humans act on the basis of decisions and other thoughts.* In short, interactionism implies that *human bodies behave in ways that violate the laws of physics.* Since there is not a shred of evidence that this is the case, we are compelled to reject interactionism just as we reject vitalism and other outmoded views that postulated various phenomena ("life" was a popular example in the nineteenth century) to be "exceptions to the laws of physics." As Kim himself puts a less detailed form of the same argument,

> There is a further assumption that I believe any physicalist would grant [and Kim is evidently a "physicalist" in this respect], namely "the causal closure of the physical domain." Roughly, it says this: *any physical event that has a cause at time t has a physical cause at t.* This is the assumption that if we trace the causal ancestry of a physical event, we need never go outside the physical domain. To reject this assumption is to accept the Cartesian idea that some physical events need nonphysical causes, and if this is true there can in principle be no complete and self-sufficient physical theory of the physical domain. If the causal closure failed, our physics would need to refer in an essential way to nonphysical causal agents, perhaps Cartesian souls and their psychic properties, if it is to give a complete account of the physical world. I think most physicalists would find that picture unacceptable.[20]

Russell's (and Kim's) argument is an *empirical* argument. It assumes that interactionism is fully intelligible (contrary to the position that I will argue for) and argues that the empirical evidence does not support it. But whether we reject interactionism on empirical grounds, as Russell did, or on the grounds that we cannot make sufficient sense of it, as I would argue we should, the fact is that scientifically minded people today do reject interactionism. So if we wish also to reject (AUTOMATA) it cannot be by simply asserting (NOT-AUTOMATA).

"i thought of what i called
'an automatic sweetheart'"

79

There are, in fact, quite a number of philosophical positions that imply that (AUTOMATA) is not true but that do not imply (NOT-AUTOMATA)—for example, reductionist physicalism, logical behaviorism, and verificationism. Philosophers who defend these positions would attack (AUTOMATA) by finding one or another thing wrong with the antecedent, which I reformulated[21] above as *Certain people do not have any mental properties, but all of their physical properties are the same as if they did and their physical environments are the same.* More precisely, such philosophers would agree that the conjunction of the denial of interactionism with the antecedent of (AUTOMATA) suffers from one or another defect—unintelligibility (according to verificationists) or self-contradiction (according to logical behaviorists) or metaphysical impossibility (according to some reductionist physicalists—as we shall see other reductionist physicalists would argue that the antecedent of (AUTOMATA) is *irrelevant* if we are interested in what happens in the actual world).

To see why this is the case, observe that if interactionism is false, and if the antecedent of (AUTOMATA) describes a state of affairs that could conceivably hold even *when* interactionism is false, then (AUTOMATA) must be true. And that would mean that James's "automatic sweetheart"—the person who has no mental properties, no "consciousness," but who behaves exactly *as if* she had such properties—is a conceivable state of affairs. Thus, a way to attack (AUTOMATA), on the assumption that interactionism is false, is to deny that the following state of affairs makes sense: the antecedent of (AUTOMATA) is true, but the people in question do not behave any differently then they would if they had their "mental properties."

Verificationism argues that the state of affairs described would be unverifiable (if the people in question acted exactly as they would have if they had their mental properties, then it would be impossible in principle to verify that they lacked them) and therefore the supposed description of this "state of affairs" ("the antecedent of (AUTOMATA) is true, but the people in question do not behave any differently than they would if it were false") is cognitively meaningless. Unlike verificationism, logical behaviorism does not necessarily assume that all meaningful propositions are verifiable in principle, but it claims that all propositions about *mental* properties are logically equivalent to propositions about (physical) behavior. So if we were to suppose that we can imagine a world in which the antecedent of (AUTOMATA) is true and interactionism is false (a world in which the antecedent of (AUTOMATA) is true, but the people in question do not behave any differently than they would if it were false), we would be supposing one can imagine that *the logically necessary conditions for the presence of mental properties are fulfilled but the properties are not present,* and this is a contradiction. So if verificationism is correct, then the conjunction of "no interactionism" with the antecedent of (AUTOMATA) is cognitively meaningless, and if logical behaviorism is correct, the conjunction is self-contradictory. If either position is correct, we can refuse to count (AUTOMATA) as a true counterfactual without being forced to accept (NOT-AUTOMATA). Unfortunately, neither verificationism nor logical behaviorism appear to be tenable positions any longer.[22]

Donald Davidson's position is that the raison d'être of talk about the mental is to enable us to "rationalize" the behavior of human agents. Moreover, he contends, this is its *whole* function; that is why there cannot be psychophysical laws. If this view is right, the conjunction of "no interactionism" with the antecedent of (AUTOMATA) describes a state of affairs in which the whole rationale for applying mental predicates applies, but those mental predicates do not "really" apply. Surely Davidson would regard this as an unintelligible suggestion!

Davidson is clearly not a verificationist, and he is certainly not a logical behaviorist, but his position has an interesting relation to both of these. Like the logical behaviorists, he believes that if you behave in all respects as if mental predicates applied to you ("all respects" here includes microphysical respects, if microphysical events can become relevant to the interpretation of your speech and other behavior), then those mental predicates *do* apply to you; although unlike logical behaviorists, Davidson does not believe that one can write down conceptual truths linking particular mental predicates to particular behavioral predicates. Like the verificationists, he believes that if a mental predicate applies to you then an observer who was "omniscient" with respect to all physical facts about you and your environment could verify that it applies to you.[23] Indeed, we might call Davidson a psychoverification-

"i thought of what i called
'an automatic sweetheart' "

ist—a verificationist about the mental. My own rejection of the intelligibility of the various AUTOMATA scenarios we have considered will, however, depart from the strategy of defending Davidson at this point. I shall not make any of the metaphysical assumptions (about the one and only purpose of talk about the mental, etc.) that figure in Davidson's metaphysics of mind.

Turning now to physical reductionism (and it is a—highly sophisticated—version of physical reductionism that Kim is defending), those who take this approach have a number of possible strategies for dealing with (AUTOMATA) and the threat it poses to the causal efficacy of the mental. The simplest is just to argue that (AUTOMATA) is *irrelevant*. After all, if it is the case *in the actual world* that our so-called mental properties are just a subset of our physical properties, then any world in which the antecedent of (AUTOMATA) is true is a world in which mental properties are very differently "realized" than they are in the actual world. Even if mental properties *would be* "epiphenomenal" in *such* a "possible world," they are definitely not in the actual world, because they are physical and physical properties are by definition not epiphenomenal.[24]

However, as I shall try to show in the succeeding lectures, reductionist physicalism is incoherent. If that is right, and we are not willing to be verificationists (or "psychoverificationists") and not willing to be logical behaviorists, on what other grounds could we possibly avoid accepting (AUTOMATA), and, with (AUTOMATA), the conclusion that since all physical events would go on in the same way even if our mental properties were stripped away, those mental properties are one and all *epiphenomenal*? How can we avoid Kim's disjunction: either our mental properties *are* physical properties in disguise, or they are epiphenomenal? (Kim tells me that he himself finds both disjuncts unattractive!)

the intelligibility of the antecedent of (AUTOMATA) reconsidered

Some would call the approach I am going to take in these lectures a Wittgensteinian approach, but even if my discussion will not be completely free of references to Ludwig Wittgenstein's later philosophy, I promise to avoid quotations from the *Investigations* and to employ Wittgenstein's own terminology as little as possible.[25] Perhaps this promise will relieve the anxieties some of you may feel! Specifically, my approach to Kim's challenging dilemma will be—not surprisingly—to question the *intelligibility* of the antecedent of (AUTOMATA). I will claim that this antecedent—once more,

(SOULLESS) *Certain people do not have any mental properties, but all of their physical properties are the same as if they did and their physical environments are the same*

—and also the conjunction of (SOULLESS) with "the denial of interactionism"—both fall short of full intelligibility.[26] And I shall argue that because neither of these supposed "possible states of affairs" is sufficiently intelligible, the question of what would happen if either of them were true is nonsensical. To draw an analogy, the statement "Cinderella's coach turned into a pumpkin" satisfies our criteria for intelligibility when *understood as an utterance in a fairy tale* (we know "what to do" with it, how to react to it, how to "play the game"); but if we detach the statement "sometimes coaches turn into pumpkins" from a very particular sort of context and try to discuss the question "What would happen if a coach turned into a pumpkin?" as if this were, for example, a serious scientific question, we would be talking nonsense. In the same way, one might enjoy a work of fiction in which someone was in love with an "automatic sweetheart," but that doesn't entail that talk of "possible worlds" in which some or all of us are automatic sweethearts makes sense.[27] But this will take a lot of unpacking, and I anticipate encountering certain misunderstandings.

The misunderstandings that I fear have to do with the erstwhile popularity and current well-deserved unpopularity of verificationism and logical behaviorism. Because the struggle against logical behaviorism that went on in the 1950s and 1960s, and the struggle against verificationism that is still going on,[28] have occupied much attention and still take up significant space in widely used collections of articles in the philosophy of mind, it is immediately expected that anyone who questions the intelligibility of a scenario like (SOULLESS) (or (SOULLESS) plus the denial of interactionism, or plus "the people in question do not behave any differently") must be a verificationist or a behaviorist. In the sequel I hope to dispel this misunderstanding by showing that there are quite different grounds for questioning the intelligibility of these scenarios, grounds

"i thought of what i called
'an automatic sweetheart'"

83

that do not turn upon a prior commitment to a philosophical theory (such as verificationism) that is supposed to yield a general method for assessing the meaningfulness of an arbitrary statement or upon a commitment to the claims of logical behaviorism. In the next two lectures I hope to show that there are closely related grounds for questioning the intelligibility of reductionism (and of antireductionism as well, for that matter) and thus for finding *both* horns of Kim's dilemma very far from fully intelligible.

the question of the "independence" of mental and physical properties

Let us consider (SOULLESS) once again:

(1) (SOULLESS) *Certain people do not have any mental properties, but all of their physical properties are the same as if they did and their physical environments are the same.*

Let us begin by looking at a prima facie reason for thinking that this makes full sense.

The following principle seems prima facie plausible:

(INDEPENDENCE) If A and B are two sorts of properties, and B-properties are not reducible to any A properties, then B properties are *independent* of A properties, in the sense that it is logically possible that the A properties should be present without the B properties.

Moreover, Kim himself clearly assumes the applicability of (INDEPENDENCE) to the case in which the A properties are the physical properties and the B properties are the mental properties in "The Myth of Nonreductive Physicalism."[29]

If we agree that this principle is correct and applicable, then, on the assumptions we are making (at this stage in Kim's argument), our mental and our physical properties are *independent*. So why *shouldn't* one be able to conceive of one sort being present without the other, and to ask what "would happen if" just as Kim does?

With this question we begin to leave the harbor and sail out into deep waters. In a way, this should not be a surprise to those of you who are familiar with the great debates in analytic philosophy in the last half-century. For

(INDEPENDENCE) assumes just the notions that Quine, in particular, attacked in his seminal papers "On What There Is" and "Two Dogmas of Empiricism": the idea of *properties* as having well-defined identity conditions and the metaphysical idea of "possibility." This is already enough to show that (INDEPENDENCE) is not a harmless truism. But my difficulties with (INDEPENDENCE) do not presuppose Quine's complete rejection of property talk and of possibility talk. I am concerned not with (INDEPENDENCE) in the abstract but with Kim's specific application of (INDEPENDENCE).

When we turn from (INDEPENDENCE) as an abstract principle to the implicit employment I believe it has in Kim's argument, we notice that one thing we must assume to use it to support the full sensicality of (SOULLESS) is that it makes sense to talk about reducibility as a relation that holds or fails to hold between mental and physical properties, that is, to suppose that we *know what we are asking* when we ask whether a given (so-called) mental property, e.g., *thinking about the beauty of the roses in Safed*, is or is not "reducible to" (or "nomologically coextensive with") a physical property. But the burden of my own arguments against "identity theories" (including my own former "functionalism") is that *the notion of identity has not been given any sense in this context.*[30] We cannot, for example (as I once thought we could),[31] employ the model of theoretical identification derived from such famous successful reductions as the reduction of thermodynamics to statistical mechanics, because that model assumes that both the reduced theory and the reducing theory" have well-defined bodies of laws. (So that a proposed statement of identity, e.g., "temperature is mean molecular kinetic energy," can be established by showing that if we assume it the laws of the reduced theory—thermodynamics, in this example—can be derived from the laws of the reducing theory.) We cannot sensibly ask whether the laws of "folk psychology" are or are not derivable from some set of assumed identities between the attributes spoken of in folk psychology and some set of computational properties (plus the description of the "program" that defines those computational properties), because, as I have argued elsewhere, the notion of a "computational property" depends essentially on *what formalism the "program" is written in,* and no one has the slightest idea what a formalism in which one can

"i thought of what i called
'an automatic sweetheart'"

write programs that reduce folk psychology might look like. As long as we have not given a determinate meaning to computational property, all this talk of functionalism is just *science fiction*. No serious scientifically discussable issue of identity has really been raised.

To be sure, Kim's purpose is not primarily to defend functionalism (although, as we shall see in a later lecture, one of his crucial arguments presupposes functionalism). What Kim proposes is rather that each mental property is "strongly supervenient" on a *physical* property, at least in the case of each species (or, perhaps, each relevant neurological "structure"). In my final lecture I shall argue that this has only the appearance of being clearer than unanalyzed talk of identity. But I shall withhold arguing this until that lecture and devote the remainder of this lecture to trying to see what follows if I am right about this.

Well, the relevance of the claim I am making to (INDEPENDENCE) is not difficult to see. Suppose we reformulate (INDEPENDENCE) as follows:

(INDEPENDENCE?) If A and B are two sorts of properties, and the question as to whether B properties are or are not reducible to any A properties has not been given any clear sense, then B properties are *independent* of A properties, in the sense that it is logically possible that the A properties should be present without the B properties.

I do not think that any philosopher would regard (INDEPENDENCE?) as having any plausibility at all! For if the question of reducibility (or nomological coextensiveness) has not been given any clear sense, then it would be natural to suppose that the question of independence has also not been given any clear sense.

What this shows, if I am right, is that if we assume (INDEPENDENCE), we have *already assumed* that all the propositions in question make full sense: the propositions about the "reducibility" or "nonreducibility" of physical and mental properties as well as the propositions about the "independence" of the mental and the physical properties. No wonder it then seems obvious that one can sensibly talk about people who are supposed to have all their physical properties and none of their mental properties!

What I want to bring into focus now and in the rest of these lectures is the way in which different philosophical pictures of how language functions

mind and body

and what meanings are (or, better, what knowledge of meanings consists in) will affect our attitudes toward just about every philosophical debate. This is something that Charles Travis, a philosopher whose work is not nearly as well-known as it should be, has written about extensively and also something that Stanley Cavell has written about at length, especially in his master-piece, *The Claim of Reason*. If you will forgive what may seem a digression, I want to say something about certain general issues raised by these thinkers before I return to the issues about reducibility and mental causation.

"words have meaning only in the stream of life"[32]

The difference between the two philosophical pictures I just referred to is laid out in a very clear way in Charles Travis's book on Wittgenstein's later phi-losophy, *The Uses of Sense*.[33] (Travis's discussion-review of Grice's philosophy of language, "Annals of Analysis,"[34] is perhaps the best short introduction to these issues as well as a powerful criticism of Grice's procedures.) Travis presents what I am calling two "philosophical pictures" as different concep-tions of what the semantics of an utterance in a natural language might be. One conception (of which Paul Grice was a leading representative) Travis calls the "classical" conception; the other—less familiar—conception, which he attributes to Wittgenstein and Austin, he calls "speaking-sensitive seman-tics," because the heart of this second conception is the claim that the con-tent of an utterance depends on the particular context in which it is spoken, on the particular "speaking."

The second conception does not deny that words have "meanings" (that is, that there is something that is rightly called "knowing the [or a] meaning" of a word and that this knowledge constrains the contents that can be expressed using the word with what can be regarded as that particular meaning). What it denies is that meaning (or the knowledge in question) completely determines what is being said (what is supposed to be true or false, or if anything *is* being said that is true or false) when a sentence is used to make an assertion.[35]

A couple of examples may clarify the issue. I certainly know the meaning of the words *there, coffee, a lot, is, on, the,* and *table*. But that knowledge by itself does not determine the content of the sentence *There is a lot of coffee*

"i thought of what i called
'an automatic sweetheart'"

on the table; in fact, the sentence, simply as a sentence, doesn't *have* a determinate content apart from particular speakings. Moreover, the truth-evaluable content of the sentence "There is a lot of coffee on the table" is highly occasion-sensitive: depending upon the circumstances, the sentence can be used to say that there are many cups of coffee on a contextually definite table (*There is a lot of coffee on the table; have some*), or that there are bags of coffee stacked on the table (*There is a lot of coffee on the table; load it in the truck*), or that coffee has been spilled on the table (*There is a lot of coffee on the table; wipe it up*), etc.

A different sort of example: I have an ornamental tree in my garden with bronze-colored leaves. Suppose a prankster paints the leaves green. Depending upon who says it and to whom and why, the sentence *The tree has green leaves*, said with my tree in mind, may be true, false, or not clearly either!

(Responding to the coffee example, a philosopher of language of my acquaintance—one wedded to Grice's distinction between the standard meaning of an utterance and its conversational implicatures—suggested that the "standard meaning" of "there is a lot of coffee on the table" is that there are many (how many?) molecules of coffee on the table. But if that is right, the "standard" sense is a sense in which the words are never used!)

The classical conception does not, of course, deny that the exact reference of some words (e.g., the tense indicators and the familiar indexicals) is speaking sensitive; but it treats speaking sensitivity as a special phenomenon, easily adjusted for. The classical picture of the semantics of a natural language is Tarskian: truth conditions are recursively associated with all the sentences of a natural language (as in Davidson's celebrated adaptation and modification of Tarski's work). The claim Travis makes is that speaking sensitivity, far from being a special phenomenon, is the norm.

Recently a good deal of literature[36] has appeared on this very phenomenon (which is now usually called context sensitivity rather than speaking sensitivity). My "coffee" and "green" examples illustrate how common nouns and adjectives may have very different reference in different contexts *compatibly* with what they "mean." To determine what is being said by "There is a lot of coffee on the table" or "The tree has green leaves now" in a particular context one needs to know the "meaning of the words," the implicit constraints on what can and cannot be said using those words, *and* to use good judgment to figure out what is being said in the given context; and, as Kant long ago said (if not in those terms), there isn't a recursive rule for "good judgment" (not one we can formulate, anyway!). As Cavell argues at length in *The Claim of Reason*, our "atunement" to another, our shared sense of what is and what is not a natural projection of our previous uses of a word into a new context, is pervasive and fundamental to the very possibility of language—without being something that can be captured by a system of "rules."

There are many other sorts of examples, besides the two I just gave. Whether a surface is "flat" or not depends on what a *reasonable* standard of flatness is in the particular context. (Against this, Peter Unger once argued[37] that only a Euclidean plane is "literally flat." [So whenever I say that a table top is flat I am speaking "figuratively"!] Note that the semantics Unger proposed for "flat" violates the Principle of Charity to the maximum extent!) Whether playing a concerto is "difficult" depends on who is asking whom (imagine a child asking a violin teacher and a professional violinist asking another). Whether a sack of sugar weighs "one pound" depends on whether the question is asked in the supermarket or in the laboratory. But it is time to say what all of this has to do with philosophy.

Consider the following scenario discussed by Wittgenstein in *Remarks on the Philosophy of Psychology*:

> 96. A tribe that we want to enslave. The government and the scientists give it out that the people of this tribe have no souls; so they can be used without any scruple for any purpose whatsoever. Naturally we are interested in their language all the same; for of course we need to give them orders and to get reports from them. We want to know too what they say among themselves, as this hangs together with the rest of their behavior. But also we must be interested in what in them corresponds to our "psychological utterances," for we want to keep them capable of work, and so their expressions of pain, of feeling unwell, of pleasure in life, etc., etc., are of importance to us. Indeed, we have also found that these people can be used successfully as experimental objects in physiological and psychological labo-

"i thought of what i called 'an automatic sweetheart'"

ratories; since their reactions—including speech-reactions—are altogether those of men endowed with souls [*seelenbegabten Menschen*]. I assume that it has been found that these automata can be taught our language instead of their own by a method very like our "instruction."[38]

Here Wittgenstein imagines that, out of the motive of exploiting and enslaving certain people, we picture them to ourselves as being precisely like the "certain people" we hypothesized above. Remember?—

(SOULLESS) *Certain people do not have any mental properties, but all of their physical properties are the same as if they did and their physical environments are the same.*

When I encounter (SOULLESS) in the context of an argument like Kim's, I confess that I am utterly at a loss what to make of it. I feel that I cannot conceive of a case in which I would use the description "these people do not have any mental properties, but all of their physical properties are the same as if they did and their physical environments are the same." And precisely because a context, a "speaking," is absent—and if we lack a context in which an utterance U makes sense, we do not provide one by just saying, "Now we are talking philosophy," or by saying, "Consider the possibility that U"!—precisely because a context is absent, I cannot say what it would be for (SOULLESS) to be *true*. Yet when I encounter 96 above in Wittgenstein's *Remarks on the Philosophy of Psychology*, I suddenly realize that there is a case in which, sadly, we might very well use such a description (or the shorter, "soulless automata"). *In that context* I understand it all too well. I understand the utterances Wittgenstein refers to ("the people of this tribe have no souls"; in 97 he adds, "If anyone among us voices the idea that something must be going on *in* these beings, something mental, this is laughed at like a stupid superstition") in the sense of being perfectly able to follow what is going on.

Does that mean that I am able to assign a "possible world" to (SOULLESS) in the context Wittgenstein has constructed? to say what it would be for the version given out by "the government and the scientists" to be *true*? Not at all.[39] That a piece of propaganda does not, on reflection, describe a state of affairs we can make sense of does not mean that it does not function effectively as propaganda. (Wittgenstein was well aware of what the Nazis said about the Jews.) One of the morals we should draw from this case is that "understanding" itself is context sensitive; in one sense, I "understand" what it means to say the people of the tribe in question are "soulless automata," I understand what the words are *doing*, what effect they are intended to have and do have, but that does not mean I understand them in the context of Jaegwon Kim's argument! Rather, to understand them in that context I would need to understand them *independently* of Kim's argument, for that argument presupposes a *prior* intelligibility of the idea that certain people are "soulless automata." (Or, more precisely, it presupposes that if we reject reductionism, then we must regard (SOULLESS) as making sense—without telling us *how* to understand the supposed "sense.")

Note that if this is right the problem with Kim's argument is not that the antecedent *couldn't* be used to make an assertion that we understand. If I were to say of a group of bureaucrats "They are quite remarkable—they do not have any mental properties, but all of their physical properties are the same as if they did and their physical environments are the same, but they are really soulless automata," I might be saying something perfectly intelligible (and something that I couldn't say just as well by saying, "They are absolutely devoid of judgment, sympathy, human understanding"). *In that context* the words that make up (SOULLESS) might have a perfectly clear content—but not one that is relevant to discussions of "mental causation." The problem with Kim's antecedent is not with the words themselves;[40] it is that we do not know what Kim means by them.

are psychological conditions "internal states"?

In the last lecture we discussed the manner in which the strange view called epiphenomenalism, that is, the view that mental states lack causal efficacy, has reappeared in contemporary debate. The epiphenomenalist scenario has always seemed rather weird, which may be why it is so hard to find an epiphenomenalist in the history of philosophy, although there are some contemporary philosophers who defend a very limited epiphenomenalism: epiphenomenalism with respect to experiential *qualia*. (These philosophers never discuss how we are supposed to be able to so much as *refer* to qualia, if qualia have no causal influence on anything else—not even on thoughts.) Leibniz, indeed, denied that there is any real "mental-physical" causation, but only by denying that there is any "real causation" apart from God's actualization of a particular possible world. (It's not so much, in Leibnizian metaphysics, that minds are causally inefficacious as that "efficacy" isn't what we suppose it to be.) Aristotle thought that the soul (*psyche*) was the form (*eidos*) of an organized living body. According to his doctrine, its functions included, in addition to what we today regard as "psychological" or "mental" ones, *digestion* and *reproduction*. Talk of a body that digested, reproduced, talked, etc., but that had no "psyche" would have seemed utterly unintelligible to an Aristotelian.[1] But Plato had a very different view.

In several of Plato's dialogues we encounter the idea of the soul as both preexisting the body and as surviving the destruction of the body, sometimes via reincarnation, sometimes by ascending to the realm of the Ideas. Such ideas were already old in Plato's time; the idea of the soul as surviving the body (though not entirely losing connection with it—which is why embalming was so important!) were central to the Egyptian religion(s), which were already thousands of years old, and, of course, the idea of the soul as having an "afterlife" was, at a later point, adopted by the monotheistic religions.

My purpose in bringing this up is not to enter into a discussion of the intelligibility of religious language, although that is something I am interested in both as a philosopher and as a practicing Jew, or of the intelligibility of religious talk about the soul, the "world to come," etc. (which also interests me, and which, like religious language in general, interested Wittgenstein as well).[2] Obviously, there is a sense in which we all "understand" religious language (as Wittgenstein remarks,[3] we can "imagine" disembodied souls; we have all seen *paintings* of them!). And, there is a sense in which the meaningfulness of religious language is deeply controversial.[4] I do not expect philosophers who are believers and philosophers who are atheists to come into agreement on this issue. What I am interested in is the *relation* between the existence of religious ways of life that include talk of "souls," "survival," etc., and the compelling illusion (for that is what I am arguing it is) that certain philosophical "hypotheses" make clear sense.

I want to spend a few pages on this topic because I believe it may shed light on (some of) the reasons for resistance to the idea that the major philosophical "hypotheses" in the philosophy of mind do not make sense. I do not want to inquire into the existential reasons for our being led into the tangles of skepticism and metaphysics at all (Stanley Cavell would claim that, at bottom, the tangles of metaphysics *are* just the tangles of skepticism); I am content to leave that to others, especially to Cavell himself. But I believe that in addition to those existential reasons (though certainly not unconnected with them) there are also deep conceptual (or "ideological") reasons for it seeming obvious to us that certain possibilities make sense that (in my view) do not. If talk

mind and body

94

of the soul and of its existence after the decay of the body has been part of our intellectual and spiritual lives for so long, it is not surprising that the meaningfulness of hypotheses concerning the "interactions" between the soul and the body, and questions as to what would happen if there were a body "without a soul," should seem to make perfect sense. (Descartes himself was a deeply religious thinker, after all.) Notice how the word *soulless* plays a key role in James's scenario of the "automatic sweetheart"![5]

A scientific analogy has occurred to me. I regard it as perfectly meaningful to conjecture that there may not be any intelligent extraterrestrials, even though that proposition, if true, could never be verified by anyone.[6] Indeed, even if there *are* intelligent extraterrestrials, *that* may not be verifiable by humans. (They may be too far away.) Yet I am confident that the question as to the existence of intelligent extraterestials makes sense, regardless of whether the answer is verifiable, because that question fits naturally into a framework that I trust, the contemporary scientific cosmology. In the same way, I suggest, the Christian and Jewish and Moslem world pictures may look like frameworks into which speculations like Descartes's fit naturally; it may seem that, short of rejecting the intelligibility of the religious world pictures entirely, one cannot question the intelligibility of the post-Cartesian hypotheses. I wish to argue that this is not the case.

But first, let me make try to make clear exactly what I am suggesting. I am saying that our reason for thinking that we can intelligibly discuss what would happen if some people were "soulless" *isn't*, at bottom, a formal reason such as the acceptance of the principle (IND) together with doubts about "identity theories" of mind and body. Such formal reasons may determine the views of a few philosophers, but I believe the widespread—indeed, the almost universal—acceptance of dualism, interactionism, occasionalism, epiphenomenalism, and reductionism as intelligible alternatives, indeed, as *the* intelligible alternatives in this area of philosophy in the modern period, has much more to do with the fact that the picture of our minds as being somehow located in our "souls"[7] rather than our bodies was *already* in place. And if we identify (as Descartes precisely wished us to do!) the post-Cartesian notion of the "mind" (*mens sive intellectus sive anima*) with the religious

are psychological conditions "internal states"?

95

notion of the "soul," that means that "Cartesian dualism" and all the questions it raises will seem as intelligible as that notion, a notion we have already accepted as fully intelligible.

Of course, religious belief is much less widespread—especially in the academy!—than it was a hundred years ago, and an atheist may well feel that the traditional notion of the soul is "nonsense." But calling something nonsense isn't necessarily denying its *intelligibility*. Indeed, most atheists seem to feel that "the existence of God," "the existence of an immaterial soul," etc., are perfectly *clear* questions to which they have given negative answers. Once a set of questions gets accepted as clear, there is real difficulty in getting anyone to accept that what one has to do is *question their intelligibility* rather than offer straightforward "answers."

But I wish to emphasize that my own questioning of the intelligibility of these philosophical questions does not stem from atheism and is not based on a rejection of religious ways of living and thinking. What I want to suggest in the next section is that religious ways of thinking (and, for that matter, the Greek philosophical ways of thinking that helped to shape the monotheistic religions ever since the classical period) do *not* support the intelligibility of the philosophical hypotheses. (I find this to be of independent interest as well as of relevance to our present discussion.)

greek (and later) views of the soul

Although it may seem obvious that the soul—if there is such a thing—is immaterial, in the strong sense of being "independent of matter," that was *not* the view of most of the Greek schools of philosophy. I have already mentioned the Aristotelian view that the soul is related to the body as form is to the matter it informs (without a soul, my body wouldn't *be* a body, in Aristotle's view,[8] and without a body the soul would be a mere concept). "Soulless body" is an oxymoron, on this conception. What is more surprising is that a number of Greek and Hellenistic philosophers embraced the concept of a *material* soul.

In particular, both the Democriteans and the Stoics thought that the soul, like the body, consists of matter—only far more "subtle" or "ethereal" matter.

Perhaps they even thought it consisted of *air!*[9] When we talk of "spirits" or "purely spiritual beings" how often do we remember that *spiritus* was "breathing, breath, air"?[10] (And although it is true that the Platonic soul was independent of matter, it does seem that it was still in some sense "substantial.")

Under St. Augustine's influence the Platonic idea that the soul has no material "substance" became dominant Christian doctrine for several centuries. But, interestingly, the great later medieval philosophers, including Aquinas, reverted more and more to the Aristotelian view, which they reconciled with the doctrine of Resurrection by positing that, at the Resurrection, God would give each person a "transformed" body, one consisting of an imperishable substance.[11]

Last but not least, it is important to note that it is not at all clear what it means to say that something is or isn't "material" (or "physical"). The Greek philosophers who talked about "soul atoms" considered themselves materialists! (And the nineteenth century spiritualists who summoned ghosts to table-rapping sessions talked about "ectoplasm," as if it were a kind of *matter* of which the ghosts consisted.) The role that may be played by talk of the soul in a particular religious form of life is so different from the role played by talk of the soul in a philosophical argument that the use of the word in the latter context simply cannot be projected in any reliable way from the former, even if the presence of the word in the former context may have, in the minds of great religious philosophers like Augustine and Descartes, played a role in legitimizing their philosophical uses of the word.

What this illustrates is that purely *religious* uses of the word *soul* (even in the context of talk of an "afterlife," "Resurrection," etc.) leave one completely free to accept or reject *philosophical* talk of the soul as "completely immaterial." Although traditional Christian pictures of the afterlife certainly supported the idea that what is ordinarily called my body is not necessary for the existence of any of my "psychological properties," a "literal" acceptance of those pictures was regarded as problematical by all the great Christian theologians (including Augustine as well as the Aristotelians); indeed, those pictures, taken "literally," would imply that the "disembodied" soul can be *painted* (and that God has fingers and toes!).[12] The idea that our mental properties belong to something "completely

are psychological conditions
"internal states"?

immaterial" was not itself a religious doctrine that Augustine simply inherited, nor a coherent part of the popular religious pictures; rather the doctrine that our mental properties belong to the soul and the soul has a certain independence of *this* body, together with the various pictures and myths in question, created a climate in which Augustine (under the influence of Neoplatonism) could introduce the philosophical doctrine as an *exegesis* of the religious doctrines and hopes. Nevertheless, I suggest that in the absence of soul talk the very idea that our mental properties might be "subtracted" from us without disrupting our bodies or altering our environments might well have seemed unintelligible. The semblance of intelligibility that philosophical hypotheses possess may, in part, be inherited from the intelligibility of the religious myths; but those myths do not depend for their *religious* functioning on their being "possible worlds in which people have physical properties and no mental properties" or "possible worlds in which there are minds with no material substance whatsoever," etc.

It may also seem that arguments like Russell's (cited) above show that the hypothesis of an "immaterial soul" controlling the body possesses scientific intelligibility: if it didn't, how could it be scientifically criticized? But what Russell's argument really refutes is the idea that there are forces acting on the body, and explaining the motion of the limbs, the words that come out of the lips, etc., that do not have sources for which momentum can be defined. This gives no *positive* meaning to "immaterial soul."

Obviously, in the context of his quarrel with Davidson, Jaegwon Kim *wasn't* asking us to imagine that there are immaterial souls. Rather (on the assumption that Davidson is right) he was asking us to imagine that there are soulless bodies that carry on just as we do. What I am saying is that one reason we are tempted to accept this as an intelligible request is that having inherited a tradition in which it is (supposedly) intelligible to think of mental properties as "housed" in an immaterial soul, it naturally seems intelligible to ask what would happen if we "subtracted" that soul.

on lacking full intelligibility

I have spoken of certain philosophical "hypotheses" as lacking *full* intelligibility. One reason for the qualifying adjective is that, of course, there *is* a sense in which I "understand" Kim's argument (just as there is a sense in which I "understand" what "the government and the scientists" are saying, what function their words have, in Wittgenstein's scenario of the soulless tribe). I "understand what is going on."[13] But "intelligibility" in *that* sense is no guarantee that what has been said is coherent enough to be described as a possible state of affairs (just as "imaginability" is, famously, no guarantee that what is said to be imagined is even logically consistent).

Another reason for speaking of (SOULLESS), etc., as lacking *full* intelligibility rather than simply as unintelligible is that, as already remarked, there are contexts in which we *can* use sentences like (SOULLESS) to say something that could correctly be called true (as when I said of certain bureaucrats that "they lack all mental properties"). And, as just discussed, there are religious sentences that are grammatically related to (SOULLESS) whose (disputed, to be sure) intelligibility may also lend a semblance of intelligibility to (SOULLESS). Indeed, as James Conant has recently argued,[14] it is typical of philosophical "nonsense" that it has, as it were, *too many meanings* rather than no meaning at all. As Conant puts it, "What Wittgenstein does . . . is to begin by showing us the diverse questions we might be asking . . . and that there is no answer to 'the question' as posed, because there is no clear question, but only a form of words hovering indeterminately between these diverse possibilities of use."[15]

In the case of (SOULLESS) and related sentences, there is an additional reason for the strong resistance one encounters (in oneself, first of all) to saying that one does not fully understand just what this "possible state of affairs" is supposed to *be*. That cause for resistance is the powerful tendency to suppose that one can *give* meaning to (SOULLESS) (or to James's "automatic sweetheart" scenario) by simply focusing one's attention on one's own "consciousness," i.e., on one's current experiences, and saying to oneself, "I mean that they don't (or she doesn't) have THIS." But a moment's reflection will establish that just being conscious doesn't suffice for having the *concept* of consciousness, nor does having experiences suffice for having the *concept* of experience. The concept is one we acquired from other people. Indeed, there is something bizarre about the suggestion that the very beings from whom I learned the word do not mean anything by it! The language is a public language, after all. Thinking "they don't

are psychological conditions "internal states"?

99

have THIS" doesn't have a determinate content unless the THIS is conceptualized and our *concepts* of consciousness, experience, etc., are all interwoven with and used in connection with the behavior of others. To suppose that other people are "soulless" is to speak outside of all the criteria that we actually have for consciousness, experience, thought, etc. (It is *sometimes* intelligible to claim that although our everyday criteria for *p* are satisfied, *p* is not *true*.[16] But one has to *tell a story* about how this is supposed to happen in each case.)

Consider, for example, the case of Wittgenstein's "soulless tribe." What would the "scientists" say if asked, "Just what is this 'soul' that the natives lack? What determines whether one has or lacks one? What is the etiology of this condition of 'soullessness'? And, by the way, how did you find out that they are 'soulless'?" It would quickly become clear that what the "scientists" are doing *isn't* "describing a possible state of affairs" but something very different.

direct realism and the inner theater conception of the mental

Since the beginnings of philosophy as a subject there has been a struggle between two very different conceptions of perception. In ancient philosophy perception was thought of as supplying us with "appearances," and the form that the struggle in question took in that period concerned the nature of these appearances. Some classical philosophers conceived of appearances as *intermediaries* between us and things external to the soul.[17] For the Democriteans, for example, appearances were affections of the senses (and ultimately of the soul, which was thought also to consist of atoms, albeit of a finer kind than bodies) and the particular sensory qualities were defined in terms of the kinds of atoms that cause them.[18] The Stoics thought of appearances as "impressions" in the soul or "alterations" of the soul (which they also conceived of materialistically).[19]

For Aristotle, on the other hand, in perception and thought the intellectual part of the soul is in *direct* contact with the properties (the "sensible form") of the things thought about. In modern jargon the Democriteans and Stoics had a "representational" theory of perception while the Aristotelians were "direct realists."

Although no modern representational theory would suppose that in perception what we are directly aware of are literally little *images*[20] in the sense of physical likenesses, Wilfrid Sellars pointed out in a famous essay[21] that the picture that underlies representational theories up to the present day is of an *inner theater* or *inner movie screen*. On this conception, the "colors we see" are not really properties of the external objects but are properties of the images on the inner movie screen; indeed, the objects we "directly see" are only objects in the inner theater or on the inner movie screen. It is this picture that so-called direct realists, i.e., defenders of what William James called "the natural realism of the common man," have always been concerned to combat; indeed, in my opinion, "direct realism" is best thought of not as a *theory* of perception but as a denial of the necessity for and the explanatory value of positing "internal representations" in thought and perception.

The disagreement between the two conceptions continued in the middle ages.[22] After Descartes, however, the situation changed drastically; direct realism virtually vanished from the scene until the early twentieth century, when William James and the American "New Realists" led by Perry defended it (in a novel form). Then it disappeared again (in spite of a strong flirtation with the American innovation by Russell in *The Analysis of Mind*), until Austin's vigorous defense of commonsense realism[23] in his *Sense and Sensibilia*. Although in the last few years both John McDowell and myself have defended varieties of "direct" (or, better, commonsense) realism, the dominant view in Anglo-American philosophy of mind today appears to be what we may call "Cartesianism cum materialism," that is to say, a combination of Descartes's own conception of the mental as kind of inner theater with materialism. Jaegwon Kim's work is perhaps the best—best, because most intelligently defended—example I know of this Cartesianism cum materialism.[24]

(It is worthwhile observing how Descartes was led to the conception of the objects of "immediate" perception as *inside* us. *Every step of the way to this conclusion was driven by a skeptical argument.* Indeed, from the insistence that when he looked out of his window at the men in the street Descartes did not see "the men themselves" but rather the coats and hats, to the conclusion that he did not see the coats and hats either but a bunch of "secondary qualities" that were not "in" the coats and hats but in his own mind, each move Descartes made has supplied the fodder for thousands of epistemology courses, all preoccupied with the idea that no one has ever "directly seen a mate-

are psychological conditions "internal states"?

rial object," and with the resultant "problem of the existence of the external world" and the "problem of other minds.")

Although I was aware of Austin's *Sense and Sensibilia* long before, it was not until I began seriously studying William James in the 1970s that I began to be convinced that these traditional problems all rested on a mistaken conception of perception. On the traditional conception, what we are *cognitively* related to in perception is not people and furniture and landscapes but *representations*. These "inner representations" are supposed to be related to the people and furniture and landscapes we ordinarily claim to see and touch and hear, etc., only as inner effects to external causes; and how they manage to determinately *represent* anything remains mysterious in spite of hundreds of valiant attempts by both "realists" and "antirealists" to clear up the "mystery." Although I will not repeat here the arguments I have offered elsewhere,[25] I believe that it is only by giving up this picture of perception as mediated by a set of "representations" in an inner theater that we will ever be able to escape from the endless recycling of positions that do not work in the philosophy of mind (not to mention traditional epistemology and traditional metaphysics)—a recycling that has been going on for at least four centuries.

kim on "internal psychological states"

The reason that I have recalled the conception of the mental as an "inner theater" is that, as we shall see, Kim's arguments for psychophysical supervenience presuppose that conception of the mental from beginning to end. Let us now examine the chain of arguments Kim offers in a paper titled "Psychophysical Supervenience."[26] Kim begins by saying that at one time many philosophers believed "something like" the following thesis:

> *The Psychophysical Correlation Thesis*: For each psychological event M there is a physical event P such that, as a matter of law, an event of type M occurs to an organism at a time just in case an event of type P occurs to it at the same time.[27]

However, this thesis cannot be true just as it stands, Kim tells us, because psychological events are usually described using concepts that do not refer to states that are strictly "internal"—concepts such that whether they apply to an organism at a time depends (conceptually) either on what happens at other times or on the existence of things outside the organism or both. For example, whether I may correctly be said to "remember that I had fruit and cereal for breakfast this morning" depends not just on my present state but on whether I did eat fruit and cereal this morning (and, perhaps, on whether I experienced that eating). As Kim puts it, "Remembering is not internal."[28] Similarly, whether I may truly be said to "know where Paris is" depends not only on my present occurrent state but on where in fact Paris is. And it has been argued (by myself, and by Tyler Burge, and by others since), that the very *meaning* of most of our words depends on features of our environment and not just on what is inside our heads, and most present philosophers of mind accept those arguments.[29] So the Psychophysical Correlation Thesis and similar theses must be restricted to psychological states of a special kind, to "internal" psychological states, before they have any chance of being true. (It is with the appearance of this notion of an internal psychological state that we begin to see the old Cartesian picture of the mind as an inner theater making a reappearance.) In fact, after a few pages devoted to explaining this point, Kim writes (p. 183):

I would suggest the following procedure. We first define the notion of an "internal property" or "internal state" of a thing, and then defend the following two theses:

The Supervenience Thesis: Every internal psychological state of an organism is supervenient on its synchronous internal physical state.

The Explanatory Thesis: Internal psychological states are the only psychological states that psychological theory needs to invoke in explaining human behavior—the only states needed for psychology.

And a little later Kim remarks (p. 186), "A moment's reflection should convince us that those who believe that our mental states are determined by the physical processes in our bodies could not have noninternal states in mind. It is not that these noninternal states are not properly psychological . . . it is

are psychological conditions
"internal states"?

just that they go beyond what is *here* and *now* in the psychological space of the organism." (Up to this point, however, Kim has not shown that there *are* such things as "internal psychological states," and the image he uses, of a "psychological space," strongly suggests the old Cartesian internal theater. We only encounter Kim's actual examples of "internal psychological states" a little later (5, pp. 188–191), when Kim defends the Explanatory Thesis.)

Kim's way of restricting the thesis is as follows. He deals first with knowing, using the following example (p. 188):

> I know that if I turn this knob counterclockwise the burner will go on. Since I want the fire to go on, I turn the knob. My knowledge that turning the knob will cause the burner to go on plays a causal role in the explanation of my action of turning the knob.

Kim deals with this example by arguing that "in fact it is only the element of belief in knowing that is causally productive of the action. As Stich says, 'What knowledge adds to belief is psychologically irrelevant.' "

Let us pause to note that there are at least two problems with this response. One problem, as we remarked a moment ago, is that it is now generally accepted that the meaning of a subject's words depends on things external to the subject's body and brain. But if that is right, then *belief* is no more a purely "internal" state than knowing is. For, if we assume the correctness of the "externalist" picture in semantics, the content of a belief itself typically depends on various facts about the "external world" (What is "the burner"? What is "fire"?—these terms have a determinate sense only by virtue of occurring in a particular context as well as in a certain general sort of environment). Although Kim does not discuss this difficulty, a remark in the preface to his book to the effect that "the position that I defend [in the essay under discussion] . . . is analogous in certain ways to the 'narrow content' approach to mental causation now favored by some philosophers," indicates that what he would say in response to this objection is that the *really* relevant "internal psychological state" (in the case of his example) is not "believing that if I turn the knob counterclockwise the burner will go on" but rather *having a belief with that "narrow content."*[30]

A second problem with this response is raised and responded to by Kim himself (pp. 188–189):

> It is true that whether or not my action succeeds in bringing about the intended result normally depends on whether the belief involved is true. Thus, whether my action results in the burner being turned on depends on whether my belief that it would go on if the knob is turned is correct. However it is not part of the object of *psychological* explanation to explain why the burner went on; all it needs to explain is why I turned the knob. . . . The job of psychological explanation is done once it has explained the bodily action of turning the knob. . . . Only *basic actions*, not "derivative" or "generated actions," need to be explained by psychological theory.

A few pages later (p. 191) "basic actions" are identified with "basic bodily movements we can perform at will." I will discuss this claim about "the object of *psychological* explanation" shortly.

What of perceptual states? Kim simply swallows the representational theory of perception whole, even employing the language of sense-datum theory (p. 190):

> When we see a tree there is some internal phenomenal state going on; some internal representation of a tree will be present in us. In the language of the sense-datum theory, we are sensing a treeish sense-datum, or we are appeared to treeishly. The Explanatory Thesis would claim that whether there is an actual tree out there, or whether we are just having this internal presentation, makes no difference to the behavior emitted [when properly described, in terms of "basic bodily movements we can perform at will].[31]

Thus, as Kim himself explains, his strategy in defense of the Explanatory Thesis is "to argue that within each noninternal psychological state that enters into the explanation of some action or behavior we can locate an 'internal core state' which can assume the explanatory role of the noninternal state"—to argue, in fact that "this internal core is the causal and explanatory core of the noninternal state. It is in virtue of this core that the noninternal state has the explanatory role that it has" (pp. 189–190). Immediately after this (p. 190), Kim asks the decisive question: "But why should we believe that there is such an internal core to every explanatory psychological state?" And after saying that "considerations of causal continuity and contiguity lead to the belief that the proximate cause of the behavior must be located within the organism emitting the behavior—that is . . . there must be a proximate causal explanation of that behavior [those "basic bodily movements"] in terms of an *internal* state of the organism," Kim asks again, "Why should we think that there must be an internal *psychological* state which will serve as proximate cause of behavior?"

His answer is (p. 190): "This is a difficult question, but part of an answer is contained in the observation that if this internal state has all of the causal powers of the corresponding noninternal psychological state in the production of behavior, then there seems to be no reason not to think of it as psychological as well."[32]

This answer is somewhat puzzling as it stands, although Kim's arguments for the supervenience thesis, which I present in the next lecture, may clarify it. Suppose an organism is in a psychological state, say, *believing that turning a particular knob will cause the fire to go on.* As we pointed out, this psychological state is not yet an "internal" state (in spite of what Kim says) because its individuation involves a particular knob, and also involves the possession of the concept "fire" (and on the "semantic externalist view," which Kim appears to accept, the meaning of a natural kind term like *fire* depends on the nature of the environment in which the subject has learned the word, and not just on what is in the head of the subject).[33] As we have already remarked, it seems that Kim's fallback position is to say that the relevant "internal" state in such a case is something like "Having a belief with the *narrow content* 'If I turn the knob the burner will go on.' " Kim wants to show that this "narrow content" can be identified with a *single* internal state.[34] So let us try and figure out how the argument just quoted might be used to argue that there is such a "state" in the case of *this* example.

Well, we are supposed to argue that, first of all, the noninternal psychological state (in this case, *believing that turning this knob will cause the fire to go on*) explains certain behavior (e.g., turning the knob, when the subject wants to heat some water) and that "the proximate cause of the behavior must be located within the organism emitting the behavior—that is . . . there must be a proximate causal explanation of that behavior in terms of an *internal* state of the organism." Second, we are supposed to argue further that "if this internal [physiological] state has all of the causal powers of the corresponding noninternal psychological state in the production of behavior, then there seems to be no reason not to think of it as psychological as well." Even if we accept this second step, for the sake of the argument, how good is the first step in the argument?

Suppose, to stick to the example, that the subject turns the knob in order to make the fire go on so that the water will get hot. We do indeed believe that some processes in the subject's brain caused the transmission of nervous impulses to the muscles, resulting in the "basic bodily movements" involved in the turning of the knob. Perhaps—although this is already problematic— we can even identify a unique minimal process in the subject's brain that was responsible for the (brain's contribution to) the causation of those basic bodily movements. But the knowledge (or, as Kim would have it, the "belief")[35] that turning the knob will make the fire go on will cause quite different behavior under other circumstances, e.g., refraining from turning the knob, saying to a child "don't touch that knob," etc. Is there any reason at all to believe that there is a common physiological event in the brain that happens in all of these cases? Note that Kim's talk of "the proximate cause of the behavior" is ambiguous as between the proximate cause of the behavior in a specific case (e.g., heating the water) and the one and the same proximate cause of the behavior in all of the cases in which a particular belief is invoked in the psychological explanation; considerations of " causal continuity and contiguity" support the assumption of a proximate cause of the behavior in the first sense, a proximate cause (but not necessarily the same proximate cause) in each specific case, but Kim's argument requires the assumption of a proximate cause of the behavior in the second, and more problematic, sense.

This completes my discussion of Kim's argument for the Explanatory Thesis. In my final lecture I shall discuss Kim's argument for the second thesis, the Supervenience Thesis.

are psychological conditions "internal states"?

107

psychophysical correlation

In my previous lectures I explained that Jaegwon Kim defends a form of what I termed reductionism. Specifically, he holds that the mental "strongly supervenes" on the physical, where strong supervenience is explained as the conjunction of two theses, namely:

The Supervenience Thesis: Every internal psychological state of an organism is supervenient on its synchronous internal physical state;

and

The Dependence Thesis: Each mental property *depends* on the corresponding physical property.

In this final lecture I shall question the intelligibility of the Supervenience Thesis. (Since the Dependence Thesis presupposes the Supervenience Thesis, I shall not discuss it separately.)

As Kim explains,[1] the Supervenience Thesis only requires that, if the person—say, myself—could be "replicated," i.e., if we could produce a synthetic human being in the identical internal *physical* state as myself in every respect, then this replica of me would also be in exactly the same internal *psychological* states. (However, Kim's argument for the Supervenience Thesis, to which he devotes the last section[2] of "Psychophysical Supervenience," would, if it were successful, establish that each internal psychological property of mine is realized by a specific physical property of mine and thus go a long way to establishing "strong" supervenience as well.) An example of a psychological state that is *not* internal, according to Kim, is "thinking of Vienna." "We put my replica in the same brain state, and he has the visual imagery that I am having—say of an old church that I was fond of visiting some years ago—and is thinking the same thoughts that I am thinking (how hot and humid that summer was in Vienna . . .). And he shares my tendency to speak of Vienna (at least to utter utterances containing the word 'Vienna') at dinner parties. Is he also thinking about Vienna? I do not think so. When I have a certain sort of visual imagery and am thinking certain thoughts, that counts as 'thinking of Vienna' because of a certain historical and cognitive relation that I have with the city Vienna, a relation that my replica lacks." (Kim tells us to suppose that his replica has never been to Vienna and has never heard of it, and that his imagery can be traced to a church in Iowa). What Kim maintains is that each *noninternal* psychological state, such as thinking of Vienna, can be factored into a state that is internal and a set of external relations ("cognitive and historical relations"), and that "supervenience" holds only for the internal part of the total noninternal psychological state.

Kim's argument for the Supervenience Thesis is quite brief, but it needs at least one premise that he himself regards as controversial and that he hesitates to accept as valid for all psychological states. Let me say again that one of the things that I admire about Kim is his willingness to rethink his views. Part of this process of rethinking is his searching out of possible weak spots in his own arguments. Necessarily, in the course of using his arguments as a target for criticism I have had to present his views without constantly reiterating that he regards various of them as possibly wrong or as depending on assumptions that may be problematic; my real "target" is, of course, not Jaegwon Kim himself but a certain philosophical approach the arguments I am criticizing represent.

Here is Kim's argument for the Supervenience Thesis quoted in full: suppose I have a "replica," as just described. Then

(3) [My replica and I] share structural, dispositional properties. Our basic physical structure is identical—at least for now—and we share the

same physical powers, capacities, and dispositions.

(4) One type of such dispositional properties would be the property of responding in certain characteristic ways to different types of internal or external stimuli. Thus my replica and I share the same system of stable lawlike relationships of the following form:

stimulus $S_1 \rightarrow$ behavior output O_1

stimulus $S_2 \rightarrow$ behavior output O_2

(5) Now the question arises how we are to *explain* these particular input-output relationships. The question arises because these particular patterns of input-output connections are not necessarily shared by other human beings (although we expect there will be similarities.

Typically, such explanations will proceed by positing certain *internal states* to mediate the particular input with the particular output associated with that input. Different organisms differ in the output they emit when the same input is applied because their internal states at the same time are different. We come now to the most controversial part of this argument, the functionalist conception of psychological states:

(6) These internal states posited to explain behavior *are* psychological states.

This is the functionalist conception of a psychological state: a psychological state is a "functional state" that connects sensory inputs and behavior outputs in appropriate ways.

(7) If a series of psychological states, together with their mutual interconnections, are posited as the best explanation of the input-output connections in my case, then, in methodological consistency, the same psychological states must be posited in the case of my replica. For he and I share the same input-output connections.

This is something like a "generalization argument" in moral theory. I think there clearly is a similar consistency requirement in the case of scientific methodology, and (7) is well justified. Of course, (7) is what needs to be established, viz. that my replica and I share the same psychological properties. Thus it follows:

(8) If two organisms or structures are physically identical, then their psychology is also identical. If two organisms coincide in the set of phys-

ical properties, then they cannot diverge in the set of psychological properties. The psychological supervenes on the physical. This completes the argument.

the foregoing arguments criticized

It may seem that we have now gotten completely away from the claim I made in the previous lectures, the claim that neither the standard problems in the philosophy of mind nor the "philosophical positions" they give rise to are really intelligible. I promise to make the connection between that claim and the issues we have been discussing in the present lecture clear in what follows.

First of all, we note that the intricate chain of theses and arguments just reviewed turns on a quite small group of key philosophical notions: "internal psychological property" (which Kim himself related to the notion of "narrow content"), "basic bodily movements" (as the "behavior emitted," which psychology explains), "internal phenomenal states" (which Kim himself relates to the sense-datum theory), and "functional state" (from my own earlier writings). I shall argue that not one of these notions is fully intelligible.

Now, there are psychological conditions, e.g., being in pain, which are in some sense "internal" to the organism. Let us grant for the sake of the argument that saying that someone is in pain does not conceptually or logically entail that the someone existed prior to the time in question or will exist in the future and does not conceptually or logically entail that anything at all "wholly disjoint from" the someone exists (although these are controversial assumptions).

Well, have I not then granted that *pain* is an internal psychological state, in Kim's sense, and hence that the *notion* of an "internal psychological state" is intelligible? Yes and no.

One way of giving the notion of an "internal psychological state" meaning *could* be to say, "I mean a condition like pain, or like having an itch, or a queasy feeling, as opposed to, to use Kim's own example, "thinking of Vienna," and this use of "internal" might well seem acceptable. Moreover, this explanation does give the notion partial meaning: we now know how we are supposed to classify the four conditions mentioned. (But do we know, just from these examples, whether *thinking about one's childhood* counts as "internal" or not?) We can agree that when we say that someone is in pain we are not "saying anything" about their existence before or after the pain, or about the existence of other things, and, to that extent, we can understand the claims that pain is not "rooted outside the objects that have it" and not "rooted outside the times at which it is had."[3] When we say that the statement that someone is in pain "does not entail" the existence of objects disjoint from the person with the pain, what we say can reasonably be taken as trivially true (unless we put a lot of philosophical *weight* on "entail," when it will become endlessly controversial!)

What I want us to attend to, however, is not whether the phrase "internal psychological condition" or "internal psychological state" *ever* has an intelligible use—of course it has!—*but whether we understand what is being claimed when it is said that, e.g.,* believing that there are churches in Vienna *is an internal psychological state with the same causal-explanatory role as the noninternal state of* knowing that there are churches in Vienna. (Note that although beliefs count as "internal psychological states" for Kim, *thinking that there are churches in Vienna* was his own example of a *noninternal* psychological state!) And I want us to think not just about what Kim is doing when he claims that belief is "internal" but about what he is doing when he refers to belief as a *state*.

Kim's claim, we recall, is that *believing that if I turn the knob the burner will go on, believing that there are churches in Vienna*, etc. (and also *remembering what I had for breakfast, seeing a tree, wanting a chocolate sundae,* or whatever the psychological state in question may be) are "states" with certain "causal-explanatory roles." In addition, Kim claims that there are strong reasons to believe that (in the case of organisms with any one particular physical structure, e.g., myself and my replica) for each one of these "states" there must be a *physical* state with the *same* "causal explanatory role." However, assuming the correctness of "the functionalist conception of psychological states," psychological states (with the possible exception of "qualia," or "phenomenal states") just *are* multiply realized "roles"; to be in a particular psychological state just *is* to be in a state (be it a physical state or a state of an immaterial "soul" or whatever) with a particular "role." Since my replica is in such a state (namely, the physical state that "realizes" the particular role in my case), and to be in a state with that role *is* to be in the psychological state in question, my replica also has the belief (or whatever the psychological state may be) as well; thus we have the supervenience of the psychological on the physical.

This argument tells us a great deal about what Kim means by calling belief a "state." According to the paper (by a former self of mine) that Kim cites to illustrate "the functionalist conception of psychological states,"[4] a given psychological state is "realized" (in each organism that is capable of being in that state) by a *particular* physical condition,[5] one and the same physical condition at every time and in every circumstance in which the organism is in the state, though not necessarily the same physical condition in the case of organisms belonging to different species. We do not, however, normally know a definition of that physical condition, nor is it necessary that we should. What we know is the *role* played by the condition (Kim's "causal-explanatory role"). How do we know that role? By knowing a "psychological theory" that *implicitly defines* that role.[6] In sum, the "functionalist conception of psychological states" posits the existence of a "psychological theory" that treats psychological conditions as theoretical entities, entities to be identified (in the case of each particular species) with physical states of a kind of organism, and posits, moreover, that vernacular psychological concepts aspire to denote such theoretical entities and to play the role of giving a causal explanation of behavior in terms of (functionally characterized) internal goings-on. To treat belief as a "state" in this sense is to treat it as a term in a (proto-) scientific theory, a term whose meaning is given by the, so to speak, "postulates" of the theory and whose function is to denote an internal condition (though not the same internal condition in all species).

When I raise the question, Is it really intelligible to think of belief as an "internal psychological state"? I mean to question both the intelligibility of thinking of belief as a "state" in *this* sense and the intelligibility of thinking of belief as "internal."

Does it really make sense to suppose that what I am doing when I ascribe a belief (or a desire, or a memory, etc.) to someone is *engaging in a bit of proto-scientific speculation about the internal causes of their behavior?* Although some functionalists[7] have supposed that the answer is "yes," the original functionalist position,[8] the one I defended in "The Nature of Mental States," was that functionalism was *not* a conceptual analysis but an empirical theory. Thus I would have agreed with the criticism implicit in the foregoing question (if we take it as a rhetorical one), that it is not the case that what we *mean* when we say, "George believes there are churches in Vienna" is that there are *physiological states common to the species to which George belongs with such-and-such causal-explanatory roles*, and George is in such-and-such a one of them; but I would have claimed that it is a reasonable *scientific hypothesis* that the "psychological states" we speak of in vernacular psychology are *identical* with physiological states characterized via their causal-explanatory roles ("functional" states). However, even this "empirical theory" version of functionalism did hold that vernacular psychology is in the business of *predicting behavior*, and of doing so by appeal to theoretical entities, "psychological states." What was said to be an empirical question was only whether these theoretical entities, the psychological states, were or were not identical with "functional states."

Strangely enough, in a footnote to another paper in the same volume,[9] Kim himself expresses disagreement with precisely this conception of vernacular psychological talk as proto-scientific theory, writing, "The right way to save vernacular psychology, in my opinion, is to stop thinking of it as playing the game that 'cognitive science' is supposed to play—that is, stop thinking of it as a 'theory' whose primary raison d'être is to generate law-based causal explanations and predictions. We will do better to focus on its normative role in the evaluation of actions and decisions." However it is *precisely* the conception of vernacular psychology as "a 'theory' whose primary raison d'être is to generate law-based causal explanations and predictions" that "the functionalist conception of psychological states" *presupposes*. And when Kim appeals to "the functionalist conception of psychological states" at a key point in the argument we are criticizing, he not only assumes this conception of vernacular psychology (since *believing* and *seeming to remember*—two of Kim's own examples of "internal psychological states" are taken from vernacular psychology) but he further assumes that it makes sense (as postulated by the functionalist program) to think of beliefs, etc., as "realized by" physical states. Indeed, this is essential to his arguments for "strong supervenience." What is, unfortunately, missing in too many discussions of functionalism is its enormous discordance with the way beliefs, etc., are *individuated*.

(Kim, however, *is* aware of the discordance, writing in the preface to *Supervenience and Mind* [p. xiii] that essay 11 in that volume ["Psychophysical Laws"] comes across "for better or worse" as a defense of Davidson,[10] and adding, "I was, and still am, ambivalent about Davidson's argument [or my version of it, anyway]; in fact, the considerations adduced in the argument are incompatible with the strong supervenience of the psychological on the physical, a thesis that I accept, at least provisionally, in several of the essays included in this volume. I must say, though, that I have not yet come across a totally convincing refutation of Davidson's argument.")

To begin with, it is generally recognized that in the case of humans *language* plays an overwhelming role, not just in the individuation of beliefs but in making it possible to have most if not all of the beliefs humans are capable of having. Take, for example, the belief that "there are churches in Vienna."[11] Pace Jerry Fodor,[12] it is unintelligible to ascribe this belief to someone unless one is prepared to ascribe a whole network of other beliefs—typically these will include the belief that Vienna is a *city*, beliefs about what a city is, beliefs about what churches are, etc.[13] (Although we might say of a chimpanzee who had learned to turn on a gas stove [a dangerous skill!] that it knew/believed that if it turned a certain knob a certain gas stove would go on, there are strong reasons not to construe this as meaning that the chimpanzee has anything like an adult human's concepts of a gas stove, or even of a knob—e.g., as an artifact made for a certain purpose—or even of fire, as a natural kind.)[14] In short, we "individuate" beliefs—determine their content—by determining what *else* the believer is prepared to say, beyond avowing the belief (if the believer *is* prepared to avow it).[15] Put this way, the point sounds verificationist, but it does not depend on any verificationist doctrine.[16] As we argued in the previous lecture, the content of *any* claim depends on the context in which the claim is made; if we cannot suppose anything about a person except that the person asserts the words "there are churches in Vienna," then the claim that the person "believes that there are churches in Vienna" has no clear content at all.

That the individuation of beliefs is "holistic" in the sense of depending on what other beliefs they "interanimate" is widely accepted. But the consequences are, I believe, often not thought through.

Here is one influential model of belief: according to a well-known paper by Hartry Field,[17] a certain stock of basic beliefs is stored in a special way (not necessarily a special *place*, of course) in the brain. More precisely, a stock of *sentences* in "mentalese" (the famous "language of thought" introduced by Jerry Fodor)[18] is stored in the "belief box." One's *beliefs* are, then, just the sentences in the "belief box" together with all the other sentences that are *obvious consequences* of these. (Field did not, however, assume that Fodor was right in claiming that the vocabulary of "mentalese" is *innate*).

A number of difficulties have been raised with this model. For one thing, it does not seem *true* that one believes all the "obvious consequences" of even one's most basic beliefs (however these might be defined). Sometimes pointing out that something is a consequence—however obvious—of a belief one has avowed will lead one to express chagrin (*How could I have missed that!*) and to withdraw the avowed belief. (And if we try to make such counterexamples unlikely or irrelevant by limiting the stock of basic beliefs and limiting the stock of inferences that are supposed to constitute the "obvious consequence" relation, it will be difficult to make it plausible that *all* of the person's beliefs *are* "obvious consequences" of so restricted a set of "basic beliefs"—but of course this is all science fiction, since neither the set of "basic beliefs" nor the "obvious consequence" relation has actually been defined at all!)

Another difficulty is that the distinction between what a person believes and what the person (or the computer) can "figure out" more or less instantly may itself be unclear. In an unpublished paper Robert Stalnaker has suggested that, in fact, the distinction may be contextual: whether we say that someone already believed something or that they figured it out on the spot may depend, among other things, on the task in question (and analogously for computers). This idea fits well with what we argued in the previous lecture; in the language we employed there, what Stalnaker is saying is that the exact content of the claim that a person believes so-and-so (and the exact content of the claim that a computer has such-and-such information available) may *depend on the context in which the claim is made in a way that is incompatible with the idea that what the claim means is that the person is in some one fixed "internal state."*

But there are, I believe, much more serious objections to Field's picture, objections that are directly connected with the fact that it entirely ignores the problem of the individuation of belief. First of all, suppose I want to know whether Alice believes that there are churches in Vienna. Suppose you tell me that "There are churches in Vienna" is included among the beliefs stored in Alice's brain in the special way Hartry Field postulated (ignoring the fact that I don't know what that special way is!). Perhaps I can now infer (or could infer if one had given some genuine scientific content to this science fiction) that Alice would probably say "Yes" if I asked "Are there churches in Vienna?" (Of course, she might say, "What are you, a nut or something?" or "Get lost" or many other things instead of "Yes.") But, *unless I know that by "Vienna" she means Vienna and by "churches" she means churches, etc., I have no basis for saying whether Alice believes that there are churches in Vienna.* The problem, in short, is that Field is talking about believing *sentences*, and what psychology—including emphatically "vernacular psychology" is concerned with is what *contents* so-and-so believes. But believing a *content*—this is what Field's model leaves out and what is so often left out of discussions in "cognitive science"—is internally related to possessing concepts. To believe that there are churches in Vienna" one must possess the concepts "church," "Vienna," "in," etc. So if "believing that there are churches in Vienna" is a functional state, it must be a state that is internally related to the possession of these concepts. But is the possession of concepts a functional state? (In my own thinking raising this question was the beginning of the end of my attachment to functionalism.)

Second, the picture of belief as a state (in the science-fiction metaphor, the state of having a sentence in one's "belief box") assumes that sentences have *fixed* truth-evaluable contents independently of context, i.e., assumes that those sentences in the "belief box" stand for *determinate* contents. But suppose the sentence "There is a lot of coffee on the table" is inscribed in the "belief box": does that mean I believe that there are lots of cups of nice hot coffee on the table? Or that I believe that there are huge bags of coffee beans on the table? Or that I believe that someone has made a mess and spilled a lot of coffee on the table? One could, of course, just postulate that sentences in *mentalese* have *context-independent* contents and that there is a sentence in "mentalese" available to symbolize any possible context-*dependent* content in a context-independent way. But then "mentalese" has to be *so unlike anything we know as a language that it becomes a mere "we know not what."* All we have to support the idea that belief is an "internal state" is science fiction — or, better, sentences that would have legitimate role as entertainment if they occurred in a work of science fiction. But when those same sentences occur in the writings of the philosophers of "cognitive science" they are profoundly confused, for they purport to have the kind of use that a scientific hypothesis has without having been given any scientific content at all.

individuating beliefs

Let us return, however, to the question of how beliefs are individuated. The task of individuating beliefs is, in general, closely related to if not the same as the task of individuating the contents of the words and sentences we use to formulate and communicate and describe beliefs; but there are many views as to how the latter task is performed and as to what the metaphysical and scientific status of the ways in which we individuate both the meanings of sentences and beliefs really is. My own view ("semantic externalism"), which most philosophers of language and mind agree with today,[19] is that the content of sentences (and, derivatively, the content of beliefs and other language-dependent psychological conditions) is at least partly dependent on the determination of the *reference* in the particular context (in technical jargon, on the "extension") of the terms used in the sentence or in the expression of belief, and that reference depends on factors that are *external* to the speaker's body and brain. Whether, for example, a speaker means *elm* when she uses the word *elm* depends, *inter alia,* on whether her word refers to elm trees, and that depends in complex ways on both her relations to other speakers (in case the speaker, like so many of us, is unable to identify elm trees reliably on her own) and on what sort of trees are in fact in the environment of the speaker and of the experts on whom the speaker relies. The speaker's neurological condition (or 'brain state") may not in principle suffice to determine whether a given speaker refers to elm trees or to beech trees when she uses the word *elm*

As to the issues about the "status" of meaning/belief talk: I think the question as to whether "meaning talk" and "belief talk" has a place in "science" depends on hopelessly ideological notions of "science" and should be rejected;[20] and as for the question of the "metaphysical status" of beliefs and meanings, if there is one thing I have learned from the classical pragmatists, Peirce, Dewey, and James, as well as from Wittgenstein, it is to take seriously—metaphysically seriously, if you like—ways of talking that are obviously indispensable to our lives and our thought.

For Quine, at the opposite extreme, neither meaning talk nor belief talk can be taken seriously when our interest is in "limning the true and ultimate structure of reality";[21] neither kind of talk has either metaphysical or scientific "status," although both kinds of talk are essential to our practical lives and thus part of "our second-grade system."[22] For John Searle, belief talk and meaning talk are to be taken fully seriously, but neither meaning nor reference depends on anything outside the head of the speaker. For Fodor (at this writing), Quine is right about meaning talk, insofar as that goes beyond the determination of the reference of our words, but he is wrong about reference. (Reference is to be taken seriously, scientifically—and for Fodor that means metaphysically.) And Fodor, like myself, is an "externalist" about reference. And I am sure there are at least a dozen other views in circulation at the present time.

It is clear, however, that *Kim*'s program of confining psychology—which he certainly takes seriously, both scientifically and "metaphysically"—to "internal states" and "basic bodily movements" depends upon finding a way to individuate beliefs *without* appealing to external factors. For if psychology has to appeal to external factors to individuate its "states," then those states are not "internal states" in Kim's sense, for, by Kim's definition of "internal," the sameness or difference of two *internal* states cannot depend on anything external to the organism and the time at which the organism is in the state(s) in question. This means that if semantic externalism is correct, and our ordinary way of individuating beliefs does depend on looking at various facts about the environment and other speakers, then Kim will need to individuate beliefs in a way that departs from that ordinary way. Those who share the desire for such a way generally appeal to "narrow content," as Kim himself remarked. But what is "narrow content"? (The "wide content" of a belief includes the reference of the terms involved, which is not "internally" fixed.)

The notion of narrow content (under the terminology "psychological state in the narrow sense") was introduced by me in "The Meaning of 'Meaning' " (although I expressed doubt there that it would prove useful in psychology).[23] Suppose that George believes that there are elms in Canada. Suppose George has a doppelgänger on Twin Earth who has a belief that he expresses by the same sentence, "There are elms in Canada." Unfortunately, one of the occasional minor differences between Earth and Twin Earth is that on Twin Earth "elm" refers to *beeches*. And, of course, on Twin Earth "Canada" refers to *Twin Canada*, not Canada. So what Twin George believes isn't that there are elms in Canada; what he believes is that there are beeches in Twin Canada. Yet Twin George could be "internally" identical to George in all psychologically relevant respects. He could even be in the same "brain state" as George, neuron for neuron.[24] In order to have a sense in which we could say that "phenomenologically" George and Twin George have the same belief, notwithstanding the difference in the "wide content" of the propositions believed, I proposed that we say that *whenever two human beings are in the same brain-state, then their beliefs have the same "narrow content."* If we can reasonably understand the "causation" of actions (or "basic bodily movements") by beliefs to be their causation by beliefs *as individuated by narrow content*, then the "internalist" program may go through. This is, I believe, what Kim was referring to when he wrote that "the position that I defend concerning the psychological import of this failure of supervenience [i.e., the fact that some psychological states are individuated in part by factors external to the organism] is analogous, in some ways, to the 'narrow content' approach to causation favored by some philosophers."[25]

But two stupendous difficulties confront this approach at once. First of all, the proposed criterion, or rather, the proposed sufficient condition for sameness of narrow content—that the two subjects be in the identical brain-state—

is one that *is never fulfilled in the real world.*[26] Second, if we say that what is needed is not "identity" of brain-state but sameness in *relevant respects*, we beg the question, which was the *existence* of internal states ("relevant respects") that can be identified with beliefs (or with their "narrow contents").

Of course, one might say, "Well, here is a criterion for having a belief with the narrow content 'There are elms in Canada,' one that does not require the *actual* existence of two individuals in the same brain-state, but only the *physically possible existence* of such:

X has a belief with the narrow content *There are elms in Canada* = df. There is a person X' in some physically possible world[27] who believes that there are trees in Canada, and such that X' and X are in the same brain-state."

But then we will have made the notion of "narrow content" wholly *parasitic* on the ordinary notion of content (i.e., on "wide content"), that is to say, parasitic on our shared sense of when people have the same belief and when they have different beliefs! No reason at all will have been given to suppose that *any* two subjects with the "same" belief in *this* sense must be in some *identical* internal physical state, or, in Kim's terminology, to suppose that belief states individuated in *this* way "strongly supervene" on (internal) physical states. (Note that it is not enough to show that if two subjects *are* in the same physical state, in all internal respects, then their beliefs—so individuated—must be the same; that much is, indeed, guaranteed by the definition; what strong supervenience requires is a sort of *converse* of this, namely, that if two subjects have the same belief, then some relevant physical state is the same, and this has not been guaranteed at all.)

However, I do not want to give the impression that the fact that the meanings of our words are partly individuated by *external* factors is the only serious problem with talk of "narrow content" (conceived of as an internal physical state or an internal computational state); an equally serious difficulty arises from the context-sensitive and "holistic" way in which we determine when two statements have the same meaning and when they have different meaning. Although we have already seen examples of this, the example that follows may help to see how the point bears on a well-known program in linguistics.

narrow content and "competence"

In various writings[28] Noam Chomsky has suggested that when a speaker understands a word, that understanding is captured by some component in the "grammar" in the speaker's brain (although Chomsky is not altogether happy with calling the component "semantic," precisely because semantics in his sense has nothing to do with *reference*).[29] If this is right, then it would seem that there is another possible route to the definition of "narrow content"; namely, just identify "narrow content" with the semantic component in the "internalized grammar." But what is this semantic component supposed to be?

Consider the word *demonstrate*, in the sense of *to give a conclusive proof from certain premises*.[30] If we ask about the syntax of the word, then we can say a good deal without fear of disagreement, e.g., that it is a verb, that its past-tense form is *demonstrated*, its participle *demonstrating*, third-person singular *demonstrates*, etc. A speaker who speaks in such a way as to manifest "tacit knowledge" of these facts has "syntactic competence" in connection with the word. Such a speaker also knows that "Helen demonstrated that the sum of the angles of a triangle is equal to two straight angles" is grammatical and that "Helen demonstrated the bottle" is ungrammatical. Chomsky's picture is that there is a more complex knowledge concerning the relationship of any word (and, a fortiori, of "demonstrating" [in this sense]) to other concepts that is tacitly possessed by *anyone* who is "competent" with the word and that constitutes the *semantical* part of the "grammar" of the word. He would admit, however, that this semantical part of the grammar has never been systematized, by himself or by anyone else.

In fact, however, *there is no fixed set of facts that is tacitly known by everyone whom we consider competent in the use of the word* demonstrate *[in the relevant sense] and that constitutes the basis on which ascribe that competence.* All of us form the past tense, the third-person singular, etc., in the same way; but we do not all manifest our "competence" with the *concept* in the same way. To be semantically "competent" one must be able to give *some* examples or other of what it is to demonstrate something; but the examples need not be at all of the same sort. One person may be hopeless at mathematics but quite able to give an example of a demonstration in theology; another may be able to think of geometrical examples but not of examples in number theory, etc. The idea that there is *a single specifiable set of skills possession of which constitutes one's "semantic competence" with the word* "demonstrate" is a theory-driven illusion.[31]

Moreover, not only does Chomsky claim that there *is* such a thing as one's "semantic" competence in connection with an arbitrary word, but he further claims that this semantic competence can be *systematized* in the way in which syntactic relations have been systematized. But, because we have no idea what our "semantic competence" is supposed to look like (apart from trivial examples of analytic truths, or allegedly analytic truths, which are all Chomsky gives in this connection), and because no one has made a single suggestion as to how to extend Chomsky's "government and binding" formalism (or any other syntactic theory) to a formalism for the supposed "semantic component," we are, once again, in the realm of *science fiction*. To say that the "universal grammar in the brain" generates the "semantic component" when the values of certain parameters have been "properly set by the environment" is to say that we-know-not-what does we-know-not-what when we-know-not-what has happened!

ascribing meaning as projection

I used an abstract verb, *demonstrate*,[32] to illustrate the point that there is no single set of skills that one must possess to be competent in the use of a word, but the point could have been illustrated with the simplest words in the language. The writings of Charles Travis are full of beautiful examples.[33] A competent speaker can use any word in an enormous variety of different circumstances, with perfect propriety, and be understood by other competent speakers. In the previous lecture I used the example of the word *flat*, which a competent speaker can apply to a Euclidean plane, but also to the landscape in Illinois. An interesting example, which I remember seeing in one of Travis's papers, is the following: there is a hovercraft containing barrels of oil entering the harbor. Is the sentence "There is a tanker in the harbor" true or false? One's first reaction might be to say, "That is a borderline case," but things are not so simple. In fact, under certain circumstances this sentence might count as clearly true (that's the kind of tanker the company is now using), under others as clearly false, and under others it might indeed be a borderline case. It is not that the sentence "There is a tanker in the harbor" can be used at any time to mean just anything; obviously not. The meanings of the words does restrict what can be said using them; but what can be said using them, consistently with the meaning of the words, depends on our ability to figure out how it is *reasonable* to use those words, given those meanings (given a certain history of prior uses), in novel circumstances. And, pace Chomsky, the idea that *reasonableness* itself can be reduced to an algorithm is a scientistic fantasy.

The same point plays a key role in Stanley Cavell's masterpiece, *The Claim of Reason*. Cavell teaches us[34] that what makes the use of words in a particular circumstance appropriate or correct in a context is the naturalness (one might also say the reasonableness) of *projecting* those words into that context (given a certain history of prior uses): that naturalness or reasonableness is not supported by something (a Platonic "form" or Aristotelian "universal") that is "wholly present in each of those instances," as medieval Realists were wont to say. Even the extension of the term (*tanker*, in the case of Travis's example) is not completely fixed by the meaning of the term but is adjusted to fit the context.

I have been talking about when we see a use of a sentence as conformant to some particular meaning, and when we do not, but virtually the same point applies to the individuation of *beliefs*. An ancient Hebrew[35] referred to the chief of a small tribe as a *melekh*. We translate the word as "king" and ascribe the belief that "Og was the king of Bashan." In 1945 English people referred to England's (figure-) head of state as "the king of Britain." What makes these both instances of believing that someone or other is a *king*? Only the naturalness of the projection! The futile search for scientific objects called "narrow contents" in the case of meanings and for "internal psychological states" in the case of beliefs are alike instances of the rationalist error of assuming that whenever it is natural to project the same words into two different circumstances there must be an "entity" that is present in both circumstances.

"basic actions"

Just as Kim insists that psychological states must be pared down to an "internal core" before they can be metaphysically and scientifically legitimized, so he insists that actions must be pared down. I shall criticize this claim as well, but at less length. I repeat the passage that was quoted in the preceding lecture:

> It is true that whether or not my action succeeds in bringing about the intended result normally depends on whether the belief involved is true. Thus, whether my action results in the burner being turned on depends on whether my belief that it would go on if the knob is turned is correct. However, it is not part of the object of *psychological* explanation to explain why the burner went on; all it needs to explain is why I turned the knob. . . . The job of psychological explanation is done once it has explained the bodily action of turning the knob. . . . Only *basic actions*, not "derivative" or "generated actions," need to be explained by psychological theory.

(These "basic actions" are also identified with "basic bodily movements we can perform at will.") The first thing to notice about Kim's claim is that it is not supported by the examination of any actual psychological theory. "Psychological theory" is, in fact, a motley. As Clifford Geertz has recently written,

> The wide swings between behaviorist, psychometric, cognitivist, depth psychological, topological, developmentalist, neurological, evolutionist and culturalist conceptions of the subject, have made being a psychologist an unsettled occupation, subject not only to fashion, as are all the human sciences, but also to sudden and frequent reversals of course. Paradigms, wholly new ways of going about things, come along not by the century, but by the decade; sometimes, it almost seems, by the month.[36]

If Kim were really claiming that *each and every one of these kinds of psychology* really concerns itself to predict basic bodily movements that an organism can perform at will, and only these, the claim would be easily falsified. But, of course, that is not what Kim is doing; what he is speaking of is a sort of "psychology" that certain philosophers dream of, a sort of psychology that, as far as I know, does not (and most likely will not ever) exist on earth. In short, Kim is "in the grip of a picture" (to use Wittgenstein's celebrated phrase), a *picture* of psychology.

Consider, for the moment, an example from the branch of psychology that might seem most amenable to Kim's description, behavioral psychology in its classical form, "rat psychology." A rat is conditioned to press a bar by arranging for it to (sometimes) receive a reward, in the form of a pellet of food, when the bar is pressed. What Kim claims is that the job of psychology is finished once it has explained the bodily action of pressing the bar. But surely this is not quite what he means to say.

It is not quite what he means to say because pressing a bar or turning a knob *aren't* just "basic bodily movements that [the organism] can perform at will." A rat cannot press a bar unless there is a *bar* there and a human cannot turn a knob unless there is a *knob* there. So these are not "internal states" at all. Can Kim mean that "the job of psychology is done" when it has explained the *movement of the limb* involved in turning a knob or pressing a bar?

That can't be right either, because (1) that same limb movement can occur when the rat is pressing something else, and the rat psychologist isn't interested in the frequency of those *other* pressings; he is interested only in the frequency of *bar* pressings, and then only in a certain environment (in respond to certain "stimuli"). *Bar pressing is an externally characterized action, not a basic bodily movement.* (Similarly, the same movement of the hand may occur when I am turning a knob that isn't attached to a burner, or turning something that isn't a knob, and the rational psychologist's [or vernacular psychological] explanation of why I turn the knob in that context isn't concerned with those other turnings. Turning a knob is an externally characterized action, not a basic bodily movement.) (2) The description of the motion, "pressing a bar," can, in fact, be realized by a whole range of *different* bodily movements. For example (if you will pardon the disgusting thought experiment), if the rat's front legs become paralyzed, or it loses them, it might wiggle up to the bar and press it with its *nose* or some other part of its body. (Similarly, humans who have lost the use of their hands might turn the knob with their toes, or with their teeth.)

Shall we say, then, that "the job of psychology" is to issue predictions of the following form?

"When the rat has *sense data*, as of the presence of a certain familiar cage including a bar, the rat will act in such a way as to produce in itself the *sense*

psychophysical correlation

data of pressing a bar with some part of its anatomy,"

Or,

"When the human has *sense data*, as of the presence of a gas stove, and the human wants to boil some water (is in a desire state with the "narrow content" *I want to boil some water*) the human will act so as to produce in itself the *sense data* of turning one of the knobs of the gas stove"?

(Recall Kim's way of dealing with "phenomenal states":

"When we see a tree there is some internal phenomenal state going on; some internal representation of a tree will be present in us. In the language of the sense-datum theory, we are sensing a treeish sense-datum, or we are appeared to treeishly.")

But rat psychology arose precisely as a reaction against introspective psychology and its internal phenomenal states! And the cognitive psychologist on the street hardly worries about reducing the claim that his subject "turns a knob" to either talk of limb movements *or* talk of sense data!

Once again, I don't want to say that Kim's claim, that psychology predicts "basic bodily movements" and not actions as normally (externally) characterized is *false*; I want to say that it only *looks* as if a clear sense has been given to "basic bodily movement" in *this* context. The *example* given, "turning a knob," turns out not to be a possible example in Kim's own sense (because his context requires that "basic bodily movements" involve nothing "distinct from" the organism, and the knob is distinct from the organism), but we cannot find a substitute example that will work. Echoing Wittgenstein's *Tractatus* (6.53), we might say that Kim has "given no meaning to certain signs in his propositions."

"internal phenomenal states"

A few years ago I devoted a whole series of lectures[37] to criticizing the idea that "When we see a tree there is some internal phenomenal state going on; some internal representation of a tree will be present in us." Indeed, I believe that this idea is responsible for the central complex of intractable "problems" and unworkable positions that has bedeviled philosophy since Descartes. But I do not have space to go over all that once again here. Instead I will simply try to expose the incoherence of one familiar argument that, I believe, is responsible for much of the appeal of the idea of "internal representations" or "sense data."

That argument may be called the "highest common factor argument."[38] In its simplest form, the argument claims that if I "have the same experience" on two occasions, say of "seeing a wall covered with roses," but on one of them I am not really perceiving what I seem to be perceiving (because, say, I am dreaming), then, still, there is quite literally *something in common* (a "highest common factor," so to speak) in the two cases, and the *something in common* cannot be external (since we have excluded that by hypothesis in one of the two cases), and so it must be an *internal* something that I experience. We can call this internal something a "representation," or we can call it by the ancient word, an *appearance*, or we can call it by the word Russell and Moore made so popular, a *sense datum*.

The opposed point of view, defended by Austin and more recently by John McDowell and by myself in the lectures I mentioned, may be called the *disjunctive view*. On this view, when I say that in both of the cases I described "I saw a wall covered with roses," all I am entitled to infer is that the following disjunction is true:

(D) *Either I really saw a wall covered with roses, or it seemed to me as if I saw a wall covered with roses.*

But I am not at all entitled to infer that there is some significant object (a wall-covered-with-roses-sense-datum or an attribute of "sensing-wall-covered-with-roses-ishly") that is literally "present in both cases."

What the highest common factor argument claims is that the disjunctive view *cannot* be right. It is, so to speak, evident—evident from the experience itself—that there *is* a highest common factor.

But let us note something about the supposed highest common factor (the "sense datum" or the "internal phenomenal state"), however: the "highest common factor" is supposed to be *necessary and sufficient* for the "appearance" in question. Indeed, it is supposed to *be* the "appearance"! If the "highest common factor argument" is right, then there are "internal phenomenal states" whose *esse* is *percipi*. If they *seem* to be the same internal phenomenal state, they *are* the same internal phenomenal state. For if there could be two different internal phenomenal states P_1, P_2 that seemed exactly the same to the subject, then the principle on which the rejection of the disjunctive view depends, namely, that *if the two occasions seem identical to the subject as far as their appearance is concerned, then an identical "highest common factor" (an identical phenomenal state) must be present* would have a counterexample.

The principle generalizes to situations in which it is not the whole scene that looks the same (or smells, or sounds, or feels the same) to the subject but only a single aspect. For example, if I look at two objects and their *color* seems identical to me, then the highest common factor argument dictates that there is a common "color quale" that I experience in both cases.

I shall now try to convince you that, appealing as the idea of a "highest common factor" undoubtedly is, it cannot be right. There cannot be phenomenal states whose *esse* is *percipi*, phenomenal states that obey the principle that *if two occasions seem identical to the subject as far as their appearance is concerned, then the subject must be in the same phenomenal state.*

The difficulty is, quite simply, that *indistinguishability in appearance is not a transitive relation, but being in the same state (i.e., in the same member of a set of mutually exclusive states) is a transitive relation.* But let me explain the difficulty more slowly.

Here is an experiment that Rohit Parikh once performed.[39] He took a can of white paint and a pack of a hundred 3" by 5" cards and painted one card with some of the paint. Then he added a *single drop* of red paint to the can and stirred well. He painted the next card with the mixture. (It was absolutely indistinguishable from the first card, "as far as the eye could tell.") He continued in this way, adding one drop of red paint to the mixture after each card was painted, using the resulting mixture to paint the next card and so on. The result was a pack of one hundred cards such that if one looked at two successive cards one could not distinguish them at all (with respect to color), but if you looked at two cards eighteen or nineteen apart in the pack you could see that the card that was later in the pack was slightly more pinkish than the card that was earlier in the pack.

Now, consider the following argument (let C_1, C_2, C_3 ... C_{100} be the hundred cards.) C_1 and C_2 look exactly the same to the subject (Rohit Parikh). So the relevant phenomenal state (the relevant "color quale") must be the same, by the highest common factor argument. Call this color quale "$Q_{1/2}$." Similarly, C_2 and C_3 look exactly the same to the subject. So the relevant phenomenal state (the relevant "color quale") must be the same, by the highest common factor argument. Call this color quale "$Q_{2/3}$." Are $Q_{1/2}$ and $Q_{2/3}$ identical or nonidentical?

If they are nonidentical, then one card, C_2, has *two different subjective colors* ($Q_{1/2}$ and $Q_{2/3}$) at the same time! But this violates the principle that an object has exactly one subjective color. Moreover, it violates the principle that drives the highest common factor argument as well, since the subject can't see any difference between $Q_{1/2}$ and $Q_{2/3}$, and *esse est percipi* is supposed to hold for subjective colors (and for phenomenal states generally). So we are forced to conclude that $Q_{1/2} = Q_{2/3}$. But similarly, we can show that C_3 and C_4 have a subjective color $Q_{3/4}$ in common, and $Q_{2/3} = Q_{3/4}$. Continuing in this way we can show that $Q_{1/2} = Q_{2/3} = Q_{3/4} = \ldots Q_{19/20}$, where, of course, $Q_{19/20}$ is the color quale that C_{19} and C_{20} have in common (if the highest common factor argument is correct). But, in Parikh's pack of cards, C_1 and C_{20} are *different* colors—they *look* different to the subject. So the color of C_{20} can't be $Q_{1/2}$, contrary to what we just showed! So the premise of the argument—the principle of the "highest common factor"—must be false!

Notice what this counterexample does *not* show. It does not show that there cannot be "phenomenal states" in quite a different sense, brain states that are somehow implicated in color perception and responsible for the ability to discriminate between different "appearances." But such states cannot obey the "highest common factor" principle. It must be possible to be in two different such states without being able to notice that one is, or otherwise to violate the idea that such states just *are* appearances. (For example, if the brain's "color recognizing devices" are neural assemblies of the kind postulated by more than one current model of the brain,[40] the simplest way to account for Parikh's little experiment is to say that different assemblies may fire both when the same card is scanned at different times, and when different cards are scanned, and that the assemblies that are capable of firing when one particular "shade of color" appears to be presented *multiply overlap*. Thus, as one successively scans C_1, C_2 . . . the cell assembly that fires keeps changing, although many of the same cells fire when two successive cards are scanned, but when such a change results in a change in "subjective color" is as indeterminate as when a man who is losing his hair becomes *bald*.) "Being able to truly say, 'It was absolutely indistinguishable' on two occasions does not license the inference to "I was in the numerically identical phenomenal state." Indeed, after we notice that the identity condition for phenomenal states is *absurd*, we realize that *we didn't know what we were talking about when we postulated them in the first place*.[41]

if not "correlation," what?

In this series of lectures I have discussed a question that has haunted philosophy since the seventeenth century, the question of "psychophysical correlation." My rejection of the "thesis" of psychophysical correlation has not been in any way, shape, or form a defense of "dualism" or "interactionism." What I have rejected is not the "thesis" of psychophysical correlation, *but the idea that the question makes sense*. I have argued that the very picture that is presupposed by the question is wrong, that is to say, the picture of our psychological characteristics as "internal states" that, qua internal states, must either be "correlated" or "uncorrelated" with what goes on inside (*literally* "inside") our bodies. I have argued that our psychological characteristics are, as a rule, individuated in ways that are context sensitive and extremely complex, involving external factors (the nature of the objects we perceive, think about, and act on), social factors, and the projections we find it natural and unnatural to make. Kim is, of course, aware of these difficulties, and the paper I have criticized today was a heroic attempt to save the traditional view of what the problem is by arguing that hidden inside our externalistically (and holistically) individuated psychological states are other, "core," states that are properly internal, as in the "inner theater" model of the mind. And if Kim could not save that view, I am sure no other philosopher has a chance!

If I have taken Jaegwon Kim as my opponent of choice throughout these lectures (this is perhaps needless to say—but let me say it once again, nevertheless!), it is for two reasons: because his presentation of the arguments I have been discussing is the one I have found by far the most challenging and because of my admiration for his philosophical intelligence and the purity of his philosophical motivation. The only thing that could, indeed, make my admiration for Jaegwon Kim even greater would be for him now to concede that my view is the right one!

part three afterwords

causation and explanation

In the course of the lectures that make up part 2 of this book I quoted with approval a saying by John Haldane to the effect that there are "as many kinds of cause as there are senses of 'because.' " But there are a number of ways of understanding this claim. One of them, which I found attractive until quite recently, would be to say that the notion of explanation has priority over the notion of causation. But this formulation now seems to me as wrong as its "opposite," that is, as wrong as the idea that the notion of causation (understood as something that is simply *independent* of our various explanatory practices) has priority over the notion of explanation. The notions of explanation and causation presuppose one another at every point; neither has "priority" in the sense of being reducible to the other. In this afterword I make some remarks about just how and why this is so.

explanatory realism and internalism (according to kim)
In his 1994 paper titled "Explanatory Knowledge and Metaphysical Dependence"[1] Jaegwon Kim proposed a distinction between two possible views of explanation that he called *explanatory realism* and *explanatory internalism*. I shall begin by explaining and discussing this distinction.

Kim distinguished two questions that philosophers may wish to ask about explanation. The first he called *the epistemological question*:

The Epistemological Question: What is it that we know—that is, what exactly is our epistemic gain—when we have an explanation of *p*?

Second, we may ask what it is that "grounds" an explanation. This Kim called *the metaphysical question*:

The Metaphysical Question: When G is an explanans for E, in virtue of what relation between *g* and *e*, the events represented by G and E respectively, is G an explanans for E? What is the objective relation connecting events, *g* and *e*, that grounds the explanatory relation between their descriptions G and E?

One possible answer to the metaphysical question, according to Kim, is to deny that there exists or needs to exist any such "objective relation." This is the answer of what Kim calls *explanatory internalism*. According to such a view, as Kim describes it, "explanation is essentially an activity *internal* to an epistemic corpus: whether or not something is an explanation—a good, 'true' or 'correct' explanation—depends on factors internal to the body of knowledge, not what goes on in the world—except, of course, for the truth of the statements comprising the explanans."[2]

The other possible answer that Kim considers is that a correct answer to a question of the form "Why did *e* occur?" must be "grounded" in some "relation" (or relations). This is the answer of *explanatory realism*. The relation that these explanatory realists (for example, David Lewis or Wesley Salmon) take to ground explanations is the causal relation: the success of an explanation is determined by its success in locating the place of an event in the causal structure of the world. For the internalists (for example, C. G. Hempel or Michael Friedman or Philip Kitcher), in contrast, as Kim puts it,

Explaining is not . . . a matter of discovering, or imparting, more propositional knowledge; explanatory activity consists in constructing derivations whose structure and steps are logically or epistemically related in certain specified ways to the rest of the belief system. To put it somewhat crudely, explanation is a matter of the shape and organization of one's belief system, not of its content.

Although I do not, in the end, find this distinction between "explanatory realism" and "explanatory internalism" helpful, figuring out why it is not as clear as it may initially look is, I think, an excellent way to come to grips with real issues. I begin with the little word *except* that occurs in Kim's explanation of internalism. On the internalist view, we recall, explanation depends on "factors internal to the body of knowledge" (on structuring the body of knowledge so that the parts stand in appropriate logical and epistemic relations) "*except*, of course, for the truth of the statements comprising the explanans."

The reason that Kim puts things this way is that he is taking Hempel to be his paradigm "internalist." In Hempel's famous paper with Paul Oppenheim,[3] a "complete" explanation was identified with a deductively valid argument whose conclusion is the fact to be explained (the "explanandum") and whose premises are the statements that do the explaining (the "explanans"). A number of logical and epistemic requirements are imposed on the structure of the argument, but in addition the premises are required to be *true*. Thus "Hempelian" explanations do fit the internalist model, as Kim defined it.

Or do they? Hempel and his coauthor also require that certain of the premises be *lawlike*, and is lawlikeness a purely "internal" property of statements?

Putting this last question aside for the moment, it is important to note that Hempel's Logical Empiricism led him to make the standard empiricist/positivist assumption that *the language of science* (which is all of "cognitively meaningful" language, according to positivists) *can be conceived of as containing neither the predicate "causes" nor any predicate which presupposes the concept of causation*. Historically speaking, this assumption goes back to Hume's view that we don't ever *observe* causation: causation must be reduced to constant conjunction, contiguity, etc., as Hume himself attempted to do, or else (as Russell proposed) we must do without the notion in proper science. (Hempel himself seems at times to have conceived of his notion of explanation as a *replacement* for the vernacular concept of causation.) If this assumption is in force, then the question that drives Kim's distinction between "explanatory realism" and "explanatory internalism" is a natural one: given that the *premises* in a

Hempelian explanation don't speak of anything causing anything else, the question arises as to whether that means that Hempelian explanations (or explanations on some other internalist model) "leaves something out" (namely, that the event described in one or more of the premises *causes* or *brings about* the explanandum), or whether this "leaving out" is an illusion, a hankering after a prescientific concept that advanced science has learned to do with out. Say that it "leaves something out," and you are a "realist" about explanation; say that nothing is left out, and you are an "internalist."

But what happens if we *don't* assume that the language of science (let alone the vernacular) can be conceived of as containing neither the predicate "causes" nor any predicate that presupposes the concept of causation? After all, our ordinary descriptions of what we observe are *loaded* with causal content. Ask people what they saw, and they will use verbs like *eat, drink, pick up, break*, and so on—and every one of these verbs semantically involves the notion of causation. It isn't just that Betty's hand came to be in contact with the vase just before the vase moved to the floor and broke into pieces; Betty *pushed* the vase (we may also say she *broke* it). Even the nouns *vase* and *hand* attribute a rich variety of causal powers. If we cannot give a single example of an ordinary observation report (let alone a nonobservational statement) that does not, directly or indirectly, presuppose causal judgements, then the idea that science (or the vernacular) could "in principle" dispense with the notion of causation should be viewed with deep suspicion. (There are also empirical findings that conflict with the idea that "we don't observe causation.")[4]

Hume would, of course, have conceded that our ordinary descriptions are loaded with causal content. The question, he—and the empiricist tradition that followed him—would have said, is how that causal content is to be interpreted. Hume would have claimed to be telling us what statements such as "Betty pushed the vase" *mean*. But Hume's explanation of what such statements mean presupposes that there is a level of observation—the absolutely fundamental level—that is free of causal hypotheses. This is the level of sense qualities. But the claim that talk about physical objects can be *reduced* to talk of sense qualities has been abandoned by virtually all[5] present-day philosophers, including, in the latter part of his life, Hempel himself.

(There is also the question—which was first raised by Kant—whether the ascription of *time order* to even sense qualities does not presuppose the objective material world and its causal structure.)

My own awareness of these points goes back to reading Elizabeth Anscombe's "Causality and Determination"[6] many years ago. I cannot resist quoting a wonderful passage (p. 137):

> First, as to the statement that we can never observe causality in the individual case. Someone who says this is just not going to count anything as "observation of causality." This often happens in philosophy; it is argued that "all we find" is such-and-such, and it turns out that the arguer has excluded from his idea of "finding" the sorts of things he says we don't "find." And when we consider what we are allowed to say we do "find," we have the right to turn the tables on Hume, and say that neither do we perceive bodies, such as billiard balls, approaching one another. When we "consider the matter with the utmost attention," we find only an impression of travel made by the successive positions of a round white patch in our visual fields . . . etc. Now, a "Humeian" account of causality has to be given in terms of constant conjunctions of physical things, events, etc., not of experiences of them. If, then, it must be allowed that we "find" bodies in motion, for example, then what theory of perception can justly disallow the perception of a lot of causality?

And she continues:

> The truthful—though unhelpful—answer to the question, "How did we come by our primary knowledge of causality?" is that in learning to speak we learned the linguistic representation and application of a host of causal concepts. Very many of them were represented by transitive and other verbs of action used in reporting what is observed. Others—a good example is "infect"—form, not observation statements, but rather expressions of causal hypotheses. The word "cause" itself is highly general. How does someone show that he has the concept cause? We wish to say: only by having such a word in his vocabulary. If so, then the manifest possession of the concept presupposes the mastery of much else in language. I mean: the word "cause" can be *added* to a language in which are already represented many causal concepts. A small selection: *scrape*,

push, wet, eat, burn, knockover, keep off, squash, make (e.g., noises, paper boats), *hurt*. But if we care to imagine languages in which no special causal concepts are represented, then no description of the use of a word in such languages will be able to present it as meaning *cause*. Nor will it even contain words for natural kinds of stuff, nor yet words equivalent to "body," "wind," or "fire." For learning to use special causal verbs is part and parcel of learning to apply the concepts answering to these and many other substantives. As surely as we learned to call people by name or to report from seeing it that the cat was on the table, we also learned to report from having observed it that someone drank up the milk or that the dog made a funny noise or that things were cut or broken by whatever we saw cut or break them.

Let us come back now to the distinction between internalist and realist views of explanation. If my answer to a request to explain why a certain vase is lying in pieces on the floor is that Betty broke it, which kind of explanation have I given? What "grounds" this explanation is obviously a causal relation: Betty's push *caused* the vase to fall and break. So the explanation is a realist one? But recall the characterization of the internalist view that we gave: "whether or not something is an explanation—a good, 'true' or 'correct' explanation—depends on factors internal to the body of knowledge, not what goes on in the world—except, of course, for the truth of the statements comprising the explanans." The "goodness" of this explanation does depend on internal factors—that citing Betty's push removes our puzzlement, for example (as just giving the magnitude of the force on the vase at a certain time would not have done). And it does not depend on any *other* factors *except* "the truth of the statements comprising the explanans." So it is also an "internalist" one! The whole way in which this dichotomy has been set up assumes that causal relations are something *over and above* what is known when we know "the truth of the statements comprising the explanans." And this is the legacy of the Logical Empiricist idea of what a proper explanans looks like!

are the realists really internalists (and vice versa)?

The distinction between internalists and realists about explanation looks even more puzzling when we examine the views of some of the people Kim cites as paradigm realists (David Lewis and Wesley Salmon, for example). Salmon does indeed hold that to answer a question of the form "Why did such-and-such an event E happen" one must provide a *cause* (or causes). But, in Salmon's[7] view (in this, Salmon is a faithful follower of Reichenbach),[8] to say that an event A caused an event B is just to make a complicated statement about relative frequencies in various sequences of events.[9] The causal relation that is the "ground" of the explanation can be brought into the explanation itself, and, when this is done, the only "external" factor that contributes to the "goodness" of the explanation will be covered by Kim's "except" clause—nothing more than "the truth of the statements comprising the explanans" is needed for a good explanation, once all the relevant facts about relative frequencies have been included, on Salmon's view.

David Lewis, to be sure, does *not* believe that causality can be analyzed in terms of relative frequency. But, according to him,[10] it *can* be analyzed in terms of counterfactuals. These counterfactual are in turn explained in terms of a rich ontology of "possible worlds" and "objective similarities." But—and this is crucial to Lewis's treatment of the *asymmetry* of the causal relation[11]— just how we *weigh* the similarities between possible worlds in assigning truth-values to counterfactuals depends on our *interests*—indeed, on our *epistemic* interests. (For example, we sometimes count sameness of laws as the more important similarity between possible worlds and sometimes count sameness of the events that have happened in the past as more important.) So is Lewis's theory perhaps really an *internalist* theory in disguise? (If, as most contemporary philosophers do, we reject Lewis's own belief in the "real existence" of possible worlds and construe them as simply possible *histories* of the world, does not the last vestige of "realism"—in Kim's special sense—not drain out of Lewis' theory?)

Lewis might of course reply that a relation can be *simultaneously* "objective" and "interest-dependent." (Our interests fix the criteria for saying that the relation holds, but that it holds *given* those criteria is a fact independent of us.) And I would heartily agree. But I am not sure that this is how Kim thinks of objectivity.

Turning to the paradigm internalist Hempel, there is also a complication. As mentioned earlier, Hempel did not only require that the premises in a "correct" explanation be *true*, he also required that certain of the premises be *lawlike*, and it is not clear that lawlikeness is a purely "internal" property of statements. Indeed, in 1954 I was party to a discussion between Carnap, Hempel, Feigl, and one or two others on the topic of lawlikeness and causation,[12] and the consensus was that the analysis of "lawlikeness" was a topic on which further work needed to be done. (Carnap thought that some nonsemantical notion—such as the notion of a "fundamental magnitude"—would have to be introduced, and Hempel did not express any disagreement.)

What is clear, once again, is the point of fundamental agreement between all these authors (and disagreement with the view expressed by Anscombe in the long quotation above). They all assume that the notion of causation will eventually be *analyzed away*. (The disagreement is about how to do this: whether one has to use Possible Worlds Semantics, or whether facts about frequencies will suffice, or facts about the "form" of the generalizations said to be lawlike (plus, of course, the truth of the generalization) can suffice, or whether one will need to appeal to metaphysical facts about the status of some of the predicates in the generalization.) Like Hume, these philosophers refuse to see ordinary descriptive predicates as *already* possessing causal content. The fight Kim is analyzing is a family fight between philosophers who share Humean suspicions about causality, and that is why it seems odd to me to describe *any* of them as "explanatory realists."

the unconsidered alternative: causation and explanation as interdependent

I agree with the view Anscombe defended. That view has four principle components: first, Anscombe claims that specific causal notions are learned as we learn the language. Without them, we could not speak of ordinary objects and ordinary goings-on at all. Second, she claims that in most cases what we see, hear, and so on cannot be described without using these specific causal notions. (So she rejects the Humean claim that we do not "observe" any such thing as causal connection.)[13] Third, she claims that the concept "caused" is an *abstraction* from these more specific causal notions. Fourth, she does not believe that the project of *analyzing* the concept "causes" (in the sense of reducing the concept to other concepts that are not already causal concepts in the way that "break" and "pick up," etc., are causal concepts) has any chance of success. Perhaps I should add a fifth component: she does not see any reason why we should commit ourselves to any such a reduction project in the first place.

But in accepting this view one must be careful not to commit the opposite error; that is, the error of supposing that one can reduce the notion of "explanation" *to* the notion of "causation." For we learn the various special causal notions that we possess by learning to answer various "why-questions," that is, by learning a motley of explanatory practices. What appeals to the slogan "meaning is use" often overlook is that, as Wittgenstein intended the remark that inspires the slogan, the ways in which we use words are not themselves describable in some one vocabulary (especially some one "scientific" vocabulary) supposed to be fixed in advance. Describing an explanatory practice requires using the concepts that are acquired with that practice (or related concepts). Causation and explanation are interdependent notions.

the hume-ayer view on mental and physical causation rejected

In part 2 of the present volume I defended the view that a given physical event (for example, water running into a bathtub) may have both a physical explanation and a "mental" explanation (the water is running because I just decided to take a bath). This is also the view of a Humean such as the late A. J. Ayer, but for a reason that I cannot accept. On Hume's account of causation, to say that an event A caused an event B is just to say that there is a regularity[14] R to the effect that (under certain specifiable conditions C) A-type events are always followed by B-type events (where the assumption I criticized above, that the "events" we speak of when we make causal claims can themselves be described without using causal notions, is of course taken by Hume to have been proved). In Ayer's view,[15] this solves the problem of how the physical event P (the water running into the bathtub) can have both a physical cause (say, the physical state S_0 of the water in the pipes, the faucet, the bathtub, and, if you like to include them, my brain and body at a suitable earlier time t_0) and a mental cause (the decision D) without requiring us to "reduce" the mental cause to the physical cause. For to say that P has these two different causes simultaneously is merely to say that D can be subsumed under two different regularities at once (under the regularity "Under conditions C_1, S_0-type events are always followed by P-type events" and under the regularity "Under conditions C_2, D-type events are always followed by P-type events" for appropriate C_1 and C_2); and why should it pose any metaphysical problem that an event can be subsumed under two or more different regularities?

To the standard objection "But how can *the same event P* (the water running) be *brought about* by two different things (the decision and the physical state S_0)?" Ayer's reply is that the notion of "bringing about" is just an "animistic" addition to the notion of causation, one that we need to throw away.

Although I agree with the conclusion of Ayer's argument: that we can speak of certain physical events, such as the water running P, alternatively (and, as the reader of part 2 will expect me to say but Ayer does not say, *depending on the context*) as having a "mental cause" such as the decision D or as having a physical cause—but again I would say that *which* prior physical event we will cite as the "cause" is a context-sensitive matter[16]—my reason is emphatically not Ayer's. I do *not* think that "bringing about" is a notion we can or should dispense with, or that causal claims do no more than subsume events under *regularities*. Part of the notion of a decision is that decisions can be *acted* upon, they can be *carried out*, and my decision to run that water, plus the fact that I carried it out, really did *bring it about* that the water is running now. The Hume-Ayer line is an easy way to defuse Kim's worry that if we allow mental causation at all (and we don't reduce it to physical causation) then we have sacrificed "the causal closure of the physical,"[17] but I have no intention of availing myself of the easy way.

reductionism and (un)intelligibility

Instead of taking the easy way, what I have argued is that the fact that there are multiple answers to a question of the form "Why did E happen?" including answers that appeal to decisions, thoughts, desires, and other "mental phenomena," *would* conflict with the "causal closure of the physical" if the question "What would happen if all the physical events were the same and the decision (or the thought, or the desire) were not to occur?" were a fully intelligible question. But it is not.

Philosopher who believe that we need to reduce the mental to the physical if the problem of "reconciling the causal closure of the physical with mental causation" is to be resolved often, in my experience, bridle at the suggestion that there is anything unintelligible about the Automatic Sweetheart scenario (which is to say, about the "what would happen if" question), although Kim himself is far more open-minded, as I know from our conversations. Yet it is easy to miss that *reductionism itself also implies that the question is not intelligible in the way we first imagine* (which is to say, not fully intelligible).

To see this, let us consider what I think is the grain of insight in Kripke's famous claim that *there is no possible world in which water is not H2O*. Although I no longer think that talk of all "metaphysically possible worlds" makes sense,[18] Kripke's argument turns on an interesting point. At first blush, it seems perfectly intelligible to say that "Water is only contingently H2O," and while there is an obvious sense in which that is true—the proposition "Water is H2O" is *epistemically* contingent, that is, it takes experiments (and not conceptual analysis) to find out that it is true—we are likely to think we can conclude that "water might not have been H20" represents a fully intelligible possibility. If someone suggests that "world in which water isn't H20" is not a description of a state of affairs we can really understand, we are likely to be offended in just the way that those philosophers who are offended by the suggestion that (modifying William James's language) "young lady whose body and brain are in the same physical condition and exhibit the same behavior as if she were conscious, but who has no mental properties at all" is not a description of a state of affairs we can really understand are offended. In Kripke's language, we are likely to think that we understand the claim that *water itself* might not have been H2O.

Against this Kripke points out that once you know that "in the actual world" water is H2O, you can easily be embarrassed if you try to describe a world in which there is "water that is not H2O." The embarrassing question you face is simply this: "Why do you describe this world as a world in which *water* is not H2O? All you have done is describe a world in which the liquid in the lakes, the liquid in our bodies, the liquid that falls in rain, etc., is a clear transparent tasteless liquid with a different chemical formula. Why don't you say that there is a possible world in which we use the word *water* for *a different liquid*—one with many properties in common with water, but certainly not water?"

Of course, Kripke also provides a *sense* of "possible"—an *epistemic* sense—in which it is "possible that water is not H2O." That is, we can describe a situation in which there is what Kripke calls an "epistemic counterpart" of water (it is even called "water") that is not H2O. But that is not what we thought we were describing when we first thought we could clearly imagine "water not being H2O."

Reductionism too is a strategy for arguing that it is not clear that the Automatic Sweetheart scenario really makes sense, even if reductionists do not always see that it is. What I claim is that we can refuse to concede that the Automatic Sweetheart scenario makes sense *without* committing ourselves to the utopian program of reducing mental predicates to physical ones. If that program were not as utopian as it is, if it were not science fiction, it would represent a way of showing once and for all that the Automatic Sweetheart scenario does not describe a possibility. I, on the other hand, have *not* offered a way of showing "once and for all" that the scenario doesn't make sense. I *do* claim that the burden of making it intelligible *to us* lies on the side of those who claim to understand it. We learn the so-called mental predicates by learning to use them in explanatory practices that involve embodied creatures. The idea that they refer to "entities" that might be present or absent *independently* of what goes on in our bodies and behavior has a long history and powerful pictorial (and not just pictorial, but religious, etc.) appeal. Yet to say that the idea "might be true" is to suppose that a clear possibility has been described, even though no way of using the picture to describe an actual case has really been proposed. The materialists are right to insist on our embodied nature; they are right to insist that the connection between mind and body is too intimate for talk of disembodied spirits, Automatic Sweethearts, the "soulless tribe," and so on, to get off the ground; but they are wrong when their scientism drives them to claim that we can only think of our mentality as something that acts *in* and *through* our bodies *if* we can reduce the terms of vernacular psychology to terms of chemistry, physics, neurology, computer science, etc.

I mentioned in part 2 that Kim himself expresses disagreement with the conception of vernacular psychological talk as proto-scientific theory in one (atypical) paper.[19] But there is a problem with saying, as he did, "The right way to save vernacular psychology, in my opinion, is to stop thinking of it as playing the game that 'cognitive science' is supposed to play—that is, stop thinking of it as a 'theory' whose primary raison d'être is to generate law-based causal explanations and predictions. We will do better to focus on its normative role in the evaluation of actions and decisions." The problem is that while vernacular psychology does not, indeed, generate *law-based* explanations and predictions, at least in the sense in which "law" is used in physics,[20] that does not mean that it doesn't also "generate" explanations and predictions. But I agree with Kim that its normative and evaluative roles are also essential.

I began by quoting with approval a saying by John Haldane to the effect that there are "as many kinds of cause as there are senses of 'because.' " And I have explained why that must not be understood as meaning that the notion of explanation has priority over the notion of causation, in a sense that would imply that one can understand the notion of explanation independently of understanding the notion of causation. Nor should Haldane's saying be taken as a claiming or presupposing that the different senses of *because* are literally different *meanings* of the word. When we speak of different "senses" of a word or phrase or sentence, what we are often doing is pointing to very different uses of the expression in question, uses we nevertheless see as projections of a single concept. (An example due to Wittgenstein:[21] there is a sense of "understanding a sentence" in which one shows one's understanding by saying the same thing in different words and another sense in which one shows one's understanding—say, if the sentence occurs in a poem—by explaining why *no* other words would do). I propose to take Haldane's pregnant remark in the following way: what he speaks of as "senses of 'because' " I propose to take as our ever expanding repertoire of explanatory practices. So understood, what the remark says is that we understand the various uses of *cause* by mastering explanatory practices. And one may add that as our repertoire of explanatory practices is indefinitely extendable, so our concept of causation (like our concept of reality, as I remarked in part 1, lecture 1) is indefinitely extendable.

I criticized the Hume-Ayer view that there is no more to causal explanation than subsumption under regularities. But that view, although erroneous for many reasons, does contain an insight: it is not otiose or redundant to have different explanations for one and the same event depending on why someone is asking "Why?" And one of the important reasons that it is not otiose or redundant is that different explanations *generalize to different classes of cases*. And Ayer was right to point out that there is no conflict or contradiction involved in being interested in an event sometimes as a member of one class and sometimes as a member of quite a different class, for example, as a mere "water running" or as *the filling of a bathtub to take a bath*.

are appearances "qualia"?

Today certain philosophers of mind and philosophers of psychology take it to be obvious that consciousness is a matter of the occurrence of qualia. Yet the term *qualia* (singular: *quale*) is hardly innocent.

a brief history of qualia-talk

The first philosopher I ever heard use the term was C. I. Lewis in his lectures on theory of knowledge at Harvard in 1949. The literature at that time generally preferred the term *sense data*, and there were many different views concerning the epistemological and metaphysical status of these entities. But *qualia* evokes a very clear image. *Qualia* is just Latin for *"qualities."* (Nelson Goodman, who was one of Lewis's students, used "qualities" interchangeably with "qualia" in *The Structure of Appearance*.) And the picture is essentially Berkeley's: the *qualities* we are aware of when we encounter an apple—the *redness* of the peel, the *white* of the inside, the *smoothness* we feel when we first pick it up—are in the mind of the beholder and not "out there." The rejection of what I have referred to in these lectures as "commonsense realism" (and sometimes by the technical term *direct realism*) is built into the term *qualia*.

Ever since Descartes's First Meditation, epistemological skepticism has been driven by the following scenario: (Scene 1) Person A has an experience (a "veridical" one) of seeing[1] some object, say a yellow door. (Scene 2) Person B (who may be person A at a different time) has a *totally* nonveridical experience (a dream or a "perfect hallucination") that is "qualitatively identical" with the experience of person A (often this "qualitative identity" is not distinguished from *indistinguishability*,[2] although Nelson Goodman was aware of the problem).[3] This scenario with its two scenes leads to the following traditional argument:[4] what we "directly perceive" is the same in the two cases (this was supposed to be evident), yet in one of the two cases the yellow door (or whatever it was) doesn't physically exist (imagine that there is nothing physically yellow in person B's environment). So what B "directly perceived" isn't physical, and, since it is the same in both cases, that means it isn't physical even in the case of person A, not physical even when the perception is veridical. The "yellow we see" (as Berkeley would say), isn't physical but mental.

To be sure, most philosophers who held to the traditional picture would at once have added that there is a "perfectly good sense" in which we *see* the physical door: namely, the sense data (qualia) we are aware of are "caused in the appropriate fashion" by the door. There is even (they would add) a sense in which the door can be said to be "yellow": namely, "It has surface properties that cause it to reflect light of such a kind that, striking the eye of a normal observer, it will cause that observer to have yellow sense data."

Other philosophers—e.g., Thomas Reid, and, I suspect, a majority of contemporary philosophers, would modify this, saying that we aren't *aware* of the yellow sense data (unless we introspect), we simply *have* them. What we are aware of (conscious of, think about) is the physical door and the physical color. But, as I argued in part 1,[5] this doesn't really change the picture: the essential part of the picture, the part that is captured by the term *qualia*, is that insofar as there is anything in the world like what we unreflectively imagine *yellow* to be (anything "sensuously yellow," as I once heard someone say), it is in our minds (or, today, our brains) and not outside.

Against this picture William James, John Austin, John McDowell (and a few other philosophers in the past century) have proposed a *disjunctive view of perception*. On this view, there is nothing literally "in common" in Scene 1 and Scene 2, that is, no identical "quality." In Scene 1 someone (person A) *sees a yellow door*. In Scene 2 it *seems to someone* (person B) that (s)he is see-ing a yellow door. On the disjunctive view "visually experiencing a yellow door" is disjunctive (or ambiguous). It can consist *either* of seeing a real door with a real color quality (yellow) or in seeming to do that. The conclu-sion that there is an HCF (Highest Common Factor),[6] a mental "color quale," simply doesn't follow from the facts of Scene 1 and Scene 2.

I have repeatedly indicated my agreement with these philosophers in this volume.[7] I believe that the traditional argument is a fallacy (call it "the HCF fallacy"). In this afterword, I want to discuss it in more detail.

there is/isn't a "common factor"

(a) First, a comment on the traditional scenario. As Austin points out,[8] dreams are not "qualitatively identical" with waking experiences. (It is far from clear how one would determine that any dream was indistinguishable from a waking experience.)[9] And Austin's skepticism as to whether halluci-nations are "qualitatively identical" with waking experiences[10] is shared by psychologists with whom I have discussed this issue. It may well be that in actual life, as opposed to science fiction (e.g., stories about Brains in a Vat, which represent technological and possibly physical impossibilities), a dream or hallucination that is "qualitatively identical" (or indistinguishable from) a waking/normal experience simply never occurs.

(b) As Austin also points out,[11] lumping illusions (e.g, the bent stick in water, trompe l'oeil paintings, the parallel lines that look to be unequal in length but are really equal) together with delusions (or with dreams) involves a number of non sequiturs. Indeed, some of the traditional illusions (the bent stick in water is an example) have a look that is quite objective (it can even be photographed).

(c) Still, I can imagine someone addressing the following objection to McDowell:

> Suppose I were a Brain in a Vat seeming to see a yellow door. (I might even have consented to this experiment and know that what I was seeing wasn't real.) Or I might have taken a drug—even if the delusion isn't perfectly iden-tical to a waking experience, it could certainly involve a yellow door.

On your account, McDowell, perception has *content*. A perception (and likewise a seeming perception) has content. In both cases—reverting to the traditional scenario, in Scene 2 as well as in Scene 1—the subject has an experience whose content "claims" that a certain part of visual space, a certain color location relative to my body, contains a yellow door. *Why isn't this common content just the HCF you deny exists?*

The answer, of course, is that McDowell does indeed insist on the existence of *this* kind of "common factor." Part of the content of a nonveridical experience can indeed be the same as part of the content of a veridical experience. Both experiences can "tell one" (incorrectly, in the nonveridical case) that there is a yellow door in front of one, for example. But, in the nonveridical case, Yellow isn't a property something we experience *has* (or a property the experience *is*) as talk of qualia suggests; it is a property the experience *ascribes* to the door. The experience *portrays the environment as containing yellow* (it "refers to" yellow, as it were); it isn't a yellow (or a "subjectively yellow") particular or universal. As William James put it, the quality is "in" the experience "intentionally," but the experience does not have it "as an attribute." Confusing having redness or hotness "intentionally" with being red or hot "adjectively" (i.e., as attributes) is the HCF Fallacy.[12]

appearances as presentations

As Richard Heck has recently pointed out,[13] the current dispute[14] about whether *all* perceptual experience is "conceptualized" frequently runs together several different issues. One issue has to do with whether experiences are just mental items with certain qualities (mental pictures, for example, as in Hume's model of the mind) or whether they have world-involving *content*.[15] This is the issue we have just addressed. There is also a dispute about whether content can be "naturalized," that is, reduced to causal covariation. I have argued in a number of places[16] that intentionality—content—cannot be reduced in this way, and also argued that the notion of causality is itself an interest-relative one[17] (and that this feature unfits it to play the role that reductionist metaphysicians want it to play), and I shall not repeat the arguments here.

But there is also a dispute over the question "Is all content *conceptual?*" The issue is far from being clear, but it obviously depends on one's requirements for being "conceptual." What Heck has pointed out is that there is a property *weaker* than conceptuality, as John McDowell conceives of conceptuality (e.g., in his disagreement over this issue with Gareth Evans),[18] which would suffice for many of McDowell's purposes. What McDowell and Evans both require for the content of a perceptual experience to be conceptual is *the availability of the concepts needed to describe that content for thinking thoughts*— not just the thought that the experience is of such and such a kind, but other thoughts involving those same concepts and *other* concepts that the subject possesses. (This is a rough statement of Evans's "Generality Constraint,"[19] which Heck formulates thus: "According to the Generality Constraint, no thinker is capable of entertaining a thought with a particular structure unless s/he is able to recombine the elements of that structure so as to form other, related thoughts.") The weaker property that Heck offers as a substitute for conceptuality in this sense is the property of *representing* (or, as I shall say, *presenting*) a part of the world (or a part of the space in the subject's neighborhood) as having certain properties. As Heck puts it:[20]

> Sense-datum views . . . are vulnerable to the objections we have rehearsed because they deny that experience has *intentional* or *representational* content. The objections exploit the fact that, on the sense-datum view, my experiences are mere subjective happenings with no bearing, as it were, on the world outside me. *Prima facie*, then, it would seem that one could avoid these objections by insisting that perceptual experience does have representational content. But non-conceptual content *is* representational content, so it is far from clear why the additional claim that experience has *conceptual* content should be required.

What drives these remarks of Heck's is the following argument of McDowell's in *Mind and World*.[21] McDowell argues (correctly, in Heck's opinion) that experiences do not merely *cause* us to have beliefs; they *justify* some (we hope a lot) of our beliefs. They bear rational relations to our beliefs, including verifying and making probable. But they could not do this if they lacked content. The experience of seeing a yellow door has a content that implies that the

second afterword
are appearances "qualia"?

belief that there is a yellow door in front of one is true. That does not mean that I must accept the belief every time I have an experience with that content. Just as I can know that someone else's report that there is a yellow door in a certain place implies that there is a door in that place and still not believe that there is a door in that place (because I don't trust the report), I can have an experience as of seeing a yellow door in that place and not believe there is (because I don't trust the experience, for one reason or another). Heck's point is that if experience is to justify beliefs then that places a constraint on the sense in which it has content (a constraint that it is not clear that causal-covariation accounts of content can meet): the content of experiences that justify beliefs must be, to coin an awkward term, *presentational*. (Heck's own term, *representational*, I find awkward because Heck himself— rightly on the view I have been defending—*rejects* the view that the *objects* of experience are representations, which he calls "the representational view." In my terminology, Heck believes that experiences *present* the world as having certain features but rejects the view that we experience representations.) Where Heck sees a lacuna in McDowell's argument is in the step from being presentational to being "conceptual" in the sense of satisfying the Generality Constraint.

It seems to me, however, not only that *many* of our experiences do have the property of presupposing conceptual capacities on our part (no one denies this, with the possible exception of Fodor), but—and this is the heart of the debate—that *such experiences are not reducible to experiences with nonconceptual content*. In particular, "seeing-as" experiences obviously involve the *concepts* we use in saying (or thinking) what the thing experienced is seen as. Seeing a duck-rabbit drawing as a rabbit without having the concept of a rabbit is an idea to which I can attach no sense.[22] And the idea that we can *reduce* the "seeing as" experience to a seeing that lacks the relevant (duck or rabbit) content plus an *inference* (an inference that the *subject* makes, not a piece of data-processing that takes place somewhere in the brain) is simply a fabulation, as Wittgenstein's discussion of the "duck-rabbit" picture was already meant to bring out.[23] My own "Girondiste" position is that while it may be that some experiential content is nonconceptual in the sense of not being conceptual*ized*, such epistemologically important content as recognizing something as an object of a certain kind is *irreducibly* conceptual.[24] And these are the experiences that we appeal to in the *justification* of beliefs.

To this, Daniel Dennett recently replied in a conversation that "talk of justification puts one in the area of rational reconstruction, and I don't know what the rules are supposed to be." I would agree with Dennett that all talk of justification, all epistemology, involves *some* "rational reconstruction," and I cannot give anyone "rules" for reasonable rational reconstruction (nor can I give anyone rules for *philosophy*!). But to conclude that all we should talk about is efficient causation is to recommend simply giving up philosophy for natural science, and that, I hope, we are not prepared to do.

Incidentally, it is frequently overlooked, if not actually denied, that part of the content of our conceptualized visual experiences is that one is *seeing* a particular look or aspect of the things in question. Contrary to a tradition that runs from Hume all the way to Carnap's *Aufbau*, when I close my eyes I do not have to *infer* that the yellow door has not gone out of existence. I *experience* my seeing the door as just that: my seeing the door, not as "the existence of visual qualia," and I experience my shutting my eyes as my own action, my avoiding seeing the door, not as some qualia going out of existence.

An example of an experience that depends upon the possession of the appropriate concepts is the following. I see a sign bearing the following letters:

STOP

as saying "stop," but someone who does not know the English alphabet may only see "something in an alphabet I don't know," and someone who knows the alphabet but not the word sees letters but not "stop," just as someone who has seen ducks but has no concept of a rabbit cannot see the famous duck-rabbit drawing as a duck. The dispute between McDowell and some of his opponents is a replay of a dispute over whether a certain basic "layer" of perceptual experience (say, the layout of colors in visual space) is nonconceptual, one in which Bertrand Russell[25] and William James took part. Russell thought that it must be possible to divide any perceptual experience into two parts, a part that is nonconceptual and a part that is "added" by conceptualization. William James's position was that while all perceptual experience has both conceptual and nonconceptual ("sensational") aspects, the attempt to divide such an experience into parts is futile. "Sensations and apperceptive idea fuse here so intimately [in a 'presented and recognized material object'] that you can no more tell where one begins and the other ends, than you can tell, in those cunning circular panoramas that have lately been exhibited, where the real foreground and the painted canvas join together."[26]

It is because it fails to take account of how much of our perceptual experience is conceptualized ("fused with apperceptive ideas," in James' terminology) that the empiricist view that what we see is simply an array of color patches is such a distortion. When I look at, say, an armchair, it may be true that I don't at that instant see the back (and I certainly don't see the stuffing); but there is, nonetheless, a most important sense in which I see it *as* an armchair, as a three-dimensional solid object, one with a back and sides that I *could see*, and with a certain softness, "comfortable looking" perhaps, as something to be sat in, and a great deal more besides. This is something Carneides and Sextus Empiricus already noted: "E.g., someone who takes in the impression of a man necessarily also gets an impression of things to do with the man and his extraneous circumstances — things to do with him like his colour, size, shape, motion, conversation, dress, foot-wear; and external circumstances like atmosphere, light, day, sky, earth, friends and everything else."[27] As Husserl puts it, perceptual experiences ("intuitions") are "the acts that in knowledge are called to the fulfillment of other intentions"[28] Explaining this passage, Charles Parsons uses an example very similar to our armchair example: "Acts of outer perception have the characteristic that they contain both fulfilled and unfulfilled intentions; for example, a perception of a cup sitting on a table will represent it as having a bottom, but since the bottom is not visible, the intention is not fulfilled."[29]

Even if we confine attention to the case in which what one is visually attending to is as simple as a color patch on a wall, similar remarks apply. The color patch will change appearance if a cloud passes over the sun, if I am viewing it by daylight. If the patch is glossy, there will be places that look almost white (if one looks at the patch with a painter's eye — or an epistemologist's), and the location of these white places will appear to change as I move. Far from showing that the patch isn't really colored as we imagine it to be (as Russell claimed in *The Problems of Philosophy*),[30] what this shows, as I argued in part 1,[31] is something that every adult human with normal vision knows very well, that colors have *looks*, looks that depend on such things as the illumination and the point from which the object is viewed. Just as the armchair has a multitude of aspects (Husserlian "unfulfilled intentions") while remaining (experientially, not just "objectively") a single armchair, so the color patch may be seen as a patch of uniform color even though it is *also* seen as having "glossy places," and even though (I am aware that) it has a multitude of other looks that will become "fulfilled intentions" if my position changes or the illumination changes. As Dewey might have put it, perception is *transactional*. We are aware of ourselves as in *interaction* with our perceptual objects. I am aware of a series of visual, tactile, etc., *perspectives* on the chair without ceasing to perceive the chair *as* an object that does not change as those perspectives change.[32]

These perspectives depend not only on the illumination and the distance and the angle from which we view the visual object (and on various familiar factors in the case of the other senses)[33] but also on our own physiological condition. Jaundice can make objects look yellow; certain drugs can alter the way colors look or cause objects to have colored "halos"; squinting can alter visual appearances, not to mention near-sightedness, astigmatism, etc.) There is a long-standing tendency in philosophy to think that perspectival properties are subjective, not really properties of "external things," but this is a mistake. (The mistake is connected with the mistake I argued against in *The Many Faces of Realism*, the mistake of denying the relativity of many of our fundamental notions to conceptual schemes.) The lines in a Müller-Lyer illusion are both of equal length when measured with a ruler *and* such as to appear of unequal length to a typical human viewer. But there is only one pair of lines—and a multitude of perceptual and other transactions we can have with them and a corresponding variety of *objectively relative* properties of *those same lines*.

some remarks about animal perception

It has been pointed out to me[34] that it seems reasonable to many cognitive scientists to say that infants and certain animals "perceive certain three-dimensional objects as such" because, for example, the subjects express surprise when, going around the object, they "notice that it isn't a three-dimensional object but only a façade." And of course I do not deny that some psychologists use the language of *perceiving* and *noticing* this way. But rather than conclude that we should either loosen the notion of conceptuality or weaken the connection between "seeing as" and "having a concept," I would respond that using these highly intentional terms in this way very often (especially in supposedly "scientific" contexts) involves a confusion between what I called "protoconcepts" in *Renewing Philosophy* and concepts in a more demanding sense. The facts, let us suppose, are these: infants and some animals exhibit (or sometimes exhibit) "startle reactions" if on going around certain objects they see the back of a façade (here I am using the verb *see* in what logicians call the "transparent" sense, the sense in which to say of a person or an animal that it sees an X-ray tube only implies that what the thing sees is in fact an X-ray tube, but doesn't imply that the subject necessarily sees it or recognizes it *as* an X-ray tube). Further, some cognitive scientists hypothesize that the brain or a part of the brain (a subpersonal processor) constructs a "3-D model" of the scene presented to the subject's eyes. These scientists would say that the failure of the 3-D model to "fit" what is seen when the rear of the façade comes into view is what causes the startle reaction. Let us suppose this is correct. The question is, does this constitute either having the concept of the thing as a "three-dimensional object" or "seeing it *as* a three-dimensional object"?

In chapter 1 of *Renewing Philosophy* I imagined that we discovered that the brains of dogs contain a "module" (or a group of modules) that facilate the recognition of the look, smell, taste, etc. of meat. I suggested that we say (in the imagined circumstance) that dogs possess a "protoconcept" of meat. Why only a *protoconcept*? I gave two reasons. The first was that the interpretation of the module as specifically a meat recognizer is *not* something that is fixed as *determinately* correct by the evolutionary history of the species. It is just as compatible with the evolutionary history of dogs either to describe the "function" of the module more broadly, for example, as a device for recognizing "stuff that looks and tastes like meat," or more narrowly, as a "nonpoisoned meat" recognizer. None of the evolutionary facts chooses between these (and, for that matter, still other) alternatives. (If we say that the "function" of the device is to recognize meat, then we will have to say that the device is "fooled" when the dog accepts a vegetarian meat substitute; if we say that its function is to recognize "nonpoisoned meat," then we will have to say that it is also "fooled" when the dog accepts poisoned meat; and if we say that its function is to recognize "stuff that looks and tastes like meat," then we will have to say that it isn't "fooled" in these cases, but these cases were not sufficiently common to negate the general contribution of the device to inclusive genetic fitness.) A mature language speaker can distinguish between thinking that something is *meat* or *nonpoisoned meat* or *stuff that looks and tastes like meat*, but canine history and behavior cannot. You don't get more determinate meaning out of "evolutionary function" than you read in (as Dennett might put it).

Second, a canine reaction, either behavioral or neurological, can be successful or unsuccessful in any given case, but it makes no sense to call it "true" or "false." A human being can imagine that a belief that was successful in every way might "really have been false." (For example, my belief that I was in my own bed when I woke up this morning was successful in the sense of being confirmed by all of my experiences, but I can imagine that someone went to enormous expense and difficulty to arrange for the entire bedroom and indeed the entire place to have been a stage setting. In that case, the belief would have been false, of course. But the dog cannot imagine that the stuff that looks and tastes just like meat "isn't really meat," as far as we now know.) To ask of a successful "protobelief" of a dog whether it was perhaps false would be precisely to assume more determinacy in a dog's "protoconcepts" than they possess.

I think that the case of the animal that exhibits a startle reaction when the object (say, a tree) turns out to be a "façade" is similar. The animal (or the prelinguistic infant) has, perhaps, a protoconcept of a solid object. There is certainly a continuum of possibilities between protoconceptual and fully conceptual behavior (and, in the case of some of the higher primates, it may be that the line is blurry). But if all there is to interpret the "protoconcept" is the "startle reaction," then I would not say that the animal or the infant "sees the thing *as* a three-dimensional object"), although I might say that it has a protoconcept, one of whose possible interpretations (perhaps the most natural one for human adults) is "three-dimensional object." We can and do "read in" this interpretation when we see the startle reaction. But there is all the difference in the world between this and fully having the concept of a three-dimensional object.

subjectivity and "inverted spectra"

In a famous thought experiment (the "inverted spectrum") first proposed by Locke, one imagines that two subjects have systematically different color experiences (my experiences on seeing the things we both call "green" are qualitatively the same as your experiences upon seeing the things we both call "red," etc.). In one recent form of Locke's thought experiment, Ned Block's "Inverted Earth,"[35] the proponent of the picture appears committed to the possibility that two subjects could be in the same internal physical state and neither misperceives his environment and yet they might have qualitatively *different* perceptual experiences. However, the question Why couldn't the qualitative character of our experiences be determined by the condition of my "immaterial soul"? or by other mysterious entities and conditions, conditions independent of our physiology and our physical environments, is one that, I argued in part 2, we have not succeeded in giving a clear sense, and I would say the same about Block's "Inverted Earth" scenario. (The "Inverted Spectrum Sweetheart" is a trivial variant of the "Automatic Sweetheart.")

It may seem, however, as if the supposedly intractable problem of "subjectivity" is left intact, even if one adopts the transactional view of perception I have been urging. If one's perception of an object can undeniably be affected by one's physiological condition, why *couldn't* it be affected in such a way that the "appearance of green" to me is the same as "the appearance of red" to *you*? This question requires closer consideration.

Here is a short piece of science fiction. On the planet Ixxz in a remote galaxy live a race of intelligent beings whose senses are much like ours apart from the sense of sight. They are not, to be sure, devoid of sight, but they discriminate only three "colors": $gray_{Ixxz}$, $white_{Ixxz}$, and *grix* (which we shall not attempt to translate). Objects we call "black" or "gray" are all reported by them to be gray$_{Ixxz}$, objects we call white (including various shades of "off-white") are reported by them to be white$_{Ixxz}$, and objects of all other colors—all red, orange, yellow, green, blue, and violet objects—are said by them to be one and the same color, the color they call "grix," and, indeed, psychological experiments performed on Ixxzians by Terrestrial scientists show that they cannot discriminate between otherwise similar objects that differ in that one is red and the other is green, or one is blue and the other is yellow, etc. In addition, the off-spectral colors (for example, brown and the various purples)[36] are seen as "grix. They also do not perceive differences in saturation and brightness apart from discriminating different shades of "gray$_{Ixxz}$."

Neurological investigation reveals that Ixxzian brains are "wired" as follows: "color" messages from the eye pass through three kinds of fibers, α, β, and γ. α-fibers are connected to an area A in the cortex, β-fibers to an area B, and γ-fibers to C. When an α-fiber from a certain part of the Ixxzian retina transmits a signal to an area A, a corresponding part of the visual field is seen as white. Similarly, β-fiber stimulation received in area B corresponds to appropriate part of the visual field being seen as gray, and γ-fiber stimulation in C corresponds to the appropriate part of the visual field being seen as "grix."

One day an Ixxzian neurologist tries the experiment of "rewiring" an Ixxzian brain so that the α-fibers stimulate area C instead of area A and γ-fibers stimulate area A instead of area C. The subject, Jaxxz, reports that all grix objects now look white (or "white$_{Ixxz}$") and all white ("white$_{Ixxz}$") objects now look grix. His "spectrum" is inverted![37] (Attempts to "switch" the α- or the γ-fibers with the β-fibers are unsuccessful, however. The reason appears to be that the β-fibers, which discriminate between different *shades* of what we call "gray," do not carry a simple "yes/no" signal, and the A and C areas cannot "read" the signal that comes from them, nor will the B area accept the simple "yes/no" signals from the α- or the γ-fibers.)

There are a number of questions that could be raised about this story, some of which I shall touch on below, but let us assume that some such story represents a conceptual possibility. What philosophical significance does this supposed possibility have?

A defender of (the materialist version of) the sense-datum theory might, of course, argue as follows: "You have to admit that in the case of the Ixxzians the subjective character of experience corresponds to something *inside the head*. For the 'spectrum inversion' shows that the 'objective colors' (i.e., the reflectance properties of the external objects, the light-rays, etc.) do not determine the subjective experience; all that matters to *that* is which area of the brain, A, B, or C, is stimulated."

To this a first reply is that of course the "character" of the experience "corresponds to" what happens in the Ixxzian brain, *in the sense that* if area A is appropriately stimulated by a fiber leading from a particular part of the retina, *it will seem to the Ixxzian* that it is seeing "white$_{\text{Ixxz}}$" in the appropriate part of its visual field, even if there is nothing white (or "white$_{\text{Ixxz}}$") "there." But the advocate of the disjunctive view certainly does not deny that it is possible for it to seem to a subject that it is perceiving white (or any other color) when it isn't really doing so. All you have done, the defender of "the natural realism of the common man" (as William James put it) will say, is to think up a fanciful case in which some perceiver is mistaken in thinking she or he perceives a certain color. But neither the natural realism of the common man nor its various philosophical defenses denies or ignores the fact that that happens.

This first reply might be countered by complicating the science fiction.

The "complication" we introduce is the following. We now imagine that in the Ixxzian embryological process the connections between the α- and γ-fibers and the A and C areas in the brain are *randomized*.[38] Thus there are two kinds of Ixxzians. An Ixxzian may be born with its α-fibers connected to area A and its γ-fibers attached to area C *or* with its α-fibers connected to area C and its γ-fibers attached to area A. (The β-fibers, which are much more complex in structure, are always attached to area B and cannot be "switched," even surgically, without destroying the relevant color vision.) In this variant of our story, *there is no area that "normally" subserves "seeing white$_{\text{Ixxz}}$"* or "seeing grix." Any two Ixxzians are as likely as not to have "inverted spectra" relative to one another. And it will not be the case that one or the other is seeing things *wrong*, at least if that means seeing things "abnormally."

I think the right line for the defender of commonsense realism is to concede that, *in the story*, neither of the Ixxzians is seeing things wrong. And, if the story represents a possibility at all, this would show that a phenomenon that (as we already remarked) exists in the Terrestrial case also exists, although in a different way, in the Ixxzian case: one's "visual perspective" may depend not only on external factors (for example, the lighting), and on the location of one's eyes, but also on internal physiological factors. What an Ixxzian sees when he looks at a white patch on a blue wall (as we would describe the object) is the way $white_{Ixxz}$ patches on a grix wall look to an Ixxzian with one of the two possible Ixxzian physiologies.

"What *is* $white_{Ixxz}$?" the reader may well want to ask at this point. The answer I would give is that while "$white_{Ixxz}$" is certainly not a well-defined *scientific* property, it is certainly a perfectly OK commonsense property given the Ixxzian perceptual apparatus. After all, Ixxzians are quite able to agree (not always, but in sufficiently many cases) on which objects, color patches, flashes of light, etc., are "$white_{Ixxz}$."

Compare the term *mountain* in our culture. Being a mountain is not a well-defined scientific property *either*, but few of us would conclude that "mountains do not really exist," and those who do conclude this are mistaken. Not all ways of conceptualizing things are scientific, but it does not follow that our commonsense ways are one and all *superstitions*.

The analogy with the term *mountain* goes somewhat further. Even though we cannot *reduce* the term *mountain* to the vocabulary of physics for a number of reasons (vagueness, the fact that it is sometimes a matter of *convention* whether something is counted as one mountain with two peaks or two mountains, etc.) we can make generalizations about mountains, and the special science of *geology* is quite happy to do that. Similarly, even though we cannot reduce either human or Ixxzian color terms to the vocabulary of physics, we can make generalizations about color, and quite a lot of scientific activity has gone and will continue to go into doing just that.[39]

But that is not the conclusion a Cartesian cum materialist will want to draw. The Cartesian cum materialist will argue as follows: "The fact (*which you accept as a fact, in this hypothetical scenario*) that two Ixxzians will have the same subjective color experience as long as the same one of the two area

A, C is stimulated *shows* that the color appearance *just is* the stimulation of the area (or stimulation of area B, in the case of grays). And something analogous must be true of human brains and human subject."

This of course overlooks the very possibility of the account I have been defending, the account on which both of the hypothetical Ixxzians are *perceiving the same color, but perceiving two different "looks" or perspectival attributes of that color.* Jaxx sees that the patch on the wall is "white$_{Ixxz}$" and also sees the particular way that a "white$_{Ixxz}$" patch looks to an Ixxian of his makeup and Jilxxx see that the patch on the wall is "white$_{Ixxz}$" and also sees the particular way that a "white$_{Ixxz}$" patch looks to an Ixxian of *her* makeup. But that does *not* mean that they are *really* aware of something inside their own brains.[40]

Those who argue that the state of the visual cortex will provide identity conditions for visual experiences when we know enough of the relevant neurophysiology frequently make the same mistake as one would be making if one took the *total* brain state to provide identity conditions for "narrow contents" (the mistake I discussed in part 2, lecture 3). For even if we were to stipulate: "Color experience X is identical with color experience Y *if* [N.B.: not "if and only if," which would clearly be false] the visual cortex is in exactly the same state when experience X is had as when it was/will be when experience Y is had," this stipulation would yield only a *sufficient* condition for "identity" of color experiences. Moreover, just as was the case with the corresponding stipulation for narrow contents, the sufficient condition is one that (in the human case) is *never realized in the real world.*

In fact, the suggestion that visual experiences are *identical* with stimulations of a neural assembly (A, B, or C) is wrong even in the Ixxzian case — wrong even if we confine attention to the Ixxzians' experiences of "white$_{Ixxz}$" and "grix," and ignore the more complex Ixxzian "gray$_{Ixxz}$" experiences, which pose the same failure-of-transitivity problems for Ixxzian philosophers to ponder that we found in the case of human color experiences. But we do not need to consider hypothetical Ixxzians to see what is wrong with the suggestion, for in the human case too there are experiences that are (reasonably) discrete; recognition of *words*, unlike recognition of colors, is usefully thought of as an "all or none" affair. And there is believed to be a particular "module" that (as a rule) gives a particular signal if and only if the subject hears what (s)he recognizes as a particular word, say *bug*. (The example comes from Jerry Fodor, who has written a book on this topic.)[41] The modules in question can be realized as very simple neural assemblies, in existing models of the brain's architecture. In *The Modularity of Mind* Fodor consistently identifies the outputs of "input modules" with *appearances*;[42] with such "phenomenologically accessible"[43] features of what we perceive as sounds, colors, etc., as well as with certain linguistic appearances. But if this were right, then one could in principle have an "appearance" in a *test tube*. For one could in principle have a neural assembly (the "module" in question) kept alive in a vat (or a test tube), supplied with nutrients and stimulated to fire by an electrode. Then there would be an appearance (say of the word *bug*) that was not *experienced* by anyone! Surely this is crazy. And exactly the same argument applies to the suggestion that the color experiences of the Ixxzians are *identical* with the outputs of the perceptual modules A, B, and C.

A significant part of the problem we face when we attempt to think clearly about mind and body comes from the tradition of speaking of "the" brain event (or process) correlated to a given mental phenomenon. In addition to the problems emphasized in connection with the propositional attitudes (believing that, thinking that, etc.) in part 2, lecture 3 above, there is a problem with this talk that affects even the most primitive mental states, say, seeing a color or feeling a pain, one to which Daniel Dennett has repeatedly called attention.[44] The problem is that there *isn't* just *one* correlated brain event. Indeed, when one says that certain events in the visual cortex, or the "firing" of certain neural assemblies, is "correlated" with a particular "experience," what one typically means is that *in the context of a normally functioning brain and nervous system* the one event happens when and only when the other does. In this sense an event E (say, a signal from one of Fodor's "modules") can be 1–1 correlated with the recognition of the word *bug and* E+M (where M is the formation of a short-term memory) can *also* be so correlated, *and* E+M+S (where S is the reception of the signal in the "speech center") can *also* be so correlated, and so on, and so on. As I remarked in part 2,[45] after philosophers have been talking for over a hundred years about the correlates of mental events, it naturally comes to seem that *identity* is what is problematic, whereas (unique) "correlation" is unproblematic. But, as I discussed at more length in *Reason, Truth, and History,*[46] the idea of a unique correlate faces enormous epistemological and metaphysical problems. Thus, in addition to all the other problems connected with the meaningfulness of "identity" in the mind-brain context that we have discussed in this volume, one must stress that if talk of "the correlate" of, say, a color experience is fundamentally unclear, as I believe it to be, then the issue of the "identity" of the experience with "the" correlate is *at least* as unclear.

A last remark on the comparison of humans with science-fiction "Ixxzians"

If we accept the story about the Ixxzians as representing a possibility, it "shows" that it is not impossible for a species to be afflicted with widespread "spectrum inversions." (In fact, as is the case in most science fiction, this story's scenario is extremely underdescribed.) In this section I wish to draw attention to a feature of our "science fiction story" that makes it difficult to draw any morals at all concerning what is possible in the human case.

I begin with a simple question. Suppose you were to replace the jack on your telephone with a connector that you could plug into the video input socket in the back of your video recorder. What would happen?

The answer (try it for yourself!) is "Nothing." The signals from the telephone line are, in effect, in code, and your video recorder is not constructed to read that code. It would not be impossible to manufacture a device which would "translate" the electrical impulses coming over the telephone wire, which are themselves coded sounds, in some systematic way into colors, but such a device would have to be specially designed for the purpose.

The relevance of this to the Ixxzian/human comparison is the following: Jerome Lettvin has shown[47] that the color information transmitted by the human eye to the brain is the result of a complex "computation" carried out by the eye itself. There isn't (of course!) a "fiber" for each possible color from each part of the retina to some part of the visual cortex as in our "Ixxzian" story. What the optic nerve transmits is *coded information*. And while certain events may disrupt that information, resulting in various conditions (forms of color blindness, flashes of color, "halos" of color around objects, etc.), it is overwhelmingly unlikely that any "rewiring" of the optical pathways could have the effect of "switching the colors around"—as unlikely as that your video recorder could "translate" the electrical impulses coming over the telephone into corresponding colors. There is no reason at all to suppose that "spectrum inversion" is a physical possibility in the human species.

the purposes of the account in this book

There are certainly many further issues that could be discussed in connection with consciousness. Let me state briefly my reasons for selecting the issues I have discussed in this book. My concern (in part 1 in particular) was with providing a way of conceptualizing our perceptual experiences that does not make those experiences into an *interface* between us and the world, a movie screen inside our own heads or minds that we directly experience *instead* of the cups and doors and cats and people and mountains and trees. Once perceptual experience is conceived of in what I called *transactional* terms, conceived of (in the successful case) as acquaintance with genuine properties of objects, one form of skepticism—the radical Berkeleyan form that claims that *it is unintelligible* how perceptual experiences (which are, on the traditional conception, all "inside") can have a unique correlation with objects that are "outside"—cannot even arise.[48] My own model-theoretic argument against realism in *Reason, Truth, and History* and in "Models and Reality"[49] were, at bottom, a form of what I just called "Berkeleyan skepticism," and I believe that there is no way to defeat those doubts if the interface conception of perceptual experience is left standing.

The fact that even if color properties (to stick to the example we have used throughout this afterword) are conceived of as properties of "external" objects they must be admitted to be *perspectival*, to have different *looks*, including looks that depend on the condition of the perceiving subject, should not be denied (as it has been, unfortunately, by certain "externalist" philosophers of mind).[50] But from the point of view of the problem of realism and antirealism, the problem that has haunted philosophy ever since Berkeley denied that we could make sense of so much as *conceiving* an "external" object, that does not affect the (dis)solution I have proposed.

In part 2 of this volume we saw issues about qualia arise in another way. The view I have long defended is that the mind is not a *thing*; talk of our minds is talk of *world-involving capabilities that we have and actitivities that we engage in*. As Dewey succinctly put it, "Mind is primarily a verb. It denotes all the ways in which we deal consciously and expressly with the situations in which we find ourselves. Unfortunately, an influential manner of thinking has changed modes of action into an underlying substance that performs the activities in question. It has treated mind as an independent entity *which* attends, purposes, cares, and remembers."[51] But the traditional view, by treating mental states as states of the "underlying substance," makes them properties of something "inside," and, if one is a materialist philosopher, that means properties of our *brains*. So the next problem naturally seems to be: "*Which* neurological properties of our brains do these mental properties 'reduce' to?" For how could our *brains* have properties that *aren't* neurological? And this is how materialist philosophers saw the problem until the advent of such new alternatives in the philosophy of mind and philosophy of language as Functionalism and Semantic Externalism.

As we saw in part 2, lecture 2, Jaegwon Kim is far too alive to the complexities of the problem to miss the fact that the mental states of "vernacular psychology" (if we prescind from the scientism of calling them "states") cannot be reduced to brain states as they stand because they contain a number of "externalistic" elements. Kim's conclusion was that his Psychophysical Correlation Thesis and similar theses must be restricted to psychological states of a special kind, to "internal" psychological states, before they have any chance of being true. So Kim was led to seek an "internal core," a core that is entirely "inside," corresponding to all the "noninternal" mental states, the mental states that we speak of in the "vernacular." The way in which qualia made their appearance in *this* context was as the supposed "internal core" of such "noninternal" mental states as seeing a white patch on a blue wall. Here, too, the problem dissolves if we reject the idea that ordinary perceptual states can be "factored," divided into qualia and various relations, relations of the mind to its qualia'and relations of the qualia to the "external world." The problem of "reducing" qualia to neural processes/states/events is as much an *artifact* of the interface conception of perception as is the Berkleyan form of the problem of realism and antirealism.

but have i ignored "the problem of consciousness"?

Some will certainly say that I have ignored a deep intractable problem, a problem about "the nature of consciousness." They will say further that even if it might have been a mistake to formulate that problem as "What is the nature of qualia?" that does not matter very much. After all, they will say, it can equally well be formulated in other ways, for example as "What is the nature of these "looks" and "appearances" you talk about?"

Indeed, there *are* difficult conceptual issues to be explored concerning the nature of consciousness.[52] But those who say that the nature of consciousness is a "mystery" (and very often also those who think that only a successful reduction of everything mental to neurophysiology-plus-computer science can solve the mystery) do not seem to be particularly interested in *conceptual* clarification.[53] What they think is that "What is the nature of consciousness" is a *factual* question,[54] one to be answered—if it can be answered at all—by *empirical* investigation. But just what is this "factual question" supposed to mean?

Too often nowadays it is assumed that a question of the form "What is the nature of X?" has only *one* meaning worth discussing, namely, "How can X be reduced to physics, chemistry, neurophysiology, etc.?" Some of the philosophers who hold that the nature of consciousness is a mystery that cannot be in any way resolved by science as we now know it, believe, indeed, that some change at the level of our fundamental physical theory will be needed before consciousness can be reduced to physics.[55] Other "mysterians" believe—pessimistically—that science would have to change in ways *that it is beyond human capacity to imagine* for the nature of consciousness to be known.[56] But what these "mysterians" share with the more optimistic reductionists is the belief that the question is a scientific one, and—when they are not outright dualists—that it would take a reduction to something like (but also unlike, in ways we cannot now imagine) physics to answer the question. But each and every question of the form "How can X be reduced to physics?" (or to one of the other sciences mentioned) has a presupposition, namely, that talk of reduction *makes sense* in the case in question.

Yet there are obviously cases in which it does not make sense. Very few would suppose that the question "How can *the subjunctive conditional* be reduced to physics?" or the question "How can the relation 'A is a good interpretation of B,' where A and B are literary texts, be reduced to physics?" have any clear sense. I would not be surprised to find that many philosophers—including some who believe that consciousness consists of "qualia" and that qualia must be reduced to brain processes—share my disbelief that *reference* and allied "intentional" notions can be reduced to a physical relation. Nor does Ruth Millikan's suggestion that *evolution* solves the problem of reducing reference to "nonsemantical" properties[57] or Paul Horwich's suggestion that "disquotation" solves the problem[58] meet with much acceptance that I can detect. Yet one does not find many "mysterians" about subjunctive conditionals or interpretation or reference. Implicitly if not explicitly, it seems to be widely understood that the questions, "What is the nature of counterfactual conditionals?" "What is the nature of interpretation?" and "What is the nature of reference?" are not questions that call for a *reduction* to physics, etc. (nor for an alteration of physics, nor for a fundamental science that we are unable to even imagine). If the same attitude is not so common with respect to consciousness, the reason, I suspect, is the enduring grip of the Cartesian picture, which makes it seem that dualism and "identity theory" (reduction) are (1) meaningful alternatives and (2) the *only* alternatives. (Mysterianism is, at bottom, just a desire that fundamental science should change in such a way that the reductionist alternative would become workable, coupled, in the pessimistic version, with the idea that it is beyond our limited human powers to make the change.) It is high time to reject both of these assumptions!

It is of course the case that questions that had no clear meaning at one time, later, as a result of new knowledge of one kind or another, came to have it.

For example,[59] the question "How can two lines that are both perpendicular to a third line still meet?" had only one answer that people living before the development of non-Euclidean geometry were in a position to understand, namely, "They can't." And if one had said, "I tell you they can. Now, tell me how?" one would have been "babbling nonsense." This is a sobering lesson from the history of science. But the moral *isn't* that *every question makes sense* but rather that the judgment that a question doesn't make sense is always a fallible, revisable judgment. (But those of us who have been willing to learn from the great American pragmatists Peirce, Dewey and James have never claimed infallible knowledge with respect to *any* question, including conceptual questions.) Throughout the lectures that comprise the body of this book I have stressed that not all philosophical questions make sense. But that does not mean that I endorse some supposed Criterion of Cognitive Significance by which one can tell once and for all which questions do and which questions do not. And neither do I conclude from our obvious fallibility in these matters that we must accept all philosophical questions and all supposed "possibilities" as having (a sufficiently clear) sense. Saying "Science may someday find a way to reduce consciousness (or reference, or whatever) to physics" is, *here and now*, saying that science may someday do we know-not-what we-know-not-how. And from the fact that those words may in the *future* come to have a sense we will understand, it no more follows that they *now* express anything we can understand than it follows from the fact that I may *someday* learn to play the violin that I can now play the violin.

In particular, I have argued that neither in the case of appearances (including looks) nor in the case of the propositional attitudes do reductionist claims make real scientific or philosophical sense. In the case of appearances I argued that the very logic of the terms to be reduced is quite different from the logic of the proposed reducing bases; *identity* (as opposed to indistinguishability) is not defined for appearances. Moreover, appearances, I also argued, are *content-bearing states*, and content (whether we call it "conceptual" in all cases, as McDowell wishes to do, or distinguish another kind of content in some cases, as Evans and Heck do) is an *intentional* notion, and the difficulties that arise in the case of the paradigm intentional notion of *reference* also arise with respect to the content of perceptual states, or so I believe.

Again, some philosphers will say—including philosophers who are sympathetic with all of the foregoing arguments—that even if I am right, that only "relocates" the mystery, but it does not eliminate it. The "mystery," as many see it, arises precisely from the fact that there are different discourses that we find, on the one hand, indispensable, but, on the other hand, not reducible to any one discourse, in particular not to the discourse of physics. The mystery, as I heard one young philosopher whose intelligence and erudition I very much respect put it, is how such things as consciousness and intentionality "emerge." But the metaphor of *emergence* is a bad one.

It is a bad metaphor because it suggests that all the true statements express-ible in the vocabulary of the "basic" sciences of physics, chemistry, biology . . . might have been true *without* there being consciousness or intentionality. In short, it suggests that we might conceivably have all been Automatic Sweethearts, and that it is "mysterious" that we *aren't*.

Of course, if calling mentality a "mystery" is just a way of saying that it is some-thing *wonderful*—something that deserves our awe and our wonder—then, in that sense, it certainly is a "mystery"—but so, in that sense, is the physical universe itself, as Einstein repeatedly reminded us. Many things deserve our wonder, but the formulation of an intelligible question requires more than wonder.

a final word

One final word. Not one word of the argumentation in this book should be construed as opposing serious research into the physical basis of our mental life. Indeed, some of the best work into that basis has been done by scientists who are well aware of the difference between finding physical processes that subserve thought, feeling, memory, perception, and so on, and reductionist claims (whether the latter take the form of insisting that thought, feeling, etc., are "identical" with brain processes or they take the "eliminative materialist" form of regarding the whole of ordinary mentalistic vocabulary as so much bosh).[60] Not only does rejecting reductionist pictures *not* entail abandoning serious scientific research but, in fact, it is those pictures that often lead researchers to misconceive the empirical problems.

Here is an example of such a misconception: on a recent trip to Europe I had a conversation with a respected neuroscientist. We were talking about *The Remembered Present*[61] by the American neuroscientist Gerald Edelman—a book I very much admire and one that is quite clear on the defects of reduc-tionism—and my conversation partner said something that puzzled me.

"I didn't find anything in the book about *consciousness*," said he.

Now the overall topic of Edelman's book is precisely the neurological basis of consciousness, and the book offers neurological models in connection with an amazing number of topics; in one case (pattern recognition) one sufficiently detailed to be modeled on a computer, while in other cases Edelman offers what are admittedly speculative ideas. In the case of pattern recognition Edelman's neural net model is biologically plausible in a way that the classical connectionist architecture is not.[62] Edelman's model recognizes that pattern recognition must be supplemented by a certain amount of recursion (something connectionists were slow to do, which exposed them to powerful criticism from Pinker[63] and others). Edelman also suggests a model for memory that features a continual revision of memory in the light of *emotion* (an idea prefigured in William James's *Principles of Psychology*, by the way). He suggsts a neural basis for the distinction between sight and the puzzling phenomenon of "blind sight." He even suggests a neural basis for the distinctive kind of self-consciousness we find in humans (and possibly in chimpanzees): the leading idea here is that self-consciousness depends on an inner model of the creature's world that includes a time-independent representation of the creature itself.

My European neuroscientific conversation partner, of course, knew what the book contained as well as I did. So in saying that it didn't contain anything "about consciousness," he was complaining, in effect, "Yes, Edelman has hypotheses about sight and the other senses, about memory, even about self-consciousness, but *where is consciousness itself?*" This is just the complaint that William James criticized in his often misunderstood essay "Does Consciousness Exist?"[64] As James saw, *there is no problem of consciousness over and above* the problems of seeing, hearing, thinking, remembering, imagining, desiring, fearing, and so on. To think otherwise is to think of consciousness as a mysterious sort of *paint* that has to be added to the brain lest we have only an Automatic Sweetheart.

It seems appropriate to close with this report of a conversation that occured only last week, because it illustrates so well the moral I had intended to draw in any case, that philosophical confusion reaches far beyond the studies of professional and amateur philosophers. Clearing up philosophical confusions is not only beneficial for our moral and political lives but also for neural science, linguistics, and the other so-called cognitive sciences. But, most of all, it is worthwhile for its own sake, as anyone who has thought deeply about any philosophical problem whatsoever should know.

notes

the antinomy of realism

Warm thanks to James Conant for his painstaking criticism of the successive drafts of this and the remaining two Dewey Lectures and for helpful suggestions. Among others who assisted with suggestions and information at one point or another are Burton Dreben, Sam Fleischaker, Richard Heck, Ernie Lepore, David Macarthur, Sydney Morgenbesser, Alva Noe, Robert Nozick, Dan O'Connor, and, as always, Ruth Anna Putnam. My apologies to anyone whose help I may have forgotten to acknowledge.

1. The term *recoil* has been used in this connection by John McDowell; cf. his *Mind and World* (Cambridge: Harvard University Press, 1994). Although I do not wish to hold McDowell responsible for my formulations in the present lectures, I want to acknowledge the pervasive influence of his work, which has reinforced my own interest in natural realism in the theory of perception—an interest that was first reawakened by thinking about the views of William James.

2. Saul Kripke, David Lewis, and Bernard Williams being, perhaps, the most influential producers of these mysterious notions at this time.

3. In this remark I do not mean to be endorsing Dewey's view of Aristotle. For a persuasive argument that Aristotle's essentialism was not the strong metaphys-

ical essentialism that the Scholastics read into him, see Martha Nussbaum's *The Fragility of Goodness*. I agree with Nussbaum that a good deal of Aristotle can be read in a less metaphysical way that the tradition has, although I have difficulty in seeing how all of Aristotle's writing can be so read. The kinship between Dewey's project and Aristotle's is especially marked in Dewey's *Experience and Nature* (New York: Dover, 1958).

4. This did not, unfortunately, keep James from his own idealist and panpsychist lapses.

5. Cf. James's letter to Dickinson S. Miller dated August 5, 1907. William James, *Letters of William James*, vol 2 (Boston: Atlantic Monthly Press), p. 295.

6. Ibid., p. 296.

7. Apart, of course, from the fact that those interests are themselves part of the world. The truth about those interests would be different were those interests different. But what the traditional realist is pointing out is that when I talk about anything that is not causally effected by my own interests—say, when I point out that there are millions of species of ants in the world—I can also say that the world would be the same in that respect even if I did not have those interests, had not given that description, etc. And with all that I agree.

8. Cf. lecture 7, "Pragmatism and Humanism," in William James, *Pragmatism*, ed. Fredson Bowers and Ignas K. Skrupselis (Cambridge: Harvard University Press, 1975); e.g., "We create the subjects of our true as well as of our false propositions." I myself regret having spoken of "mind dependence" in connection with these issues in my *Reason, Truth, and History* (Cambridge: Cambridge University Press, 1981)!

9. On this, cf. my "Is Semantics Possible?" and "The Meaning of 'Meaning' " in my *Philosophical Papers*, vol. 2, *Mind, Language, and Reality* (Cambridge: Cambridge University Press, 1975).

10. Note that James's example of classifying beans does not challenge the first of these assumptions. This may possibly reflect the fact that in James's metaphysics there is, if not exactly a totality of all "objects," still an *etwas*—"pure experience"—tbat all conceptualizations are constrained by but that cannot itself be captured by concepts. This element in James's thinking is not one with which we should have any sympathy.

11. In particular, the criterion originally proposed by Donald Davidson—namely, that two events are identical if they have the same effects and the same causes—is powerless to resolve any of the cases in which the boundaries of an event are unclear. To see this, imagine, for example, that a philosopher who thinks that events must have definite "identity criteria" is unsure whether the event of sugar being rationed in 1942–1945 was a *part* or an *effect* of World War II!

12. My objection to "Quine's criterion of ontological commitment," as this view is called, is that ontological commitment—"commitment to the existence of a kind of object"—only seems to be a determinate sort of "commitment" because it is assumed that *exist* is *univocal*: assumed, that is, that I am saying the same sort of thing when I say that the brick houses on Elm Street exist and when I say that prime numbers greater than a million exist, notwithstanding the enormous differences between the uses of words (in the case of this example, between the use of words in empirical description and in mathematics). Of course, it would be wrong to register that difference by saying, flat-footedly, that *exist* has several different meanings, in the sense of deserving several different dictionary entries. But the assumption that the meaning of words, in any conventional sense of that phrase, determines exactly what is *said* on each occasion of the use of the words reflects a picture of how language functions that I would argue is deeply misguided. (Quine would of course agree with this last remark—which makes it all the more puzzling that he is gripped by the picture of *exists* as univocal!) I think it is helpful to distinguish, in this context, between the "sense" of a word and its "meaning." In this connection, see my "Reply to Conant" in *Philosophical Topics*, vol. 20, no. 1, *The Philosophy of Hilary Putnam* (Spring 1992).

13. The cost is high because, if "mereology" is taken to be a system of superlative new truths about "the furniture of the world," it is metaphysically profligate. This objection does not arise, of course, if we are willing to regard "mereological sum" talk as merely an *extension* of our customary talk about objects. No one can challenge our right to introduce new ways of talking (although Alva Noë has asked for what purposes *this* talk is a *useful* extension). But then my point about the extendability of our notion of an "object" will have been granted. In fact, this one extension does not by itself provide a sufficiently large totality of "objects" (or "entities") for the reconstruction of all our predications and all our universal and

existential generalizations. The sky is not a mereological sum of objects in the paradigmatic sense of the term (animals, vegetables, rocks, hills, etc.), nor are events, nor are mirror images.

14. For a fuller discussion of the strangeness of quantum mechanical knowledge, see the title essay of my *Realism with a Human Face* (Cambridge: Harvard University Press, 1990).

15. My use of the distinction I draw here and elsewhere between looking at the role a notion like "reality" plays in our actual lives and construing it in the way philosophers are so often tempted to do is helpfully discussed by James Conant in his introductory essay to my *Words and Life* (Cambridge: Harvard University Press, 1994).

16. That those immediate objects were conceived of in so many different ways (Cartesian "ideas" or Humean "impressions" or Machian "sensations" or Russellian "sense data") can be taken to be a sign that the classical theorists had a constant struggle to formulate their own assumption in a coherent way.

17. I neglect here the Berkleyan subjective idealist alternative to the Cartesian account.

18. The idea that the mind is neither a material nor an immaterial organ but a system of capacities is strongly urged by John McDowell in "Putnam on Mind and Meaning" in *Philosophical Topics, The Philosophy of Hilary Putnam*. McDowell draws, in turn, on the insights of Gareth Evans in *Varieties of Reference* (Oxford: Oxford University Press, 1982), a book whose importance I regret having failed to appreciate when I reviewed it in the *London Review of Books* some years ago.

19. These were published by Harvard University Press under the title *Mind and World*.

20. The reason the name "direct realism" is unhappy is that, as John Austin points out at length in *Sense and Sensibilia* (Oxford: Oxford University Press, 1962), there is a good deal that is question begging in the traditional epistemologist's use of "direct" and "indirect."

21. See John Searle's *Intentionality*, p. 37, for an example of the sort of move I criticize here.

22. I use shudder quotes here because the terms *internal* and *external* introduce a false picture of the mind—the picture of the mind as something "inside"

one. Note that that picture is not overcome by rejecting dualism—on the contrary, the popular tendency to just identify the mind and the brain makes it seem that the picture is literally true!

23. Cf. William James's *The Works of William James: Essays in Radical Empiricism*, ed. Frederick Burckhardt and Fredson Bowers (Cambridge: Harvard University Press, 1976), and "James's Theory of Perception" in my *Realism with a Human Face*.

24. Note that even the materialist version conceives them so; it is just that for this version alterations of our brain states is what affectations of our subjectivity *are*.

25. Many years after the publication of the New Realist manifesto in 1910, Perry and Montague are reported to have asked each other "Whatever became of our program of reform?" Cited in Herbert W. Schneider, *A History of American Philosophy*, 2d ed. (New York: Columbia University Press, 1963), p. 512.

26. Strawson argues that perception is a causal concept in Peter Strawson, "Perception and Its Objects," in G. F. McDonald, ed., *Perception and Identity: Essays Presented to A. J. Ayer* (Ithaca: Cornell University Press, 1979), on the ground that comon sense has it that we normally have experiences because of the presence of their objects, and—according to Strawson—this is itself tantamount to the causal theory of perception.

27. "Realism and Reason" is collected in my *Meaning and the Moral Sciences* (London: Routledge and Kegan Paul, 1978).

28. "Models and Reality" is collected in my *Philosophical Papers*, vol. 3, *Realism and Reason* (Cambridge: Cambridge University Press, 1983).

29. Cf. p. 24 in "Models and Reality."

30. For a detailed account of those reasons see "The Meaning of 'Meaning' " (collected in my *Mind, Language, and Reality*) and my *Representation and Reality* (Cambridge: MIT Press, 1988).

31. Cf. my "Does the Disquotational Theory of Truth Solve All the Problems?" collected in my *Words and Life* for this reading of Wittgenstein, as well as chapters 7 and 8 of my *Renewing Philosophy* (Cambridge: Harvard University Press, 1992).

32. Although some have objected to even speaking of a "paradox" here, on the ground that Skolem did not derive (and did not claim to have derived) a *contradiction* from the assumptions of intuitive mathematics in the way that Russell did

with *his* celebrated paradox, it does seem fair to speak of an "antinomy" here if one is attracted to a Platonist philosophy of mathematics—one upon which mathematics refers to a collection of "abstract objects," a collection of *things* that, mysteriously, we know about without having any causal interaction with them at all. For if one wants to hold *that* view *without* postulating magical powers of mind to enable us to know of those objects, then the natural move is to say that our understanding of what those objects are is constituted entirely by our intellectual grasp of *truths* about them, the truths of mathematics.

33. Contrary to what is often claimed, the problem does not disappear if we formalize mathematics in Second Order Logic; rather it simply reappears as the problem of the existence of unintended interpretations of Second Order Logic itself.

34. See, for example the appendix to my *Reason, Truth, and History*.

35. For details, see *Reason, Truth, and History* (chapter 2 and the appendix.) Readers who have some acquaintance with mathematical logic may also want to consult "Models and Reality"

36. Some readers, misled by a careless reading of a sentence in "Realism and Reason," started referring to what they took to be my new position, as first put forward in those two essays, as "internal realism." I used the term *internal realism* in "Realism and Reason" as a name for the position I held in "The Meaning of 'Meaning' " and in my "functionalist" writings. In *Realism and Reason internal realism* was not a term for my new position; it was rather a term for a kind of scientific realism I had already accepted for some years, for a position (I now argued) both realists and antirealists could accept. But I soon discovered that everyone else was using the term as a name for my new position (or for whatever they took that position to be). Even though I had modified my position in certain ways between those two essays and *Reason, Truth, and History*, in that work I capitulated to the fashion of calling whatever Putnam's new position happened to be "internal realism." I should also mention that Gary Ebbs (cf. his paper in *Philosophical Topics, The Philosophy of Hilary Putnam*), has found the label to be one that misleads my readers, and I agree.

37. For Dummett, a sentence is, in general, either (conclusively) verified or it isn't (apart from vagueness). For me, verification was (and is) a matter of *degree*. For an account of the misunderstandings evoked by my use of the term

ideal epistemic conditions in *Reason, Truth, and History,* see the preface to *Realism with a Human Face,*

38. Cf. M. Dummett, *Truth and Other Enigmas* (Cambridge: Harvard University Press, 1978).

39. This aspect of Dummett's view may perhaps spring from his expressed desire to carry Brouwer's intuitionist logic, a logic designed by Brouwer in connection with an antirealist philosophy of mathematics, over to empirical language. The simplest possible way to make such a carryover is to extend the notion of "proof," which is the basic notion in the intuitionist semantics for mathematical language, to a broader notion of "conclusive verification" applicable to mathematical and nonmathematical language alike, and this is the way Dummett suggests.

40. This reply is given in the last chapter of *Representation and Reality* .

41. Am I then giving up "internal realism"? Well, while in *Reason, Truthm, and History* I identified "internal realism" with what I am here calling "moderate verificationism," in *The Many Faces of Realism* (LaSalle, Ill.: Open Court, 1987) I identified it with the rejection of the traditional realist assumptions of (1) a fixed totality of all objects; (2) a fixed totality of all properties; (3) a sharp line between properties we "discover" in the world and properties we "project" onto the world; (4) a fixed relation of "correspondence" in terms of which truth is supposed to be defined. I rejected those assumptions not as false assumptions but as, ultimately, *unintelligible* assumptions. As will become clear in the sequel, I still regard each and every one of those assumptions as unintelligible, although I would argue for that conclusion in a different way. So whether I am still, to some extent, an internal realist is, I guess, as unclear as how much I was including under that unhappy label.

42. A paradoxical feature of this view is that according to it affectations of our subjectivity are identical with physical states of our brains, and, hence, with something *objective*. But this is a feature of any materialist view that tries to have "qualia" and "naturalize" them too. Cf. note 22 above.

43. The same picture appears in "Computational Psychology and Interpretation Theory" (collected in my *Philosophical Papers,* vol. 3, *Realism and Reason*) and also in "Reference and Understanding" in *Meaning and the Moral Sciences* (this last was written just before my turn to "internal realism").

44. An epithet once applied to behaviorist philosophies of mind by Ayer.

45. See, for example, Daniel Dennett's "The Absence of Phenomenology," in Tapscott and Gustafson, eds., *Body, Mind and Method: Essays in Honor of Virgil Aldrich* (Dordrecht: Reidel, 1979).

46. There is, I think, another reason that I did not take the question of the *objects* of perception to be a serious issue when I was arriving at my so-called internal realism. It seemed to me then that even if one *did* take a "direct realist" view, the same issues would simply rearise with respect to the "theoretical entities" of physics; with respect to electrons, quarks, electromagnetic fields, etc. It seemed to me that even if the line between "observables" and "unobservables" is somewhat arbitrary, the problems I described in "Models and Reality" would arise *wherever* one drew "the line."

I think that this idea too seemed compelling largely because of my allegiance to "functionalism," to the computational conception of the mind, and to the Cartesian cum materialist epistemology that went with that conception of the mind. If perception requires "qualia" or "sense data," construed as mere affectations of one's subjectivity, and the mind (including its "qualia") is identical with the brain, and "qualia," of course, have to be identified with something physical, then they cannot be identified with anything *outside* the brain. As we have seen, there is, on this conception, a fundamental difference between my perception of my "qualia," which lie inside my own "mind," and my perception of objects, which are "outside." I could, and in fact did, grant that the notion of "observation" could be extended to include observation with the aid of instruments (in "Models and Reality"), but I could not grant any significance to this concession in connection with the "antinomy" that I was trying to overcome, since I could not grant any significance to even the fact that we normally speak of perception as being of things that we perceive *without* the aid of instruments. The problem that really bothered me was not that "the problem would arise anyway wherever one drew the line between observables and unobservables" (although that is the way I thought about it); the real source of the problem, although I failed to recognize it, was that *one* "place to draw the line," namely, at *qualia*, seemed to have absolute metaphysical priority.

the importance of being austin

1. In these lectures I include relations under the term *properties*; that rela-

tions are metaphysically as fundamental as properties was long denied, and it was not till the work of Frege and Russell that philosophical opposition to that idea finally crumbled.

2. Cf. "Putnam's Paradox," *Australasian Journal of Philosophy*, vol. 62 (September 1984), pp. 221–236. It is unclear, at least to me, how the singling-out of the "elite classes" is supposed to occur. Readers of Lewis often assume that the elite classes must be the ones that obey nice "laws"; however, this doesn't really make sense as an interpretation of what Lewis has in mind, because (1) the model theoretic arguments I gave in my *Reason, Truth, and History* (Cambridge: Cambridge University Press, 1981) show that there are nonelite classes that obey the very same laws in our world the elite classes do (Lewis is quite clearly aware of this); and (2) Lewis's elite classes are classes of things in different worlds, and there are infinitely many worlds in which they do not obey nice laws and in which the members of various nonelite classes do.

3. Many terms have been used for what I called "sense data": *impressions, sense-impressions, sensations*, the German word *Empfindungen, experiences, qualia, raw feels*.

4. Cf. my "Changing Aristotle's Mind" (with Martha Nussbaum) and "Aristotle After Wittgenstein," collected as chapters 2 and 3 of *Words and Life* (Cambridge: Harvard University Press, 1994).

5. Cf. Aristotle, *De Anima*, chapter 4 (429a 14–17).

6. The roots of this conception are to be found in Descartes and Locke, but these thinkers thought that at least some of our sensory ideas "resemble" their causes.

7. On the enormous influence of that new psychology on the thought of the time, see Walter Jackson Bates's *From Classic to Romantic: Premises of Taste in Eighteenth-Century England* (New York: Harper and Row, 1961).

8. See John Carriero, "The First Meditation," *Pacific Philosophical Quarterly*, 58 (1987).

9. Cf. Edmund Husserl's *The Crisis of the European Sciences and Transcendental Phenomenology*, trans. David Carr (Evanston, Ill.: Northwestern University Press, 1970).

10. For a criticism of the idea that modern science definitively rules out the possibility of identifying colors with *objective* properties, see Jonathan Westphal's *Colour:*

Some Philosophical Problems from Wittgenstein (Oxford: Blackwell, 1991). See also chapter 5 of my *Renewing Philosophy (Cambridge: Harvard University Press, 1992).*

11. Reid understood what was happening, and (both in the *Inquiry* and in the *Intellectual Powers*) he called for a return to a direct realism akin to that of, e.g., Aquinas. On this see John Haldane's "Reid, Scholasticism, and Current Philosophy of Mind" in M. Delgarno and E. Mathews, eds., *The Philosophy of Thomas Reid* (Dordrecht: Kluwer Academic, 1989). If, nevertheless, I do not count Reid as a genuine advocate of what I am calling "natural realism," it is because, on my reading at least, he retains the idea that sensations are nonconceptual and internal "signs" (as opposed to *sensings* of what is *there*) as an essential part of his epistemology and ontology. Similar remarks apply to Peirce's calls for "direct realism" (indeed, Peirce cites Reid as a model).

12. William James, *The Works of William James: Essays in Radical Empiricism,* ed. Frederick Burckhardt and Fredson Bowers (Cambridge: Harvard University Press, 1976).

13. Husserl, *The Crisis of the European Sciences.*

14. Stated so briefly, this can sound like positivism; but the key to reading the *Crisis* is to appreciate that it is nothing of the sort. Compare Wittgenstein's remark in Ludwig Wittgenstein, *Lectures on the Foundations of Mathematics,* ed. Cora Diamond (Chicago: Chicago University Press, 1989), p. 252, about the importance of remembering that the "particles" of modern physics are not like a "grain of sand."

15. I am thinking of Kripke's *Wittgenstein on Rules and Private Language* (Cambridge: Harvard University Press, 1982).

16. The reader may also may want to consult the papers collected in part 4, "Essays After Wittgenstein," of my *Words and Life.*

17. I have been told that those who have had hallucinations and later regain their mental balance report that the "quality" of hallucinations is not at all like that of everyday perception. This is something that Austin conjectures may well be the case. Note, however, that Austin does not absolutely deny the logical possibility that a dream experience or a hallucination could be "qualitatively" indistinguishible from a waking experience.

18. Cf. John Austin, *Sense and Sensibilia* (Oxford: Oxford University Press,

1962), chapter 2, for a discussion of this argument.

19. Ibid.

20. I use *nonphysical* in connection with early to mid twentieth-century metaphysics and epistemology to cover both theories on which the postulated "objects" of "nonveridical experiences" (the "sense data," in Moore and Russell's terminology) are mental and theories according to which they are something "neutral" (which, in certain "nonveridical" cases, does not happen to be part of anything physical, although in other cases it is).

For an account of James's view, see my "James's Theory of Perception," collected in *Realism with a Human Face* (Cambridge: Harvard University Press, 1990). Although James does think that some bits of "pure experience" are involved in imagining, dreaming, etc., it does not seem that he thinks our relation to them is necessarily one of perception. Rather, holding a "bundle theory of the mind" as he does, he thinks that these bits of pure experience are *parts* of our minds. Austin does not think that seeming to perceive something physical is really standing in a relation to something else, mental or "neutral." He simply denies that *seeming to perceive* objects of one kind (say "middle-sized dry goods") must really be perceiving (or standing in some other cognitive relation) to objects of another kind ("sense data").

21. Cf. Hans Reichenbach, *Experience and Prediction* (Chicago: University of Chicago Press, 1938), who identifies sense data with brain states, as well as the response to *Sense and Sensibilia* by R. J Hirst, "A Critical Study of *Sense and Sensibilia*," in K. T. Fann, ed., *A Symposium on J. L. Austin* (London: Routledge, 1969).

22. Note that my sense datum epistemologist has shifted from speaking of "directly" perceiving to "immediately" perceiving, as a partial concession to Austin. (On this use of "immediately" see *Sense and Sensibilia*, pp. 14–19.) In fact, my imagined sense datum epistemologist has made some further concessions to Austin and James, e.g., in not speaking of sense data as "mental."

23. Cf. Nelson Goodman, *The Structure of Appearance* (Cambridge: Harvard University Press, 1941), 4th ed. (Dordrecht and Boston: Reidel, 1977).

24. Perhaps this is the reason that most traditional sense datum epistemologists did not explicitly make the rejoinder I suggested on their behalf. Nevertheless, in exploring the options open to such theorists, the use of an appeal to what is plau-

sible/implausible at a crucial stage in the argument implicitly concedes that the theory is supposed to be an explanatory hypothesis. The more common line was to claim that we are "immediately aware" that when we dream we are aware of *something*; to claim, that is, that the *analysis of the experience of dreaming (imagining, having an illusion, hallucinating, etc.) into the form* perceiver—relation of immediate awareness—object or objects *is as much an experiential certainty as the fact that when we dream we seem to be seeing real objects*. But this is just a mistake. Denying that there are any objects I am really aware of (or "immediately perceive") when I dream is not denying that I seem to myself to be aware of objects—not of sense data, but of persons, places, etc. Note that in ordinary language, it would be perfectly in order to say "I wasn't aware of anything—I was sound asleep," even if I remembered having dreamt, and also in order to say, "In the dream, I suddenly became aware that the building was shaking." Just as from the fact that we can speak of "fictional characters" doesn't mean that there really are such objects as "fictional characters" (even if some "ontologists" like to claim it does), the fact that we can speak of the objects we were aware of in our dreams doesn't mean that there really were any objects we were aware of.

25. Cf. Richard B. Brandt, "Doubts About the Identity Theory," in Sydney Hook, ed., *Dimensions of Mind* (New York: New York University Press, 1960).

26. Earlier, in my series of "functionalist" papers, beginning with "Minds and Machines," I had used the idea of "theoretical identity" to support identifying propositional attitudes with computational states of the brain. For an account of my history as a philosopher of mind, see "To Functionalism and Back Again," in Samuel Guttenplan, ed., *A Companion to the Philosophy of Mind* (Oxford: Blackwell, 1994).

27. The position I am arguing for rejects this dichotomy from the start, of course.

28. For a more precise formulation, see *Representation and Reality* (Cambridge: MIT Press, 1988), pp. 76–80.

29. Cf. my *Representation and Reality*; *Renewing Philosophy*; "To Functionalism and Back Again" (cited in noted 26 above); "Functionalism: Cognitive Science or Science Fiction" in David M. Johnson and Christina Erneling, eds., *The Future of the Cognitive Revolution* (Oxford and New York: Oxford University Press, 1997); and chapters 21, 22, 23, and 24 of *Words and Life*

(Cambridge: Harvard University Press, 1994).

30. Cf. chapter 3 of my *Renewing Philosophy*, and Loewer's "From Information to Intentionality," *Synthese*, vol. 70, no. 2 (February 1987), pp. 287–316.

31. For the reasons for this, and the resulting change in the statement of functionalism, see my "The Nature of Mental States," collected in my *Philosophical Papers*, vol. 2, *Mind, Language, and Reality* (Cambridge: Cambridge University Press, 1975).

32. Jerry Lettvin has developed an impressive theory of visual perception in which much of the computation takes place directly in the human eye—not in the brain proper!

33. That content depends on what is in the organism's environment ("semantic externalism") is argued in my *Representation and Reality*.

34. See Donald Davidson, *Essays on Actions and Events* (New York and Oxford: Oxford University Press, 1980).

35. For a discussion this negative side of Davidson's position, see my "Computational Psychology and Interpretation Theory," in *Realism and Reason*, and my "Information and the Mental," in *Essays on Truth and Interpretation*, ed. E. Lepore (Cambridge: Blackwell, 1986).

36. Cf. Quine's "Events and Reification" in E. Lepore, ed., *Actions and Events: Perspectives on the Philosophy of Donald Davidson* (Oxford: Blackwell, 1986), pp. 161–171, and "Reply to Quine on Events" (in which Davidson concedes that Quine is right), Lepore, *Actions and Events*, pp. 172–176.

37. In his "Reply to Quine on Events," cited in the previous note, Davidson actually adopts Quine's suggestion for a criterion of event identity (same space-time region), but this is subject to familiar counterexamples as well as to the problems just noted in connection with the same causes–same effects criterion.

38. Here again I follow the lead of John McDowell in *Mind and World* (Cambridge: Harvard University Press, 1994).

39. There are exceptions to this claim. Russell, for example, was increasingly attracted to the view that all qualities were in something "neutral" out of which both minds and material things could be "constructed." As early as *The Problems of Philosophy*, sense data (e.g., the colors I perceive) are not in themselves mental, but my awareness of them (the "sensation" as opposed to the

"sense datum") *is*. The sense data are in this sense already "neutral." This "neutral monism" seems to disappear from Russell's philosophy of perception by the time he writes *Our Knowledge of the External World*. For an account of Russell's views, see Morris Weitz's "Analysis and the Unity of Russell's Philosophy" in *The Philosophy of Bertrand Russell*, ed. P. A. Schilpp (Chicago: Open Court, 1944).

40. The view that it is a "large-scale mistake" to think of the world as *colored* is defended by Bernard Williams in his *Descartes: The Project of Pure Enquiry* (New York: Penguin, 1978). For a detailed examination of Williams's arguments, see chapter 5 of my *Renewing Philosophy*.

41. Cf. Dewey, *Experience and Nature* (New York: Dover, 1958).

42. Peter Strawson's paper, "Perception and Its Objects," was published in G. F. MacDonald, ed., *Perception and Identity: Essays Presented to A. J. Ayer* (Ithaca: Cornell University Press, 1979).

43. See, in particular, my *The Many Faces of Realism* (LaSalle, Ill.: Open Court, 1987).

44. This point is taken from Strawson, "Perception and Its Objects."

45. Russell, who had a conception of sense data as "neutral" objects, would, of course agree with this remark, but for the wrong reason!

46. On Russell's view, according to which sense data are not necessarily correlated to brain states (because they can exist "independently" of being perceived, according to the strange sort of "realism" he and Moore advocated), but are still not properties of the physical table, their scientific status is even *more* problematical.

the face of cognition

1. My reasons for rejecting the project of reducing intentionality to causal connections are set forth in *Renewing Philosophy* (Cambridge: Harvard University Press, 1992), especially the first four chapters. See also "The Question of Realism" in my *Words and Life* (Cambridge: Harvard University Press, 1994) for a discussion of the tendency of philosophers to oscillate between these two positions.

2. The identification of "mind" and "soul" and "intellect" was a novelty of Descartes's view. Cf. my "How Old Is the Mind," collected in *Words and Life*.

3. See "To Functionalism and Back Again," in Samuel Guttenplan, ed., *Companion to the Philosophy of Mind* (Oxford: Blackwell, 1994), and

Representation and Reality (Cambridge: MIT Press, 1988. In these writings I argued in detail that the psychological descriptions in which propositional attitudes figure cannot be reduced to the computational description of the brain, important as the project of constructing such a description may be.

4. Saul Kripke, Michael Dummett, Richard Rorty, and Crispin Wright have all contributed to this current.

5. On this, see John Haldane's "Whose Theory? Which Representations? — Reply to Robert Stecker," *Pacific Philosophical Quarterly*, vol. 74 (1994).

6. Ludwig Wittgenstein, *Philosophical Investigations*, p. 194.

7. This interpretative claim has been made, for example, by Norwood Russell Hanson in *Patterns of Discovery* (Cambridge: Cambridge University Press, 1958), chapter 1.

8. Cf. Wittgenstein, *Philosophical Investigations* 503ff. Charles Travis, *The Uses of Sense* (Oxford: Oxford University Press, 1989), contains an excellent discussion of the ways in which Wittgenstein's use of *Satz* (translated as "proposition" by Anscombe, but often read as "sentence" by analytic philosophers) involves a rejection of the standard sentence/proposition (in the sense of the "sense" or Fregean *Sinn* of a sentence) dichotomy.

9. In Richard Rorty, *Contingency, Irony, Solidarity* (Cambridge: Cambridge University Press, 1989), he repeatedly refers to language users as producers of "marks and noises."

10. E.g, in Wittgenstein, *Philosophical Investigations* §190–198.

11. Just as there is a sense of *see* in which one could see the surrender without knowing that it was a surrender one was seeing, there may be a sense of *imagine* in which one could imagine the surrender without knowing that it was the surrender one was imagining (although I find this doubtful); but in the full achievement sense of imagining, imagining that one was seeing (in the full achievement sense of "seeing that") the Germans surrender to Eisenhower at that time and place, one has to have the knowledge of what a surrender is to imagine the surrender.

12. The third "Lecture on Religious Belief," in Ludwig Wittgenstein's *Lectures and Conversations on Aesthetics, Psychology, and Religious Belief*, ed. Cyril Barrett (Berkeley: University of California Press, 1966). Wittgenstein had already written the first hundred and thirty or so sections of *Philosophical Investigations* at this time.

13. They like to say that these assertability conditions are "fixed by communal norms"; on this, see Stanley Cavell's discussion of Kripke's interpretation in *Conditions Handsome and Unhandsome* (Chicago: University of Chicago Press, 1988).

14. "Commanding, questioning, recounting, chatting, are as much a part of our natural history as walking, eating, drinking, playing." Wittgenstein, *Philosophical Investigations* §25.

15. Ibid. 95.

16. In John McDowell's *Mind and World* (Cambridge: Harvard University Press, 1994), he mars an otherwise fine defense of a direct realist view of perception by suggesting that animals do not have *experiences* in the same sense that humans do. What leads McDowell to this—in my view, erroneous—idea is his failure to see that the discriminatory abilities of animals and human concepts lie on a continuum. And he fails to see this because his dependence on Kant's discussion leads him to impose much too high requirements on having both concepts and percepts. ("No percepts without concepts" may be right if one is sufficiently generous in what one will count as a concept, but not if—as McDowell does—one requires both self-consciousness and the capacity for critical reflection before one will attribute concepts to an animal—or a child.) Another possible (but less likely) source of McDowell's error may be the thought that the "discriminatory abilities" of animals are to be identified with *physical and chemical reactions*—that is, that reductionism is the right stance to take with respect to the psychological predicates we apply to animals but not to humans.

17. For my reasons for distinguishing between human concepts and animal "protoconcepts," see chapter 2 of *Renewing Philosophy*.

18. For example, see the discussion of the difference between the human concept of meat and what a dog's protoconcept of "meat" might be in *Renewing Philosophy*.

19. A simple example: a dog may be able to see a sign that says STOP, but even if it is taught to "discriminate" that sign as pigeons are taught to discriminate various objects and various groups of objects, it will not experience the sign as *saying*, "Stop!"

20. Aristotle, *Nichomachean Ethics*, book 1, chapter 3.

21. For my reasons for calling such talk utterly empty, see *Representation and Reality*, and "To Functionalism and Back Again," cited in note 3.

22. See Michael Dummett's *The Logical Basis of Metaphysics* (Cambridge:

Harvard University Press, 1991).

23. A. Tarski, "The Concept of Truth in Formalized Languages," reprinted in his *Logic, Semantics, Metamathematics* (Oxford: Oxford University Press, 1956).

24. If the sentence S is not in English, then we must write the translation of the sentence S into English in the blank.

25. Jan Wolenski, a scholar who has spent many years studying the history of Polish logic and philosophy, has informed me that at the time he wrote "The Concept of Truth in Formalized Languages" Tarski held that nothing much could be said about what understanding a sentence consists in. The idea that Tarski agreed with logical positivist accounts of language is just wrong, according to Wolenski. In "The Concept of Truth" itself, Tarski employs the notion of "ascribing concrete, and, for us, intelligible meanings to the signs" quite uncritically. See *Logic, Semantics, Metamathematics*, pp. 166–167; see also Jan Wolenski, "Tarski as a Philosopher," *Poznan Studies in the Philosophy of the Sciences and the Humanities*, vol. 28 (1993), pp. 318–338.

26. Paul Horwich, a well-known deflationist, sums up the position thus in a recent review: "It is a mistake to think that truth is a substantive property with some unified underlying nature awaiting philosophical articulation. Rather, our truth predicate is merely a logical device enabling simple formulations of certain kinds of generalizations. . . . And the concept of truth is entirely captured by stipulating the equivalence schema, "The proposition that p is true if and only if p"—where p can be replaced by any declarative sentence." "In the Truth Domain" (a review of Crispin Wright, *Truth and Objectivity*), *Times Literary Supplement*, July 16, 1993, p. 28.

27. See, for example, Paul Horwich, "Wittgenstein and Kripke on the Nature of Meaning," *Mind and Language*, vol. 5, no. 2 (Summer 1990), pp. 105–121. Horwich writes, "The communal disposition to use a word in a particular way should not be regarded as simply the disposition to treat certain sentences as definitely and permanently acceptable and others not. In addition there are dispositions to sanction various levels of confidence (*cashed out as 'betting behavior'*) in the truth of certain sentences—where the appropriate degrees of belief are *a function of observable circumstances*" (p. 112; emphasis added). Horwich has published a book-length defense of deflationism titled *Truth* (Oxford: Blackwell, 1990). Note that when Horwich says that this theory is not "committed to verifi-

cationism" (p. 114), all he means is that he is prepared to say that a sentence can be said to be true or false even if its verification conditions do not determine that it is "determinately" true or false—indeed, this follows from the decision to retain the Principle of Bivalence as a logical truth; Horwich's account of *what understanding consists in* is precisely Carnap's, down to the identification of confidence with "betting behavior."

28. According to Horwich ("In the Truth Domain"), one of the purposes of what he calls the "truth predicate" is to enable us to make the generalization "All propositions of the form 'p or not p' are true," where p is "any declarative sentence." In particular, even if *p* is a sentence whose truth value we might consider inde-terminate—e.g., "A broken chair is still a chair"—logic forces us to say that the sentence *is* true or false, on Horwich's account. Cf. Horwich, *Truth*, pp. 80–88.

29. If I distinguish here between Dummett himself and the position he calls "global antirealism," it is because Dummett frequently expresses some dissatis-faction with the counterintuitiveness of global antirealism and some uncertain-ty as to its correctness. But, I would argue, it is because he structures the debate in the way I describe that he sees no satisfactory alternative to global antirealism.

30. Cf. R. Carnap, "Truth and Confirmation," in H. Feigl and W. Sellars, eds., *Readings in Philosophical Analysis* (New York: Appleton-Century-Crofts, 1949), for as clear and powerful a statement of what has come to be called "deflationism" as has ever been given.

31. As pointed out in note 27, Horwich believes that there are "substantive" things to be said about degrees of warranted assertability—e.g., that they are deter-mined, at least loosely, by "communal standards" and that they establish legitimate "degrees of confidence" that are in turn to be interpreted as "betting behavior."

32. Wittgenstein, *Philosophical Investigations* §195.

33. I fell into this error myself in my previous published criticisms of defla-tionism ("On Truth" and "Does the Disquotational Theory of Truth Solve All Philosophical Problems?" both reprinted in *Words and Life*).

34. In this connection, see Cora Diamond's discussion of the "sense" of riddles, in "Riddles and Anselm's Riddle," *Proceedings of the Aristotlean Society*, suppl. vol. 60 (1977), reprinted in her *The Realistic Spirit* (Cambridge: MIT Press, 1991).

35. I borrow this use of "correspond to a reality" from Wittgenstein's *Lectures*

on the Philosophy of Mathematics, ed. Cora Diamond (Chicago: Chicago University Press, 1989), lecture 25.

36. That our abilities to follow a rule, to understand words, to refer, etc., are not freestanding abilities is, of course, a constant preoccupation of Wittgenstein's *Philosophical Investigations*, but even this preoccupation has been subjected to reductionist misunderstandings. Wittgenstein's point is not that all these abilities presuppose a large number of, for example, "habits," in a *behaviorist* sense of "habit," or a large number of "conditioned responses." Even if that is true (as a causal statement), the fact is that the description of our abilities at such a behavior-scientific (in fact, quasi-biological) level makes their *normativity* completely invisible. When Wittgenstein speaks of our "natural history" in 25 he refers to "commanding, questioning, recounting" as "parts" of it; he does not attempt to *reduce* commanding, questioning, recounting to more "primitive" notions, as a Skinnerian psychologist would.

37. See Michael Dummett, *The Logical Basis of Metaphysics* and *Truth and Other Enigmas* (London: Duckworth, 1978), essays 1, 10, 11, 13, 17 and 21.

38. For example, John McDowell, in "Putnam on Mind and Meaning," in *Philosophical Topics*, vol. 20, no. 1, *The Philosophy of Hilary Putnam* (February 1992); and John Haldane in his 1989 paper "Reid, Scholasticism, and Contemporary Philosophy of Mind," in M. Dalgarno and E. Mathews, eds., *The Philosophy of Thomas Reid* (Dordrecht: Kluwer, 1989); and "Putnam on Intentionality," *Philosophy and Phenomenological Research*, vol. 52 (1992).

39. Cf. my "The Question of Realism," collected in *Words and Life*.

40. Hilary Putnam, "What Theories Are Not," collected in my *Mathematics, Matter, and Method* (Cambridge: Cambridge University Press, 1975).

41. My current view on the interpretation of quantum mechanics is that the quantum theories are best thought of as describing real physical things—not just the behavior of measuring instruments—but Bohr and Reichenbach were right in holding that they only describe the behavior of those things *while they are interacting in certain ways with macroscopic things* (when they are being "measured," in quantum mechanical jargon). How quantum mechanical "particles," "fields," etc., act when they are not being measured can be "pictured" in various incompatible ways (Many Worlds Interpretation, Bohm's Hidden Variable

Interpretation, etc.), all of them paradoxical and none of them (at least none of the ones so far proposed) compelling. Cf. the title essay of my *Realism with a Human Face* (Cambridge: Harvard University Press, 1990), and my exchange with Michael Redhead in *Reading Putnam* (Oxford: Blackwell, 1994).

42. E.g., "Two Dogmas of Empiricism," in W. V. Quine, *From the Logical Point of View* (Cambridge: Harvard University Press, 1961). See also my "Meaning Holism" in L. E. Hahn and P. A. Schilpp, eds., *The Philosophy of W. V. Quine* (LaSalle, Ill.: Open Court, 1986).

43. In Michael Dummett, "Wittgenstein's Philosophy of Mathematics," *Philosophical Review*, vol. 58 (1959), pp. 324–348. Reprinted in Dummett, *Truth and Other Enigmas*.

44. "The Face of Necessity," chapter 9 of her *The Realistic Spirit*.

45. For Tarski's probable views, see note 25 above.

46. Note that from the fact that a "that-clause" is a *nominalization*, it does not follow that we have to postulate an *object* that it names. Davidson (who is following Tarksi here) is right in maintaining that the connection between the "fact," if it is a fact, that Lizzie Borden committed the famous murder (or whatever the example in question may be) and the truth of the sentence we are using as an example can be stated as a simple biconditional: "Lizzie Borden did commit the famous murder" is true if and only if Lizzie Borden did commit the famous murder; and that biconditional does not contain a that-clause. Even sentences with (apparently) ineliminable that-clauses, e.g., "John believes that Lizzie Borden did commit the famous murder," do not have to be interpreted as asserting a *relation between a belief and a proposition* (contrary to the view of Jerry Fodor). The tendency to postulate entities whenever one finds quantifiers used is the legacy of Quine's "criterion of ontological commitment"; my reasons for rejecting the whole idea of such a criterion are briefly stated in note 12 to lecture 1.

47. In "A Comparison of Something with Something Else," collected in *Words and Life*, I argue that Tarki's so-called truth definitions are at best *extensionally correct*: they do not yield correct characterizations of truth under counterfactual circumstances, and they certainly do not tell us what "true" *means*.

48. "This is how things are" was given as the general form of propositions in Wittgenstein's *Tractatus Logico-Philosophicus* (New York: Humanities Press, 1951).

49. See, for example, Wittgenstein's distinction of two very different notions of "corresponding to reality" in lectures 25 and 26 of *Lectures on the Philosophy of Mathematics*. Among other things, Wittgenstein says that "This chair is blue" (imagine he had a blue chair in front of him) corresponds to a reality, but he can only say to what reality by using the sentence itself. He also says that while the sentences of arithmetic do not correspond to a reality in *that* sense, the *practice* of arithmetic does, in a different sense, correspond to a "diffuse empirical reality."

50. Note that in §138 of *Philosophical Investigations* Wittgenstein *rejects* the idea that "the meaning of a word I understand fit[s] the sense of a sentence I understand," saying, "Of course, if the meaning is the *use* we make of the word, it makes no sense to speak of such 'fitting.' " A similar contrast between thinking of meaning as use and thinking of the possibilities of use as fixed by the ways in which meanings "fit" or fail to "fit" one another is already drawn in Desmond Lee, ed., *Wittgenstein's Lectures, Cambridge, 1930–1932* (Totowa, N.J.: Rowman and Littlefield, 1980).

51. Cf. Wittgenstein, *Philosophical Investigations* §7

52. As I pointed out earlier, Wittgenstein thinks of a "sentence" (*Satz*; translated as "proposition" by Anscombe) *neither* as a sentence in the sense in which logicians speaks of "sentences," that is, a mere string of marks or noises, *nor* as a "proposition" in the sense in which some philosophers do, i.e., as a "sense" (in abstraction from the sign design that carries that sense). Wittgenstein rejects that kind of "sentence/proposition" distinction. Deflationists read the formula "p is true = p" as meaning that to produce the mark or noise *p is true* is equivalent to producing the mark or noise p; but Wittgenstein is not talking about writing *marks* or producing *noises*.

53. See Paul Horwich's formulation of deflationism quoted in note 26.

54. Although Tarski never pretended to be a philosopher of language, his profound logical investigation into the Liar paradox and the other so-called semantical paradoxes (investigations that built on the techniques Gödel used to prove the celebrated Incompleteness Theorem) convinced him that, on pain of paradox, we may only regard "true" as a well-defined concept when that predicate is restricted to a single "language," a single determinate totality of propositions, and that the judgment that a member of the totality is itself true or false may not

belong to the totality on pain of contradiction. An immediate corollary of this Tarskian view is that the totality of possible propositions is inherently unsurveyable. For details, see the discussion of the Liar paradox, and the version known as the "strong Liar," in the title essay of my *Realism with a Human Face*. Today not all logicians agree with Tarski that a consistent language may never contain its own truth predicate; but the "non-Tarskian" ways of avoiding the Liar paradox that have been proposed by Kripke and others still have the property that the semantics of a consistent language cannot be completely given *in* the language itself. As Kripke has put it, "The ghost of the Tarskian hierarchy is still with us." Of course, *Wittgenstein's* reasons for regarding language as an ever growing body of ways of speaking and thinking, with an unpredictable variety of ways of "corresponding to reality," do not have to do with the problem of the formal antinomies that concerned Tarski.

55. Rush Rhees, who understood Wittgenstein's philosophy as well as anyone, once wrote, "If anyone does ask, 'What are moral statements like?' I should think one ought to begin by giving examples of them. But often writers on ethics do not do this. You mention 'Honesty is good.' I cannot remember ever hearing anyone say this, unless it be in a philosophy discussion. And I cannot imagine just the circumstances under which anyone *would* say it." *Without Answers* (London: Routledge and Kegan Paul, 1969), p. 103.

56. For a discussion of Wittgenstein on religious language, see chapters 7 and 8 of my *Renewing Philosophy*.

57. Wittgenstein, *Remarks on the Foundations of Mathematics*, ed. G. H. von Wright, R. Rhees, and G. E. M. Anscombe (New York: Macmillan, 1956), §46 ("A motley of techniques of proof") and §48 ("I want to give an account of the motley of mathematics").

58. Note that the reason this is clear in context is certainly not that the context makes it perfectly precise! It is that exactness has no place here—and, as Wittgenstein says (*Philosophical Investigations* §69), "You still owe me a definition of exactness."

59. Wittgenstein, *Philosophical Investigations* §422 to §427.

60. Cora Diamond, "Riddles and Anselm's Riddle," p. 261.

"i thought of what i called 'an automatic sweetheart'"

1. William James, *The Works of William James*, ed. F. Burkhardt, F. Bowers, and I. Skrupskelis, vol. 2, *The Meaning of Truth* (Cambridge: Harvard University Press, 1975), p. 103, n. 2.

2. René Descartes, *Descartes: Selected Philosophical Writings*, ed. John Cottingham, trans. John Cottingham, Robert Stoothoff, and Dugald Murdoch (Cambridge: Cambridge University Press, 1988), p. 44. I thank Steve Gerrard for calling my attention to this passage.

3. There are considerably more entries under "Davidson" in the index to *Supervenience and Mind* than under the name of any other philosopher.

4. "Strong supervenience" of a domain of properties A on another domain of properties B requires not only that every property in A *covary* with a corresponding property in B, but that the obtaining of any property in A *depends on* the obtaining of the corresponding B property. The nature of this dependence is something that Kim tries to explicate (e.g., by requiring that it involve the decomposition of the objects characterized by A properties into constellations of objects that can be described in the vocabulary to which the B properties belong), but he is not himself wholly satisfied by any of the existing explications.

5. "Psychophysical Laws," chapter 11 of Jaegwon Kim, *Supervenience and Mind* (Cambridge: Cambridge University Press, 1993). In the introduction to the volume Kim writes concerning this paper, "For better or worse, the paper comes across, I think, as a defense of Davidson. I was, and still am, ambivalent about Davidson's argument. . . . in fact, the considerations adduced in the argument are prima facie incompatible with the strong supervenience of the mental on the physical, a thesis that I accept, at least provisionally, in several of the essays in this volume. I must say, though, that I have not come across a totally convincing refutation of Davidson's argument" (p. xiii).

6. Kim refers in particular to my "The Nature of Mental States," reprinted in my *Philosophical Papers*, vol. 2, *Mind, Language, and Reality* (Cambridge: Cambridge University Press, 1975).

7. Kim, *Supervenience and Mind*, p. 273. Kim correctly points out that the functionalism I espoused in "The Nature of Mental States" *presupposes* the nature of such "species-specific bridge laws." In my *Representation and Reality*

(Cambridge: MIT Press, 1988) I argue that such "species-specific bridge laws" can no more be found that can global laws of the form P↔M.

8. Although she does not refer to Davidson by name, Elizabeth Anscombe's "Causality and Determination" (her inaugural lecture at Cambridge) contains powerful counterexamples to any position that entails that every true singular causal statement must be backed by a lawful regularity. This lecture is reprinted in Ernest Sosa, ed., *Causation and Conditionals* (Oxford: Oxford University Press, 1970); and also in *The Collected Philosophical Papers of G. E. M. Anscombe*, vol. 2, *Metaphysics and the Philosophy of Mind* (Minneapolis: University of Minnesota Press, 1981).

9. Jaegwon Kim, "The Myth of Nonreductive Materialism," *Supervenience and Mind*, p. 269.

10. Ibid., pp. 269–270.

11. There are, however, other arguments by Kim that seem to me telling against the adequacy of Davidson's account. Specifically, it does seem that while mental events can cause physical events on Davidson's account, the fact that those mental events bear mental *predicates* plays no role in explaining why they do. This flows from Davidson's commitment to the idea that it is *strict laws* and only strict laws that ground causal relations. See the articles by Davidson, Kim, McLaughlin, and Sosa in John Heil and Alfred Mele, eds., *Mental Causation* (Oxford: Clarendon, 1993).

12. Cf. part 1, lecture 2 of this volume, "The Importance of Being Austin: The Need for a Second Naïveté."

13. Reprinted in Sosa, *Causation and Conditionals*.

14. A further problem with Davidson's account of causality is that not all physical laws are *causal* laws, and Davidson offers no way of distinguishing between a connection between events that is genuinely causal and one that is nomological without being causal.

15. "That matter cannot, by transposition of its particles, *become* what we call consciousness is an admitted truth; that mind cannot *become* its own occasions or determine its own march, though it be a truth not recognized by all philosophers, is in itself no less obvious." (p. 206) "To ask for an efficient cause, to trace back a force or investigate origins, is to have already turned one's face in the direc-

"i thought of what i called
'an automatic sweetheart'"

tion of matter and mechanical laws: no success in that undertaking can fail to be a triumph for materialism. . . . Spirit is useless, being the end of all things; but it is not vain, since it alone rescues all else from vanity." (p. 212). Both quotations are from volume 1 (*Introduction and Reason in Common Sense*) of Santayana's *The Life of Reason* (New York: Scribners, 1927).

16. "Postscripts on Supervenience," *Supervenience and Mind*, 2, pp. 167–168.

17. But neither he nor I can remember the place! In "Reductionism and the Nature of Psychology" (1973), collected in my *Words and Life* (Cambridge: Harvard University Press, 1994), I defended the view that explanations seek their own level; explanations in terms of microcausation do not conflict with, e.g., psychological explanations because *they generalize to very different classes of cases*, and since one case may belong to many different generalization classes, it may have simultaneously more than one explanation. In conversation Jaegwon Kim has told me that he is now considering the view that *explanation* is the fundamental notion and not causation, and that thinking in this way may make it intelligible that one and the same event can have different "causes." I discuss this view in part 3, first afterword.

18. Note that (AUTOMATA) and (NOT-AUTOMATA) are contraries, not contradictories.

19. In his *A History of Western Philosophy* (New York: Simon and Schuster, 1945), p. 568.

20. Kim, "The Myth of Nonreductive Materialism," p. 280.

21. The term *antecedent* is, of course, taken from propositional calculus. When we deal with counterfactual conditionals, however, grammar requires us to change the mood of the verbs in the antecedent to the indicative (in this case "did" to "do" and "were" to "are") when we consider the antecedent as an independent statement.

22. For discussion of classical verificationism and logical behaviorism (especially their Logical Positivist forms) see "What Theories Are Not," chapter 13 in my *Philosophical Papers*, vol. 1, *Mathematics, Matter, and Method* (Cambridge: Cambridge University Press, 1975), and the essays collected as chapters 11, 16, and 22 in my *Philosophical Papers*, vol. 2, *Mind, Language, and Reality*. A contemporary form of verificationism due to Michael Dummett is criticized in part

1, lecture 3 of this volume, "The Face of Cognition."

23. This assumption figures explicitly in Davidson's "A Coherence Theory of Truth and Knowledge," in Dieter Henrich, ed., *Kant oder Hegel* (Stuttgrat: Klein-Cotta, 1983).

24. Alternatively (but more controversially), the reductionist physicalist can build on ideas put forward by a philosopher who is himself an opponent of this sort of reductionism: Saul Kripke. In his brilliant and widely influential *Naming and Necessity* (Cambridge: Harvard University Press, 1980), Kripke claimed that when we discover that a certain stuff or a certain property or magnitude has a nature that is describable in the language of physics or chemistry—when we discover, for example, that water is H2O or that light is electromagnetic radiation with a wavelength in a certain part of the electromagnetic spectrum or that temperature is mean molecular kinetic energy—we also discover what that stuff or that property or that magnitude is *in any metaphysically possible world*. If we accept Kripke's claim (but see "Is Water Necessarily H2O" in my *Realism with a Human Face*), then it follows that *there is no possible world in which water is not H20*. A fortiori, any counterfactual with the antecedent, "If water were not H2O" is problematic. And similarly for counterfactuals with such antecedents as "If light were not electromagnetic radiation" and "If temperature were not mean molecular kinetic energy." And, similarly, if our mental properties are in fact reducible to physical properties in the way in which light, water, and temperature are all reducible, then any counterfactual with an antecedent such as "if our mental properties were not reducible to physical properties" or "if our mental properties were all absent while our physical properties remained"—in particular, the counterfactual (AUTOMATA) itself—is problematic. For, on this view, if as an empirical fact our mental properties *are* reducible to physical properties (which Kripke himself does not believe), then the antecedent of (AUTOMATA) posits a *metaphysical impossibility*.

25. I shall avoid Wittgenstein's characteristic terms (e.g., *language game*) as much as possible in these lectures, not because I am critical of Wittgenstein's own use of these terms but because so many competing exegeses of them are now on the market that their use in philosophical writing that is not specifically about Wittgenstein is likely to create rather than dissipate confusion.

"i thought of what i called
'an automatic sweetheart'"

26. Cf. Stanley Cavell's distinction in *The Claim of Reason*, e.g., in chapter 8 (Oxford: Oxford University Press, 1979) for the distinction between simply "making sense" and "making *clear* sense" (194 ff.). My notion of lacking *full* intelligibility is influenced by Cavell's discussion, but he should not be held responsible for it.

27. I will discuss later a remarkable suggestion Wittgenstein makes, that the idea that "nothing mental" goes on in certain people, that they are "automata," might be accepted by us because they are "a tribe we want to enslave." "The government and the scientists give it out that the people of this tribe have no souls; so they can be used without scruple for any purpose whatever." *Remarks on the Philosophy of Psychology*, vol. 1 (Chicago: University of Chicago Press, 1980, 1988), pp. 20–22.

28. Cf. part 1, lecture 3 of this volume.

29. Kim, "The Myth of Nonreductive Physicalism," *Supervenience and Mind*, pp. 280–282, for example.

30. Cf. part 1, lecture 2: "The Importance of Being Austin: The Need for a Second Naiveté," in the present volume, and also my "Functionalism: Cognitive Science or Science Fiction?" in David M. Johnson and Christina Erneling, eds., *The Future of the Cognitive Revolution* (Oxford and New York: Oxford University Press, 1997).

31. E.g., in "The Nature of Mental States."

32. Ludwig Wittgenstein, *Last Writings on the Philosophy of Psychology*, vol. 1 (Chicago: University of Chicago Press, 1982, 1990), 913. In vol. 2, p. 30, Wittgenstein writes, "What goes on within also has meaning only in the stream of life."

33. Charles Travis, *The Uses of Sense* (Oxford: Oxford University Press, 1989).

34. Charles Travis, "Annals of Analysis," *Mind*, vol. 100.398 (April 1991), pp. 237–263.

35. In "The Method of the *Tractatus*," forthcoming in *Wittgenstein in America*, ed. by Timorthy McCarthy and Peter Winch (Oxford: Blackwell), James Conant argues that a similar conception is already at work in Wittgenstein's *Tractatus*, contrary to the many attempts to view the early Wittgenstein as holding a view of language more like Rudolf Carnap's.

36. The appendix to Kent Bach, "Semantic Slack: What Is Said and More," in S. Tsohatzis, *Foundations of Speech-Act Theory: Philosophical and Linguistic*

Perspectives (London: Routledge, 1994), contains a useful list of types of "semantic underdetermination." I am indebted to Steven Gross for this reference; Gross's unpublished dissertation, "Essay on Linguistic Context-Sensitivity and Its Philosophical Significance," Ph.D. diss., Harvard University, May 1998, is an important contribution to the topic.

37. The context-*in*sensitivity of such "absolute" terms as *flat* was defended by Unger in chapter 2 of his book, Peter Unger, *Ignorance: A Case for Scepticism* (Oxford: Oxford University Press, 1975). David Lewis, in response, advocates a context-sensitive approach in his "Scorekeeping in a Language Game," *Journal of Philosophical Logic* (1979) — reprinted in his *Philosophical Papers*, vol. 1. Incidentally, Unger no longer endorses the view that *flat* context-insensitively expresses a property only ideal geometric surfaces possess. In his book *Philosophical Relativity* (Minneapolis: University of Minnesota Press, 1984), he hypothesizes that there's no fact of the matter as to whether his earlier view or Lewis's view is correct. (Thanks to Steven Gross for these references.)

38. Wittgenstein, *Remarks on the Philosophy of Psychology*, vol. 1 93–101; I quote only 96.

39. In vol. 2 of *Remarks on the Philosophy of Psychology*, 47 (p. 10), Wittgenstein says that "we construct things like the 'soulless tribe' — which drop out of consideration in the end. That they dropped out had to be shown."

40. The actual words that Kim used to formulate what I call "Kim's conditional" were "[You would not disturb a single causal relation if] *you randomly and arbitrarily reassigned mental properties to events, or even removed mentality entirely from the world.*" Kim, *Supervenience and Mind*, pp. 269–270.

are psychological conditions "internal states"?

1. Cf. "How Old Is the Mind?" in my *Words and Life* (Cambridge: Harvard University Press, 1994).

2. Cf. chapters 7 and 8 of my *Renewing Philosophy* (Cambridge: Harvard University Press, 1992).

3. Ludwig Wittgenstein, *Philosophical Investigations* (Oxford: Blackwell, 1953), part 2, iv, p. 178.

4. I discuss this topic in the following papers (in addition to the chapters in

"i thought of what i called
'an automatic sweetheart'"

Renewing Philosophy cited in the previous note): "Negative Theology," *Faith and Philosophy*, vol. 4 (October 1997); "God and the Philosophers," *Midwest Studies in Philosophy*, vol. 21 (1997); and "Questions for an Analytical Thomist," *Monist*, vol. 80, no. 4 (October 1997).

5. Note that Wittgenstein also employs the word in the passage about the "soulless tribe." (Neither James nor Wittgenstein thought the idea is, in the end, fully intelligible by the way, though for very different reasons.)

6. Cf. part 1, lecture 3: "The Face if Cognition," in the present volume; and "Pragmatism," *Proceedings of the Aristotelian Society*, vol. 95, part 3 (1995), pp. 291–306.

7. Descartes was the first, to my knowledge, to *identify* the mind and the soul.

8. A "dead body" is a body only homonymously, for an Aristotelian.

9. A suggestion advanced by Gisela Striker, in conversation.

10. Similar examples might be given from Jewish sources. As Paul Franks pointed out to me, although we are now inclined to read words like *nephesh* and *neshamah* as meaning the soul in some Platonic or Cartesian sense, there is no evidence that this is what they meant in biblical or even Talmudic times. Literally, *neshamah* means "breath" and *nephesh* seems to mean "neck" (according to Semitic cognates), both of which (as Franks says) "are material necessities of life."

11. Cf. Carolyn Bynum, *The Resurrection of the Body in Western Christianity* (New York: Columbia University Press, 1995).

12. In Judaism speculation about the afterlife is relegated almost entirely to "aggadah," or, traditions that are not legally binding; when "halakha" (the Law) is at stake, the Talmud generally avoids it.

13. This is also the answer to a question I often get asked in this connection, "Why *isn't the context of Kim's argument* enough to determine the content of (SOULLESS)?" That context *is* enough to enable me to "understand what is going on," but just about any supposition can be "intelligible" in that sense, however incoherent. E.g., if you want a "philosophical argument" in the context of which the supposition that *rocks feel pain* is "intelligible," consider the argument I sketch for a metaphysical realist in chapter 4 of *Reason, Truth, and History* (Cambridge: Cambridge University Press, 1981), pp. 95–101. Or think of David Lewis's argument that possible worlds are "real." Indeed, philosophy has the two

are psychological conditions "internal states"?

interesting features that, on the one hand, *anything* can count as "intelligible" in the context of some argument or other (in this respect, philosophy is like *fiction*), and yet every great philosopher suggests that some other philosopher's arguments involve unintelligible suppositions!

14. Cf. James Conant's "The Method of the *Tractatus*," and my "Was Wittgenstein *Really* an Antirealist About Mathematics?" both of which are forthcoming in *Wittgenstein in America*, ed. Timothy McCarthy and Peter Winch (Oxford: Blackwell).

15. James Conant, "On Wittgenstein's Philosophy of Mathematics II," *Proceedings of the Aristotelian Society*, vol. 47, part 2 (1997).

16. Cf. Stanley Cavell, *The Claim of Reason* (Oxford: Oxford University Press, 1979), on "criteria" (the discussion runs through all of part 1).

17. I use "soul" for the Greek "psyche," in spite of the considerable differences between the later conceptions of the soul or mind and the various Greek conceptions of the *psyche*.

18. This is Democritus's view as reported by Theophrastus, *De Sensibus*, ed. G. M. Stratton (London 1917; repr. Chicago: University of Chicago Press, 1967). For a penetrating and philosophically sophisticated discussion of the state of our knowledge of Democritus's views and what those views were likely to have been, see Mi-Kyoung Lee, "Conflicting Appearances," Ph.D. diss., Harvard University, 1996.

19. The Stoics standardly described a phantasia as an impression ($\tau\acute{\upsilon}\pi o\varsigma$—as from a signet ring in wax), and Sextus Empiricus (*Adversus Mathematicos* VII, 288ff) reports a long debate among the Stoics about the appropriateness of his description, Chrysippus objecting that one could not imagine several conflicting "impressions" arising simultaneously and proposing to speak of "alterations" in the soul instead. Communication from Gisela Striker.

20. But Kosslyn comes close! Stephen M. Kosslyn, *Image and Mind* (Cambridge: Harvard University Press, 1980).

21. Wilfrid Sellars, "Empiricism and the Philosophy of Mind," *Minnesota Studies in the Philosophy of Science*, vol. 1, *The Foundations of Science and the Concepts of Psychology and Psychoanalysis*, ed. Herbert Feigl and Michael Scriven (Minneapolis: University of Minnesota Press, 1956).

are psychological conditions
"internal states"?

22. Cf. John Haldane's account in "Reid, Scholasticism, and Current Philosophy of Mind," in M. Delgarno and E. Mathews, eds., *The Philosophy of Thomas Reid* (Dordrecht: Kluwer, 1989).

23. The view of perception Austin defends in *Sense and Sensibilia* is, in fact, closer to "the natural realism of common man" than is James's own "radical empiricism." Cf. my "Pragmatism and Realism," *Cardozo Law Review*, vol. 18, no. 1 (September 1996).

24. Cartesianism cum materialism is not a new position; this conception, indeed, appeared immediately after Descartes's own philosophy—the idea that one can save everything that is sound in Descartes's thought by simply identifying the Cartesian mind/soul/intellect with the *brain* was advanced or endorsed by La Mettrie, Diderot, and others.

25. In my Dewey Lectures, collected as part 1 of this volume, and in "Pragmatism and Realism."

26. Collected in Jaegwon Kim, *Supervenience and Mind* (Cambridge: Cambridge University Press, 1993).

27. Ibid., p. 178.

28. Ibid., p. 185.

29. Cf. my "The Meaning of 'Meaning,' " collected in my *Philosophical Papers*, vol. 2, *Mind, Language, and Reality* and my *Representation and Reality* (Cambridge: MIT Press, 1988).

30. In a later section of this lecture I shall argue that the only identity conditions that have been given for "narrow content" are hopelessly parasitic on the identity conditions for so-called wide contents, that is, on the meanings of our beliefs as determined by our informal procedures of interpretation of discourses, and that this has fatal consequences for Kim's program. Incidentally, the philosopher Kim cites in his footnote to this sentence about an approach to mental causation "now favored by certain philosophers," Jerry Fodor, has recently abandoned the notion (in *The Elm and the Expert* [Cambridge: MIT Press, 1994])!

31. Kim's treatment of memory in *Supervenience and Mind*, p. 189, resembles his treatment of perception: in this case what the Explanatory Thesis would claim is that whether I actually remember having had fruit and cereal for

are psychological conditions "internal states"?

breakfast or only "seem to remember" it makes no difference to the behavior emitted.

32. At this point Kim adds, "And in many cases we can identify the internal psychological core of a given noninternal psychological state, as we have done in the cases of knowing and remembering."

33. Cf. Putnam, "The Meaning of 'Meaning.' "

34. Note, by the way, that the above way of identifying the psychological state via its "narrow content" refers to the words "If I turn the knob the fire will go on," that is to say, not just the *noise*, but the *words*, i.e., the utterance *as that utterance is used in the English language*, and the "English language" is just as much something "external to the organism" as fire is.

35. Kim regards knowing as "noninternal" and belief as "internal." Cf. next lecture.

psychophysical correlation

1. In "Psychophysical Supervenience," chapter 10 of Jaegwon Kim, *Supervenience and Mind* (Cambridge: Cambridge University Press, 1993).

2. Ibid., 6, pp. 191–193.

3. These notions are employed by Kim in defining "internal" state.

4. "The Nature of Mental States," in my *Philosophical Papers*, vol. 2, *Mind, Language, and Reality* (Cambridge: Cambridge University Press, 1975).

5. For a criticism of this condition—one that Kim appeals to in a number of the papers collected in *Supervenience and Mind*—see chapter 5 of *Representation and Reality (Cambridge: MIT Press, 1988).*

6. Cf. *The article titled "Putnam, Hilary" in Samuel Guttenplan, ed., A Companion to the Philosophy of Mind* (Oxford: Blackwell, 1994), for particulars and criticism.

7. I am thinking of David Lewis, whose views are discussed in chapter 5 of *Representation and Reality*.

8. For an account of the development and present forms of functionalism see (in addition to the article cited in note 6) the articles "Functionalism (1)" by William Lycan and "Functionalism (2)" by Ned Block in Guttenplan, *A Companion to the Philosophy of Mind*.

9. Jaegwon Kim, "Mechanism, Purpose, and Explanatory Exclusion,"

are psychological conditions
"internal states"?

Supervenience and Mind; cf. p. 263, n. 46.

10. Donald Davidson has long objected to the idea that psychological states correspond to physical states, appealing precisely to considerations about how psychological states are individuated. See his *Essays on Actions and Events* (Oxford: Oxford University Press, 1980).

11. Kim discusses this example in *Supervienience and Mind*, pp.181-91.

12. In *Holism: A Shopper's Guide* (Oxford: Blackwell, 1992) Fodor and Ernest Lepore argue that the possession of any concept presupposes the possession of no other concepts!

13. Fodor and Lepore confuse several issues here. One is the issue of whether the subject must have any one particular belief for us to ascribe the belief that there are cows in Romania (my example, not theirs); a second is the issue of whether some of the beliefs that are usually thought to be conceptually connected to the belief that there are cows in Romania are *analytic*; and the third, the one we are discussing, is whether one could believe there are cows in Romania while having or not having any other beliefs at all. The position I take above is compatible with holding that, e.g., we might be able to make sense of someone's believing that there are cows in Romania while *not knowing that Romania is a country* (but there would have to be a "story" about just what the person thought). It is not compatible with the Fodor-Lepore position, according to which there could be an organism that had the beliefs that there are cows in Romania and *no* other beliefs at all.

14. For a discussion of the differences between human and animal belief see chapter 2 of my *Renewing Philosophy* (Cambridge: Harvard University Press, 1992).

15. In some cases—and not only "self-deception" cases, by any means—we may ascribe a belief to someone who does not avow it; not everyone is good at verbalizing what they believe.

16. To spell this out: the suggestion that someone believes that there are churches in Vienna but does not have *any* of the other beliefs that would justify a reasonable interpreter in attributing the concepts "church" and "Vienna" isn't just an *unverifiable* suggestion; it is an unintelligible one.

17. Hartry Field, "Mental Representation," *Ernkenntnis*, vol. 13 (1978).

18. Jerry Fodor, *The Language of Thought* (New York: Crowell, 1975).

19. With the conspicuous exception of John Searle. See my introduction to Andrew Pessin and Sanford Goldberg, eds., *The Twin Earth Chronicles* (Armonk, N.Y. and London: Sharpe, 1996).

20. I argue this in "The Idea of Science," chapter 26 of *Words and Life* (Cambridge: Harvard University Press, 1994).

21. Cf. Quine's celebrated *Word and Object* (Cambridge: MIT Press, 1960), p. 221.

22. Quine, *Ontological Relativity and Other Essays* (New York: Columbia University Press, 1969), p. 24.

23. Cf. "The Meaning of 'Meaning,' " collected in *Philosophical Papers*, vol. 2, *Mind, Language, and Reality*, p. 220.

24. It might be objected that the *appearance* of Twin Earth "elms" isn't the same as that of Earth elms. But George and Twin George are both city dwellers, and neither has actually *seen* an elm/Twin "elm."

25. Kim, *Supervenience and Mind*, p. xii.

26. Even identical twins don't have the same neuronal structures! This follows from "neural Darwinism": cf. *Neural Darwinism* (New York: Basic, 1987), and for a short and readable summary, chapter 3 of Gerald Edelman, *The Remembered Present* (New York: Basic, 1989).

27. I confine the quantification to *physically possible* worlds not only because of my doubts about "metaphysical possibility" but to avoid the problem that belief itself might have a different *nature* in some "possible worlds" if the laws of nature are allowed to be sufficiently different.

28. In Noam Chomsky's *Language and the Problems of Knowledge* (Cambridge: MIT Press, 1988) he writes that there is a "language organ" in the brain that may be thought of as "a complex and intricate network of some sort associated with a switch box consisting of an array of switches which can be set in one of two positions." (Chomsky also says that this network *is* "the system of principles of universal grammar"!) When the "switches" in the child's brain have been "set" by experience, "the child has command of a particular language and knows the facts of the language: *that a particular expression has a particular meaning and so forth*" (pp. 62–63; emphasis added).

29. Noam Chomsky, "Explaining Language Use," *Philosophical Topics*, vol.

20, no. 1.

30. I.e., not in the sense of "demonstrate how to do something," e.g., tie a bow tie.

31. I have been asked whether this is a "verificationist" argument. In addition to what I said above about this, let me add that if the suggestion isn't simply that beliefs are "atomistic" but rather that, in spite of the fact that having a belief is internally related to having suitable *other* beliefs (*which* other beliefs are suitable depends of course on the context!), there may still be a single "neural state" such that when one is in that neural state one always has one of the total networks of belief that would count as possessing the belief that there are churches in Vienna *and* possessing all the concepts required for that, and, conversely, such that whenever one has one of those total belief networks one is in that very same neural state. I can only say that none of the states so far suggested as "belief states" (e.g., having a sentence in mentalese in a "belief box") has the requisite properties, and the idea of a *neural* state that can account for such a diverse collection of cognitive structures is presently another example of a "we know not what." Is saying that alleged "scientific hypotheses," to which no determinate scientific content has been assigned, cannot be truth-valued, "verificationism"?

32. One of my reasons for using this example is a connection with Gödel that I spell out in "Reflexive Reflections" (in *Words and Life*) and in the forthcoming second edition of *Representation and Reality*.

33. Charles Travis, *The True and the False* (Amsterdam: John Benjamins, 1981); "On What Is Strictly Speaking True," *Canadian Journal of Philosophy*, vol. 15 (1985); *The Uses of Sense: Wittgenstein's Philosophy of Language* (Oxford: Oxford University Press, 1989).

34. Stanley Cavell, *The Claim of Reason* (Oxford: Oxford University Press, 1979), chapter 7.

35. Numbers 21:33–35.

36. Clifford Geertz, "Learning with Bruner," *New York Review of Books*, vol. 44, no. 6 (April 10, 1997), p. 22.

37. The Dewey Lectures 1994, collected as part 1 of this volume.

38. The term was introduced by John McDowell, "Coherence, Defeasibility, Knowledge," *Proceedings of the British Academy* (1982), pp. 457–479.

39. Parikh has written on the logic of vagueness. I do not know whether he has

ever written up this particular experiment, which he described in a lecture about twenty years ago.

40. I have in mind both connectionist models and the models described by Gerald Edelman in *The Remembered Present*. Although these models are different from a biological point of view, in both sorts of models pattern recognition is affected by properly connected cell assemblies. (In Edelman's model, supported by biological data, the assemblies may also gain and lose cells over time.) Note also that if we are talking about *perceiving* colors then something beyond these cell assemblies must be involved, namely, whatever is involved in having the requisite *color concepts*. For both these reasons—that these assemblies do not correspond in any one-one way to "appearances" and that having an appropriate assembly fire is only a necessary condition for perceiving a particular shade, and not a necessary one—taking these *neural* states to be "internal psychological states" in Kim's sense would simply amount to labeling a piece of neurology "psychology" (misleading the consumer).

41. In the second paper I ever published, "Reds, Greens, and Logical Analysis," *Philosophical Review*, vol. 65 (1956), pp. 206–217, I proposed to avoid the problem of nontransitivity (which I was aware of long before Parikh's elegant experiment was performed) by defining Ex,y (x is exactly the same color as y) in terms of Ix,y (x is indistinguishable from y with respect to color) as follows:

$Ex,y = df (z)(Ix,z \leftrightarrow Iy,z)$.

But this proposal fails because of the *vagueness* of the predicate "Ix,z." Not only is it quite probably vague just when two *physical* items are "indistiguishable with respect to color," but whether two "phenomenal items" (which may be separated with respect to time) are *indistinguishable* has frequently no clear answer at all. No neural criterion will help here, because the relevant neuronal connections change with time. One cannot try causing the cell assembly connected as it was earlier to fire and then try causing it to fire connected as it was later and "compare the results," because the cells (assuming they are even the same cells!) cannot be connected both ways at one and the same time. Memory is no help, because calling up a memory of a visual scene activates the cell assemblies one possesses *when the memory is called up*; there is no way of comparing the neural events themselves for "subjective quality." If someone insists that nonetheless

there is a fact (an unverifiable one) as to whether my "subjective color experience" at two different times is *indistinguishable* even in cases in which I can make
no judgment, that cannot be a *physical* fact, and so it will be of no help to Kim's
argument for psychophysical correlation. But what except an unshakable attachment to sense datum theory could make one think there is such a fact?

first afterword: causation and explanation

This afterword was inspired by the discussions in my seminar on "Perception and
Consciousness" in 1998. I am grateful to the students in that class for probing discussions. In particular, Jennifer Lackey's fine paper on explanation and causation
forced me to rethink my views on the subject. I am also grateful to Yemima Ben-
Menahem for helping me to avoid an error!

1. Kim's paper appeared in Enrique Villanueva, ed., *Philosophical Issues*,
vol. 5 (Atascadero, Cal.: Ridgeview, 1994), pp. 51–69. It is Jennifer Lackey who
called this paper to my attention.

2. Ibid., p. 57.

3. C. G. Hempel and P. Oppenheim, "Studies in the Logic of Explanation,"
Philosophy of Science, vol. 15 (1948), pp. 135–175; collected in C. G. Hempel,
Aspects of Scientific Explanation (New York: Macmillan, Free Press, 1965).

4. See M. W. Morris, R. E. Nisbett, and K. Peng, "Causal Attributions Across
Domains and Cultures," in D. Sperber, D. Premack, and James Premack, eds.,
Causal Cognition (Oxford: Oxford University Press, 1995), pp. 577–612; and see
"Visual Perception of Causation" in the same volume, pp. 591–599.

5. I say "virtually all" out of caution, not because I actually know of any living
phenomenalists.

6. This paper (Anscombe's Inaugural Lecture at Cambridge University in
1971) is collected in *The Collected Philosophical Papers of G. E. M. Anscombe*,
vol. 2, *Metaphysics and the Philosophy of Mind* (Minneapolis: University of
Minnesota Press, 1981).

7. Wesley C. Salmon, "Why Ask 'Why': An Inquiry Concerning Scientific
Explanation," in *Hans Reichenbach: Logical Empiricist* (Dordrecht and Boston:
Reidel, 1979).

8. For a description of Reichenbach's view of causation see "Reichenbach's

Metaphysical Picture, collected in my *Words and Life* (Cambridge: Harvard University Press, 1994).

9. In his 1984 *Scientific Explanation and the Casual Structure of the World* (Princeton University Press), Salmon does, however, acknowledge that the statement about relative frequencies in question has *counterfactual* components, and he seems to acknowledge that counterfactual conditionals are not reducible to statistical statements. (I say "seems to" because saying that counterfactuals are "scientifically indispensable" [op. cit., 149] is not quite the same as "irreducible."

10. See David Lewis, *Philosophical Papers*, vol. 2 (Oxford: Oxford University Press, 1986), part 6: "Causation."

11. Lewis's discussion of this assymmetry can be found in chapter 17, "Counterfactual Dependence and Time's Arrow," ibid., together with the postscripts to that chapter.

12. This discussion took place in Carnap's lodgings in the Institute for Advanced Study on January 2, 1954.

13. As in the words we already quoted, "As surely as we learned to call people by name or to report from seeing it that the cat was on the table, we also learned to report from having observed it that someone drank up the milk or that the dog made a funny noise or that things were cut or broken by whatever we saw cut or break them."

14. Both Hume and Ayer are aware than not *any* regularity will do, of course, and the point at which their theories run into trouble is the difficulty of finding additional conditions (e.g., Hume's "contiguity") that (a) do not presuppose the notion of causality; and (b) are sufficient to exclude all cases of coincidence and other noncausal regularities from counting as cases of causation. The consensus for some time, even among empiricists, has been that this project cannot be carried out.

15. E.g., in *The Foundations of Empiricial Knowledge* (London: Macmillan, 1940), A. J. Ayer writes, "If a question as to the cause of a sense-datum [*sic*] is to be admitted at all, it must be understood as a question of correlating the sense-datum with other sense data, in such a way as to make its occurrencce inferrible by the use of extrapolable laws" (p. 224). Physical causation is only a special case of "causation by sense data," on Ayer's view, because physical objects themselves—he held at this time—are simply constructions out of sense-data.

16. With regard to the context-sensitivity and interest-relativity of "causes," see

my *Renewing Philosophy* (Cambridge: Harvard University Press, 1992), pp. 47–48 and 61–66; *Meaning and the Moral Sciences* (London: Routledge and Kegan Paul, 1978), pp. 41–45; *The Many Faces of Realism* (LaSalle, Ill.: Open Court, 1987), lectures 1 and 2; and "Is the Causal Structure of the Physical Itself Something Physical?" collected in my *Realism with a Human Face* (Cambridge: Harvard University Press, 1990).

17. On p. 147 of his *Philosophy of Mind* (Boulder, Col.: Westview, 1996), Kim writes, "If x is a physical event and y is a cause or effect of x, then y, too, must be a physical event." This form of the "causal closure" principle seems much to strong to me. Interestingly, in the very next sentence Kim states a "somewhat weaker" requirement: "If a physical event has a cause at time t, it has a physical cause at t." And he adds, "Thus if the closure principle, in either form, holds, to explain the occurrence of a physical event we need never go outside the physical domain." This conclusion of Kim's evidently follows only if what explanation we "need" is itself not an interest-relative matter.

18. See "Is Water Necessarily H2O" in my *Realism with a Human Face*.

19. Jaegwon Kim, "Mechanism, Purpose, and Explanatory Exclusion," *Supervenience and Mind* (Cambridge: Cambridge University Press, 1993), cf. p. 263, n. 46.

20. A remark on the notion of "law" that I cannot resist making:, even if it *is* a digression: the orthodox view among writers in the philosophy of mind is that a law is a generalization that (1) is confirmable by observing instances that fall under it; and (2) supports counterfactuals. It seems to be thought that *this* is the notion of law that is used in physics. But the idea that physical theories can be stated in an *extensional* language is a fundamental mistake. I would argue that dynamical theories, for example Newton's or Einstein's or quantum mechanics, involve the *modal* notion of physical possibility from the very beginning. ("Phase space," "configuration space," Hilbert space, etc., are devices for representing *spaces of physical possibilities*, not mere "generalizations" in the extentionalist sense.) The generalizations of vernacular psychology are not and do not pretend to be laws in this sense at all. I don't doubt that they are confirmable by instances—unlike, by the way, the Schrödinger equation! (whose "instances" involve the psi-function, which itself makes no sense unless one already has

assumed the Schrödinger equation or one of its relativistic variants)—and that they support counterfactuals, but so does an ordinary dispositional statement such as "George always twitches when you mention his mother," which no one would call a "law." The idea of trying to say what a "law" is in these epistemic/linguistic terms is a hangover from Logical Empiricism.

21. Cf. Wittgenstein, *Philosophical Investigations*, 531.

second afterword: are appearances "qualia"?

Warm thanks to Hilla Jacobson for her critical reading of drafts of this afterward, and for many excellent and substantive suggestions.

1. Although it is supposed to be the case that the same argument applies to hearing, smelling, touching, etc., it has often been remarked that the literature on perception tends to focus, overwhelmingly, on the sense of sight—the sense that does not involve any manipulation or alteration of the object. This may be a further reason that the case for skepticism is made to seem so compelling.

2. Recall our discussion of indistinguishability and identity in connection with appearances in part 2, pp. 128ff.

3. In Nelson Goodman, *The Structure of Appearance* (Cambridge: Harvard University Press, 1941), 4th ed. (Dordrecht and Boston: Reidel, 1977), pp. 196ff. Note that "matching" is Goodman's term for what we have called "indistinguishability."

4. John Austin, in *Sense and Sensibilia* (Oxford: Oxford University Press, 1962), quotes several contemporary authors who offer this argument, and rebuts it with extraordinary care (and wit).

5. See part 1, lecture 1, this volume, especially pp. 10-11.

6. The term *Highest Common Factor* was introduced by McDowell in "Coherence, Defeasibility and Knowledge."

7. Especially in part 1 (the first three sections of lecture 2) and, more briefly, in part 2, lecture 2 (the section titled "Direct realism and the inner theater conception of the mental").

8. Austin, *Sense and Sensibilia*, pp. 48–49.

9. Recently I had a dream in which I "knew that I was dreaming," and was *trying to tell if the dream was just like a waking experience* (!). (In the dream, I decid-

ed that it *wasn't*.)

10. I take this to be the significance of Austin's remark about "seeing pink rats in D.T.s." Austin, *Sense and Sensibilia*, p. 49.

11. Ibid., pp. 20–25.

12. The use of the terms *intentionally, adjectively,* and *as an attribute* in this connection can be found in William James, "Does Consciousness Exist," in *The Works of William James: Essays in Radical Empiricism,* ed. Frederick Burckhardt and Fredson Bowers (Cambridge: Harvard University Press, 1976). See pp. 17–18.

13. Richard Heck, "Nonconceptual Content and the 'Space of Reasons,' " unpublished ms.

14. Participants in this dispute include, in addition to McDowell, the late Gareth Evans, Christopher Peacocke, and Martin Davies.

15. For Hume, of course, this was a false dichotomy: for an idea to have "content" was just for it to *resemble* an impression. As Elijah Milgram has put it (in his Harvard Ph.D. dissertation, "Instrumental Practical Reasoning," 1991), Hume's "semantics" was pictorial. But *we* no longer believe that resemblance is intrinsically referential.

16. See "Is the Causal Structure of the Physical Itself Something Physical?" collected in my *Realism with a Human Face* (Cambridge: Harvard University Press, 1990). Fodor is one of the best known "naturalizers"; I discuss Fodor's attempts in chapter 4 of *Renewing Philosophy* (Cambridge: Harvard University Press, 1992).

17. In my *Renewing Philosophy*, pp. 47–48 and 61–66; *Meaning and the Moral Sciences* (London: Routledge and Kegan Paul, 1978), pp. 41–45; *The Many Faces of Realism* (LaSalle, Ill.: Open Court, 1987), lectures 1 and 2; and "Is the Causal Structure of the Physical Itself Something Physical?" collected in my *Realism with a Human Face*.

18. John McDowell's disagreement with Evans on this issue is the subject of lecture 3 of his *Mind and World (Cambridge: Harvard University Press, 1994).*

19. *Gareth Evans, The Varieties of Reference* (Oxford: Oxford University Press, 1982).

20. In the ms. cited in note 13.

second afterword
are appearances "qualia"?

21. This argument is already announced on the first page of the introduction to McDowell, *Mind and World*, and runs through the whole book.

22. Hilla Jacobson asks, "What should we say about a creature who saw ducks before and can recognize them, but never saw a rabbit, and notices that sometimes instead of seeing a duck he sees another—unfamiliar looking—creature, one whose ear is in that place, etc. He has concepts like 'eyes' and 'ears,' but no concept of a rabbit. Does he see the rabbit differently than we do?" I think the answer should be, "Of course he does." Consider a different case: suppose someone has never seen a rabbit, but sees an *unambiguous* drawing of a rabbit. If the drawing is in color (say, the wonderful Dürer drawing), it might well be that he now knows what a rabbit looks like (or at least what one rabbit looks like) and sees it just as we do, in one sense of "sees it just as we do." (I say, "in one sense," because when I see a rabbit I see it as a kind of animal that is timid, that hops, that freezes when startled, etc., and he doesn't. The phenomenal "meaning" of a rabbit is different when one knows more about a rabbit than just what it looks like in the sense in which the Dürer drawing tells you what it looks like.) But if the drawing is a simple line and a dot, then, whether it can also be seen as a "duck drawing" or not, it would be little short of miraculous if he saw it as a rabbit even in the sense of seeing it as an animal that the Dürer drawing accurately depicts.

23. Wittgenstein, *Philosophical Investigations*, pp. 194–199.

24. All *I* mean by being "conceptual" is that it makes no sense to ascribe the experience in question to someone who lacks the concepts in question; this involves no causal hypotheses of any kind. I find McDowell's talk of our conceptual powers being in play uncomfortably reminiscent of faculty psychology.

25. In Bertrand Russell, *The Analysis of Mind* (New York: Macmillan, 1921), chapter 8. Russell's term for the conceptual element in experience was *mnemic*, because this element, he thought, depends on the *memory* of prior experiences.

26. James, *Essays in Radical Empiricism*, p. 16.

27. Sextus Empiricus, *Against the Professors* 7.176–184. Sextus Empiricus is here explaining the position of Carneides, but he voices no disagreement at *this* point.

28. Edmund Husserl, *Logische Untersuchungen*, 1, 9 and 14, in Husserl, *Husserliania*, ed. E. Panzer, Vols. 19.1 and 19.2 (The Hage: Nijhoff, 1984), cited in Charles Parsons, "Intuition and the Abstract in *Philosophie in*

Synthetischer Absicht" (Stuttgart: Klett-Cotta, 1998), p. 162.

29. Ibid.

30. Bertrand Russell, *The Problems of Philosophy* (Oxford: Oxford University Press, [1912] 1980), pp. 2–3.

31. Cf. part 1, lecture 2, p. 39, this volume.

32. Hume was, of course, aware of this: much of his psychology was an attempt to explain this as an all-but-irresistible illusion.

33. The way in which sensations of hot and cold are perspectival was a staple of seventeenth- and eighteenth-century writing about perception; a familiar example was that if one of my hands has been warmed and the other chilled, the same object may feel warm to the chilled hand and cool to the warmed hand. This was taken to show that what we feel is not a property of the object felt, but what was missed was that this is not the same as showing that what is felt is *subjective*. For if we suppose that what the nervous system detects (and is evolved to detect) is not *temperature* but *heat flow*, then this is perfectly in order: heat is flowing from the warmed hand *to* the object and *from* the object to the chilled hand.

34. By Hilla Jacobson.

35. N. Block, "Mental Pain and Mental Latex," in Enrique Villanueva, ed., *Philosophical Issues*, vol. 7, *Perception* (Atascadero, Cal.: Ridgeview, 1996), pp. 19–49.

36. The purples, by the way, run from violet to blue without passing through the spectrum — a fact that was not appreciated until the nineteenth century.

37. Of course, it is isn't really a "spectrum." I should really speak of a "color switch," but because the thought experiment in the case of humans is so constantly referred to as a *spectrum inversion*, I shall use that term also for the imagined color switch in the case of the Ixxzians.

38. That different subgroups in a population may have different visual "wiring" is at least suggested by the fact that there exist tribes in which color-blindness is extremely common. Cf. Oliver Sacks, *The Island of the Color-Blind* (New York: Knopf, 1997).

39. See Jonathan Westphal, *Colour: A Philosophic Introduction* (Oxford and Cambridge, Mass.: Blackwell, 1991).

40. In conversation, Tyler Burge appealed to the case of Donald Davidson's

"Swamp Man" (a duplicate of a human being who comes into existence out of the matter in a swamp by a quantum-mechanical "fluke" of almost zero probability) to pose a difficulty for the positions I am arguing for. The difficulty was supposed to be that since (both Davidson and I agree) *there are causal constraints on reference,* and the Swamp Man has, at the moment of his "spontaneous creation" no prior history of causal interaction with *anything,* we cannot say that Swamp Man has any concepts at all. Yet (Burge believes) it would be absurd to say Swamp Man has no *experiences.* My reply is that the moment Swamp Man begins experiencing anything he also begins to be in causal interaction of an information-carrying kind with the objects of that experience, and this is enough to bestow some minimal content on the concepts he uses in connection with that experience.

41. Jerry Fodor, *The Modularity of Mind* (Cambridge: MIT Press, 1983), p. 79.

42. Indeed, I once heard a lecture by Fodor in which he referred to the outputs in question by precisely this term: *appearances.*

43. Fodor, *The Modularity of Mind,* pp. 93–94.

44. Cf. Dennett's *Brainstorms* (Cambridge: Bradford, 1978), chapter 11 (chapter 8 is also relevant to this topic), and his *Content and Consciousness* (Boston: Little, Brown, 1991).

45. Part 2, lecture 3, this volume.

46. Hilary Putnam, *Reason, Truth, and History* (Cambridge: Cambridge University Press, 1981), chapter 4.

47. Jerome Lettvin, "XIV. Neurology," in *Quarterly Progress,* report no. 87 (Cambridge: MIT, Research Laboratory of Electronics, 1967). A similar view is presented by David Hilbert, *Color and Color Perception: A Study in Anthropocentric Realism* (Stanford: Center for the Study of Language and Information, 1990).

48. The seemingly less radical version of skepticism that doesn't deny that we *may* be in touch with the "external world" but "only" challenges our claim to *know* that we are is discussed by me in "Strawson and Skepticism," in Lewis E. Hahn, ed., *The Philosophy of P. F. Strawson: The Library of Living Philosophers,* vol. 26 (Chicago and Lasalle, Ill.: Open Court, 1998), and "Skepticism," in Marcelo Stamm, ed., *Philosophie in Synthetischer Absicht: Synthesis in Mind* (Stuttgart: Klett-Cotta, 1998).

second afterword
are appearances "qualia"?

I say "seemingly" less radical, because this "epistemological" form of skepticism often presupposes the same picture of experience that the "radical" version does.

49. Hilary Putnam, "Models and Reality" in the *Journal of Symbolic Logic*, vol. 45 (1980), pp. 464–482; collected in my *Philosophical Papers*, vol. 3, *Realism and Reason (Cambridge: Cambridge University Press, 1983).*

50. Externalists typically hold that the "external" property (which they conceive of as nontransactional) suffices to determine the particular look. Any admission that looks depend on the condition of the perceiving subject is taken by them to amount to accepting that there is "mental paint"—that is, adopting some form of interface conception). I believe that the picture of the represented property as a transactional one reconciles a representational externalist view according to which qualitative character is identified with the represented external property with the view that the looks/qualitative characters depend on conditions of the perceiving subject. Accepting it as an undeniable fact that physiological condition participates in the determination of qualitative character/looks is not the same thing as conceding that qualitative character/looks are *inside* our brains.

Among the externalists are Dretske, Harman, Tye, and Lycan, and among their writings on the subject the following are especially important: F. Dretske, *Naturalizing the Mind* (Cambridge: MIT Press, 1995), especially chapter 5, "Externalism and Supervenience," pp. 123–168; see also Dretske's "Phenomenal Externalism" in Villanueva, *Perception*, pp. 143–158; G. Harman, "The Intrinsic Quality of Experience," in J. E. Tomberlin, ed., *Philosophical Perspectives*, vol. 4, *Action Theory and Philosophy of Mind*, (Atascadero, Cal.: Ridgeview, 1990), repr. N. Block, O. Flanagan, and G. Guzeldere, eds., *The Nature of Consciousness* (Cambridge: MIT Press, 1997), pp. 663–675; M. Tye, *Ten Problems of Consciousness: A Representational Theory of the Phenomenal Mind* (Cambridge: MIT Press, 1995, see especially chapter 5, section 4, "Can Duplicate Brains Differ Phenomenally," pp. 150–155; W. Lycan, *Conscious Experience* (Cambridge: MIT Press, 1996).

51. John Dewey, *Art as Experience*, in *John Dewey: The Later Works, 1925–1953*, vol. 10, *1934* (Carbondale, Ill.: Southern Illinois University Press, 1991), p. 268.

52. One such issue, whicht Hilla Jacobson called to my attention, is the

neglected—and intricate—connection between being conscious of something and having pro or con attitudes (desiring, liking, disliking, finding the thing attractive or repulsive, fascinating or boring, etc.). She is planning to explore this issue in her Ph.D. dissertation.

53. An exception is Joseph Levine, who is taken to be a mysterian, but who does emphasize that the problem is a conceptual one in the sense that it is our very concept of consciousness that (according to him) makes phenomenal consciousness fundamentally inexplicable. Levine however takes standard scientific reductions to be *the* model for explanation. Hilla Jacobson pointed out to me that it is possible to view his arguments as showing that, in the case of qualia, talk of reduction doesn't have sense, or has a different sense than talk of reduction in other cases. Two papers in which he argues for the existence of an "explanatory gap" are J. Levine, "Materialism and Qualia: The Explanatory Gap," *Pacific Philosophical Quarterly*, vol. 64 (1983), pp. 354–361; and J. Levine, "On Leaving Out What It's Like," in M. Davies and G. W. Humphries, eds., *Consciousness* (Oxford: Blackwell, 1993), pp. 121–136; repr. Block, Flanagan, and Guzeldere, *The Nature of Consciousness.*

54. "How can I speak of 'conceptual' issues after Quine's attack on the analytic-synthetic distinction?" some will ask. The answer is that conceptual truths need not be conceived of as analytic, nor our knowledge of conceptual truths as something immune from revision. There are real limits to what we can make sense of. That those limits may sometime prove "casual" (the phrase is James's) does not make them philosophically insignificant or nonexistent.

55. This is the position of Roger Penrose, in *Shadows of the Mind* (Oxford: Oxford University Press, 1994), and Galen Strawson in *Mental Reality* (Cambridge: Bradford and MIT Press, 1994).

56. This is the position of Colin McGinn, in *The Problem of Consciousness* (Oxford: Blackwell, 1991), and probably of Noam Chomsky, who views *reference* as an inexplicable mystery in "Explaining Language Use," *Philosophical Topics*, vol. 20, no. 1, *The Philosophy of Hilary Putnam* (Spring 1992), pp. 205–233.

57. See my *Renewing Philosophy*, chapter 2, for a discussion of Millikan's various views.

58. See part 1, lecture 3, this volume.

second afterword
are appearances "qualia"?

59. I first used this example in "It Ain't Necessarily So," *Journal of Philosophy*, vol. 59, no. 22 (October 25, 1962), collected in my Philosophical Papers, vol. 1, *Mathematics, Matter, and Method* (Cambridge: Cambridge University Press, 1975).

60. Thus Paul Churchland, the outstanding representative of this school, has written, "The real motive behind eliminative materialism is the worry that the 'propositional' kinematics and 'logical' dynamics of folk psychology constitute a radically *false* account of the cognitive activity of humans, and of the higher animals generally. . . . The worry about propositional attitudes, in short, is . . . that they are too much like (the avowedly nonexistent) phlogiston, caloric, and the four principles of medieval alchemy" (!). Paul Churchland, "Activation Vectors Versus Propositional Attitudes: How the Brain Represents Reality," *Philosophy and Phenomenological Research*, vol. 52, no. 2 (June 1992).

61. Gerard Edelman, *The Remembered Present* (New York: Basic, 1989).

62. D. E. Rumelhart, and J. L. McClelland, and the PDP Research Group, *Parallel Distributed Processing: Explorations in the Microstructure of Cognition* (Cambridge: Bradford and MIT Press, 1986), vol. 1; (Cambridge: Bradford and MIT Press, 1987), vol. 2.

63. Steven Pinker and Alan Prince, "On Language and Connectionism: Analysis of a Parallel Distributed Processing Model of Language Acquisition," *Cognition*, vol. 28 (1988), pp. 73–193.

64. James's "Does Consciousness Exist," *Essays in Radical Empiricism*.

index

Grice, Paul, 87, 88

Haldane, John, 77, 137, 149–50
Hallucination, 26, 152, 153
HCF (Highest Common Factor),
153–54; HCF argument, 129–31
HCF Fallacy, 153, 154
Heck, Richard, 154, 155, 156, 173
Hempel, C. G., 138, 139, 140, 143, 144
Hobbes, Thomas, 23
Horwich, Paul, 53, 55, 172, 193nn26,
27, 194n31
Hot and cold, are perspectival, 219n33
Human being who lacks all mental prop-
erties, 73–74, 76, 78, 80, 83, 84, 90,
91; see also Automatic sweetheart
Hume, David, 23, 29, 139, 140, 144,
145–46, 150, 157; model of mind,
154; psychology of, 219n32
Husserl, Edmund, 24, 38, 158, 159

Idealism, 18, 23, 44
Identity, 173; across metaphysically pos-
sible worlds, 4; in mind-brain con-
text, 168
Identity theories, 85, 86, 95, 172; empti-
ness of, 30–38
Illusions, 25, 27, 153
Imagining, 45–46, 48, 191n11
Impressions, 9, 10, 43, 45
Incompleteness theorem, 197n54
(INDEPENDENCE), 84–87
Intelligibility, 205n13; antecedent of
(AUTOMATA), 80, 82–84; of inter-
nal psychological states, 112–14; of
philosophical hypotheses, 96,
98–100; of reductionism, 84; of reli-
gious language, 95, 96, 98, 99; of
Supervenience Thesis, 109–33
Intentionality, 154, 173–74; reducing to
causal connections, 43–44, 190n1
Interactionism, 78–80, 95, 132; rejec-

tion of, 79, 80, 81, 83
Interface: between cognitive powers and
external world, 10, 11, 18; between
mind and external objects, 43, 44,
45, 59; perceptual experiences as,
169, 170
Internal core state, 105–6, 125, 132, 170
Internal phenomenal states, 112, 113,
128–32
Internal psychological states, 109–10,
111, 120, 125, 132, 170, 212n40;
intelligibility of, 112–14; Kim on,
102–7
Internal realism, 13, 17–18, 182n36,
183n41, 184n46
Internal representations, 128, 129
Internal states, psychological conditions
as, 93–107
"Inverted Earth," 162
Inverted spectra, subjectivity and,
162–69
Inverted spectrum puzzle, 40–46
"Inverted Spectrum Sweetheart," 162

Jacobson, Hilla, 221n52, 222n53
James, William, 10, 11, 27, 28, 38–39,
41, 44, 101, 102, 120, 147, 152, 154,
157, 158, 164, 172, 175, 177n1,
222n54; account of perception, 24;
automatic sweetheart, 73, 76, 80, 95,
99; metaphysics, 178n10; natural realism, 15; pragmatism, 9; realism, 5–6
Judaism, 205n12

Kant, Immanuel, 89, 140, 192n16
Kim, Jaegwon, 74–75, 76, 77–82, 83,
84, 90, 91, 98, 99, 122, 128, 146,
147, 149, 170; application of
(INDEPENDENCE), 85, 86;
Cartesianism cum materialism, 101;
explanatory realism/internalism distinction, 137–42, 143, 144; on inter-

Visual imagery, 45, 110
Visual perception, theory of, 189n32
Visual perspective, 165

Williams, Bernard, 177n2, 190n40
Wisdom, John, 41
Wittgenstein, Ludwig, 6, 11, 14, 15, 24, 25, 41, 44–48, 49, 54, 58, 82, 89–91, 120, 126, 128, 145, 149, 156, 195n36, 203n35; automata, 203n27; on language, 198n54; later philosophy of, 87; on philosophy of mathematics, 61, 62–64; on religious language, 94; soulless tribe, 89–90, 99, 100; on truth, 64–69
Wolenski, Jan, 193n25
Words, 9; contents of, 119–20; correspond to properties, 21; interpretation of, 17; meanings of, 6–7, 46, 87–91, 103, 104, 122, 125, 179n12; recognition of, 166–68; role in thinking, 46–47; understanding of, 123–24; use of, 145
Wright, Crispin, 191n4